“Tikkun Olam”

"Tikkun Olam" —To Mend the World

A Confluence of Theology and the Arts

Edited by
JASON GORONCY

Foreword by Alfonse Borysewicz

PICKWICK *Publications* • Eugene, Oregon

"TIKKUN OLAM"—TO MEND THE WORLD
A Confluence of Theology and the Arts

Pickwick Publications
An Imprint of Wipf and Stock Publishers
199 W. 8th Ave., Suite 3
Eugene, OR 97401

www.wipfandstock.com

ISBN 13: 978-1-61097-922-1

Cataloging-in-Publication data:

"Tikkun Olam"—to mend the world : a confluence of theology and the arts. Edited by Jason Goroncy ; with a foreword by Alfonse Borysewicz.

xxiv + 208 pp. ; 23 cm—Includes bibliographical references and index.

ISBN 13: 978-1-61097-922-1

1. Art and religion—Christianity. 2. Christianity and the arts. I. Title.

BR115 A8 T49 2014

Manufactured in the USA

In memory of the child artists
of Terezín Ghetto, 1941–1945

Consider the wounds under water.
Consider how mountains are torn
Consider the holes in volcanoes.
Consider how old men are born.

—Glenn Colquhoun

Contents

Contributors

ALFONSE BORYSEWICZ

Alfonse Borysewicz, born and raised in Detroit, survived those years and moved to New York City, where he has resided for twenty-five years with his wife, daughter, and son. Exhibiting widely with his paintings, he has recently focused on placing work with churches that compliment their liturgical cycles. He also teaches philosophy and theology.

LIBBY BYRNE

Libby Byrne is an artist, art therapist, and theologian. Her images are internal landscapes that map and record the landscape of the inner journey. Libby's work is a meditation on that which is shared in the human experience and offers the viewer an opportunity to "know" and "be known" on the journey to wholeness. Libby is regularly engaged to develop liturgical images that feed the spiritual health of congregations and communities. These images challenge and engage people with questions of ultimate concern. Over the past decade Libby has worked as an Art Therapist in the public health sector in Melbourne, with a particular focus in Palliative Care. Libby has specialized in assisting people to use art as a means of honoring and reflecting on significant life experiences as well as creating opportunities to develop meaningful and personal ritual in and around the experience of death. Libby now works as an Associate Lecturer, teaching in the Art Therapy Programs at La Trobe University in Melbourne, Australia. She is currently enrolled with the MCD University of Divinity, developing PhD research into an art-based theological method of inquiry. Based in Whitley College, this work is a visual exploration of "Healing Art and the Art of Healing."

JULANNE CLARKE-MORRIS
Julanne Clarke-Morris is currently editor of *Anglican Taonga*, the pro vincial magazine of the Anglican Church in Aotearoa, New Zealand and Polynesia. She holds a degree in theology from the University of Otago and an Honours Diploma in Fine Arts from the Otago School of Fine Arts. Her MA in Fine Arts (Virtual Realities) is from Ireland's National College of Art and Design (National University of Ireland). She has travelled extensively in Europe and Asia researching liturgical and visual arts in various tradi tions, including through the Asian Christian Art Association and through an Erasmus exchange in Greece. She has lived and worked as a teacher, artist and editor in Japan, Ireland and Switzerland, and she currently lives in Dunedin, Aotearoa New Zealand.

JOHN DENNISON
John Dennison is a literary scholar and poet. He holds a degree in English and Classics from Victoria University of Wellington, and degrees in English and Theology from the University of Otago. In 2011 he completed a PhD at the University of St Andrews on the prose poetics of Seamus Heaney, now in preparation as a monograph. He is married to Jannah; they have three sons, and live in Wellington, New Zealand.

WILLIAM DYRNESS
William Dyrness is Professor of Theology and Culture at Fuller Theological Seminary in Pasadena, California. After his studies at Fuller, the Univer sity of Strasbourg in France, and the Free University of Amsterdam, he has taught for over 30 years at the Asian Theological Seminary in Manila, New College Berkeley (California) and, since 1990, at Fuller. His recent publica tions include *Senses of the Soul: Art and Visual in Christian Worship* cade, 2008); *A Primer on Christian Worship* (2009); *Poetic Theology: God and the Poetics of Everyday Life* (2011); and *Senses of Devotion: Interfaith Aesthetics in Buddhist and Muslim Communities* (Cascade, 2013).

ALLIE EAGLE
Allie Eagle is a trained painter and art teacher who has worked in both secondary and tertiary institutions. She runs her own atelier on the west coast of Auckland and is preparing for a major travelling exhibition. She was a leading exponent of the woman's art movement in New Zealand. In the 1970s, her provocative and avant-garde installation work helped es tablish lesbian feminist politics as one of the key ideologies that drove the establishment of a recognizable position from which many New Zealand

women felt they could speak. Since that time Allie's ideas and concerns have undergone a radical reappraisal. In 1980 a life changing spiritual experience saw her critically reconsider many of the views she had previously held adopting instead a Christian framework as her primary motivational focus. This crisis of faith encouraged Allie to revisit and challenge many of the feminist themes she had earlier explored in her life and work as an artist. Although none of Allie's passion or commitment to social activism has dissipated, her existential "change of mind" and decision to go back and think again recognizes the underlying creative necessity for all ideologies to be constantly reviewed and tested.

JASON GORONCY
Jason Goroncy is Lecturer and Dean of Studies at the Knox Centre for Ministry and Leadership in Dunedin. His research interests lie chiefly in the areas of Christian doctrine, theological anthropology (particularly around theologies of childhood, disability and death), the work of P. T. Forsyth, and theological aesthetics. His publications include *Hallowed Be Thy Name: The Sanctification of All in the Soteriology of Peter Taylor Forsyth* (2013) and *Descending on Humanity and Intervening in History: Notes from the Pulpit Ministry of P. T. Forsyth* (Pickwick, 2013).

STEVEN GUTHRIE
Steven R. Guthrie, Associate Professor of Theology at Belmont University, Nashville, Tennessee, was formerly research fellow and then lecturer in theology at the Institute for Theology, Imagination and the Arts, University of St. Andrews. His publications include *Creator Spirit: The Holy Spirit and the Art of Becoming Human* (2011); *Resonant Witness: Conversations between Music and Theology* (edited with Jeremy Begbie, 2011); and *Faithful Performances: Enacting Christian Tradition* (edited with Trevor Hart, 2007).

TREVOR HART
Trevor Hart is Professor of Divinity and Director of the Institute for Theology, Imagination and the Arts in the University of St. Andrews. He has lectured and published widely on the relationship between theology and imagination, and the material for these lectures is closely related to a forthcoming book on divine and human creativity. He is an ordained priest in the Scottish Episcopal Church, and enjoys the opportunity for ministry in a local parish alongside his full-time role as a university teacher. He is married to Rachel, and they have three children (two grown, and one rapidly growing!). When time permits, Trevor enjoys watching Scotland play

rugby, hillwalking, and learning to play the violin again. He studied theology first at the University of Durham (where he learned to bring constructive Christian theology and English literature into a fruitful conversation) and completed his doctoral thesis on the christology of the eastern fathers at the University of Aberdeen. He taught systematic theology in Aberdeen for nine years before moving to St. Andrews in 1995.

CAROLYN KELLY
Carolyn Kelly grew up in Northland and Auckland where she studied English, and later taught in secondary schools. Her BD is from the University of Otago, and PhD (Divinity) from the University of Aberdeen, Scotland. Carolyn lives in central Auckland and is working as a university chaplain whilst completing ordination training with the Presbyterian Church of Aotearoa-New Zealand. She is married to Mark, and together they have three young-adult children.

JOANNA OSBORNE
Joanna Osborne is a PhD candidate at the University of Otago, with an interest in theology and art history. She holds a BFA in photography from the Dunedin School of Art, and exhibits occasionally.

MURRAY RAE
Murray Rae is Professor of Theology at the University of Otago, and Head of the Department of Theology and Religion, where he teaches courses in systematic theology and ethics. His research interests include the work of Søren Kierkegaard, theological hermeneutics, Maori engagements with Christianity, and theology and the built environment. He is editor of the *Journal of Theological Interpretation* monograph series and his publications include *Mana Maori and Christianity* (2012); *Kierkegaard and Theology* (2010); *History and Hermeneutics* (2005); and *Kierkegaard's Vision of the Incarnation* (1997).

JONATHAN RYAN
Jonathan Ryan is part of the missional community, Servants to Asia's Urban Poor, in which he currently serves as the New Zealand coordinator. He also serves as an ordained minister at Highgate Presbyterian Church in Dunedin. His academic background includes degrees in music and history (Victoria University, Wellington) and in theology (Regent College, Vancouver), and he has an ongoing interest in the vocation of the church in contexts of poverty and marginality.

Illustrations

Foreword

Alfonse Borysewicz

I awoke to the news of another mass shooting in the United States, this time at a cinema. Once again, the news was met with outpourings of grief and shock, and with the same reluctance to engage with the questions that similar prior events had brought to the surface. Unfortunately this plague will be repeated soon enough in some other form and at some other place; it is just a matter of time. Until such time, Bernard Lonergan offers solace and a remedy for action as he persuades the reader to brave the journey in the odyssey of self-understanding: "[T]he desire to know is . . . the dynamic orientation manifested in questions for intelligence and for reflection."[1] It takes little effort and rational inquiry for the *why* questions, those questions that concern the sheer fact of evil, to reach the surface and, for many, to give voice to either blame or denial of God. Simone Weil says that it is "impossible to love God if one regards God as responsible for everything. Those who have attempted to do so and have revolted against God have been unwilling to appreciate the absurdity and the subtlety of the act of creation."[2]

And so the cry *tikkun olam*, to mend the world—a cry most responsibly shaped by that brand of divine love of which St. Paul speaks in the hymn of Philippians 2 wherein "Christ reveals that God's power, indeed the triune nature, is made known to the world in the act of self-emptying."[3] Mother Teresa's Sisters of Charity demonstrated that self-emptying in a very real way for me. In 1979, when I was a young seminarian in Detroit,

1. Lonergan, *Insight*, 660.
2. Miles, *Simone Weil*, 36.
3. Fowl, *Philippians*, 96–97.

a city drowned in racial and economic distress, I met Mother Teresa as she arrived to open a house for her Sisters in an inner city parish where I lived and worked. My job was to paint the meager house in which her congregation would reside. I remember how she calmed the press down by her humble demeanor, speaking so quietly that they had to shut up to hear her. The more I reflect on this moment, the more I marvel at how her house in Detroit incarnated that self-emptying of which St Paul spoke. Is this much different from the moment narrated in the Gospel of John when Jesus met the Samaritan woman at the well? Our Savior meets the Samaritan woman and offers her first conversation and then nourishment. This is the well where artists and others now meet, where they can drink the beauty and truth of "God-with-us" and quiet the noise of lost cultures.

Almost a century ago, Robert Frost wrote of the arts: "The person who gets close enough to poetry, he is going to know more about the word belief than anybody else knows, even in religion nowadays."[4] Frost identified three types of belief. The first was self-belief: knowledge (and confidence) of oneself that he or she will bring themselves into fulfillment, into acceptance. Second, the belief in someone else: a relationship that will be brought into fulfillment (or contrary, into disappointment and failure). And, finally, a literary belief (or, we could add, a belief in painting, or music, or dance, etc.): "Every time a poem is written, a short story is written, it is written not by cunning, but by belief." Frost then proceeds to suggest that these three types of belief "are closely related to the God-belief, that the belief in God is a relationship you enter into with Him to bring about the future."[5] Is mending the world not in fact the gift of restoring the future to it, of bringing the future into a holy alliance with the past and the present through the act of belief given form in, among other human pursuits, the fine arts? Is not a work of art something that may invite one into the fullness of life—the gift of time, space and relationship? Is not that the meaning of the story of the woman with the alabaster jar at Bethany that Jonathan Ryan reflects on so insightfully in this volume? By pouring her perfume on the head of Jesus, this "waste" unites us to the reality of the moment with the pregnant possibility of the future.

4. Thompson, *Robert Frost*, 364.

5. Ibid., 365.

Image 1: Anselm Kiefer, *20 Jahre Einsamkeit* (1971–91) (1993). Mixed media, 380 x 490 x 405 cm. Marian Goodman Gallery, New York.

Almost twenty years ago I entered an exhibition of the German painter Anselm Kiefer. Packed to the ceiling of the Marian Goodman Gallery in New York were dozens of the artist's paintings, totally trashed with real but dead sunflowers squashed between them. Like the spectators in St Mark's account, I thought: "Why this waste?" (Mark 14:4)—such an assortment of worked paintings purposely destroyed and abandoned. But on closer inspection of Kiefer's *20 Jahre Einsamkeit (1971–91)*, I was awed by this abandonment that revealed a Nietzsche-like critique of our civilization that in turn opened the doors to the reality of grace. So Simone Weil: "Only by the supernatural working of grace can a soul pass through its own annihilation to the place where alone it can get the sort of attention which can attend to truth and to affliction. It is the same attention which listens to both of them. The name of this intense, pure, disinterested, gratuitous, generous attention is love."[6]

6. Miles, *Simone Weil*, 71–72.

The same "waste" question can be asked about the installation "Re membering" by Chinese artist Ai Weiwei. Using nine thousand backpacks on the museum's outside walls, Weiwei brought awareness of the thousands of school children killed in the 2008 Sichuan earthquake. The artist hears the cry of the victims and their lovers as they highlight the government's role in poorly-built school buildings and the corresponding cover up. And one recalls Yahweh's cry to Cain: "What have you done?" (Gen 4:9).

Image 2: Ai Weiwei, *Remembering* (2009). Backpacks. Haus der Kunst, Munich.

This same cry is taken up by the Dardenne Brothers in their film *Kid with the Bike*, and in "the effort of resurrection"[7] in Tarkovsky's film *The Sacrifice* in which a once silent "Little Man" discovers his voice. At the end of the movie, as his father is being taken away in an ambulance, "Little Man" is found beneath the dead tree with his watering can, asking: "In the beginning was the Word. Why is that, Papa?"

Tarkovsky's answer comes in the accompanying music of Bach's St Matthew Passion—an Epiphany is at hand. We will not be alone, we will not be abandoned. As Karl Barth insists, God will "transform the reality of the creature, in a transformation which includes death, dissolution and new creation, but He will not destroy it; He will not take it away again. He will never be alone again as He was before creation. Nor will the creature be again as it was prior to creation."[8]

7. Turovskaya, *Tarkovsky*, 149.

8. Barth, *CD* 3/1, 43.

The contributors to this book seek to stay alive between the questions and the answer. They have labored to offer us their reflections on realities that have been made and that are still being made anew. The result is a prayer to stir us awake. We need such books.

Bibliography

Barth, Karl. *Church Dogmatics 3/1: The Doctrine of Creation*. Edited by G. W. Bromiley and T. F. Torrance. Translated by J. W. Edwards, O. Bussey, and H. Knight. Edinburgh: T. & T. Clark, 1958.

Fowl, Stephen E. *Philippians*. Grand Rapids: Eerdmans, 2005.

Lonergan, Bernard. *Insight: A Study of Human Understanding*. Collected Works of Bernard Lonergan 3. Toronto: University of Toronto Press, 1992.

Miles, Sian. *Simone Weil: An Anthology*. New York: Grove, 1986.

Thompson, Lawrence R. *Robert Frost: The Years of Triumph, 1915–1938*. New York: Holt, Rinehart & Winston, 1970.

Turovskaya, Maya. *Tarkovsky: Cinema as Poetry*. London: Faber & Faber, 1989.

Preface

This book first emerged out of a stimulating symposium and art exhibition purposed to explore the theme of *tikkun olam*, and grew to include some further contributions from those with an interest in the subject. The initial conversations were the collaborative brainchild of Murray Rae, Joanna Osborne, Peter and Jessica Crothall, Kevin Ward, and myself and were engaged in with that intensity of enthusiasm and grace dreamt of by every conference organizer and exhibition curator. The symposium and exhibition were made possible by the support of the Department of Theology and Religion of the University of Otago, the Knox Centre for Ministry and Leadership, the Temple Gallery, and by a refreshingly heterodox "congregation" of artists and theologians. I am grateful to Mike Crowl, Catherine van Dorp, Chris Green, André Muller, Jill Pope, and Graham Redding who were kind enough to cast their eyes over and to offer constructive suggestions about various parts of the manuscript.

Jason Goroncy
Dunedin

Introduction

Jason Goroncy

Mise-en-scene

In W. H. Auden's poem, "In Memory of W. B. Yeats," written in February 1939 just a month after Yeats's passing, we read:

> You were silly like us; your gift survived it all:
> The parish of rich women, physical decay,
> Yourself. Mad Ireland hurt you into poetry.
> Now Ireland has her madness and her weather still,
> For poetry makes nothing happen: it survives
> In the valley of its making where executives
> Would never want to tamper, flows on south
> From ranches of isolation and the busy griefs,
> Raw towns that we believe and die in; it survives,
> A way of happening, a mouth.
> . . .
> Follow, poet, follow right
> To the bottom of the night.
> With your unconstraining voice
> Still persuade us to rejoice.
>
> With the farming of a verse
> Make a vineyard of the curse,
> Sing of human unsuccess
> In a rapture of distress;
>
> In the desert of the heart
> Let the healing fountain start,
> In the prison of his days
> Teach the free man how to praise.[1]

1. Auden, "In Memory of W. B. Yeats," 82–83.

Here Auden suggests that among poetry's gifts—gifts that poets, and other artists too, are not infrequently "hurt . . . into" from "ranches of isolation and the busy griefs"—is a proclivity to bear witness to how things are and not merely to how they might appear to be. Such a proclivity involves a telling of the truth about those largely untampered-with and untraversed spaces of our world, about what is present but underexposed or disregarded, and even, Auden hints, to lead with "unconstraining voice" the way toward healing and toward a renewed sense of enchantment, freedom and praise beyond the pedestrian and clamorous. It seems too, to press further, that among poetry's concerns, as Rowan Williams reminds us, is not so much a "celebratory sense of being at home in the world," but rather an "acute awareness of the world not being at home in itself,"[2] an awareness about which the responsible artist has a marked sense of personal complicity. The world, in other words, is dislocated. And artists, like theologians and other endangered species, are called to "survive" in order to speak responsibly to that dislocation, to speak with fidelity not only to time but also to eternity, and to acknowledge the meaningful relation of both to human being in the world and, in so doing, dignify the human condition.

"The serious artist," writes Williams,

> should easily comprehend the passion with which Job turns away from the neat, facile explanations, solutions and evaluations which his comforters import into his disordered experience. The brutal and overwhelming monologue which Yahweh addresses to Job and his friends is essentially a long statement of the utter alienness and inaccessibility of the order of the world to the mind of [human beings], the impossibility of an ordered linguistic picture of it. If there are things which God alone sees ("Where were you when I laid the foundations of the earth?"), how can speech about them ever be possible? The morning stars and the sons of God who stand at the creator's side are entitled to their shouts of joy at the world; but [humanity] is not so graced. Can you draw out leviathan with a hook? can you harness the monsters? Then the extraordinary volte-face: let Job intercede for his friends, because he has "spoken well of me," and they have not. Job, with savage persistence, has demanded justice, vindication, *justificatio*, but he has not looked for it *in* the world, in the language of [human beings]. God is not a [human] who can give a conversational reply (9.32), yet Job continues to demand an answer; he refuses both resignation to the world as it is, and facile justification of the world

2. Williams, "Poetic and Religious Imagination," 178.

> as it is, because his instinctive and most basic conviction is that "the world is not enough" . . . Mere resignation is a betrayal; structuring and explanation is a blasphemy. What is left, then, if the world is neither to be accepted nor to be rationalized? What remains is Job's *protest.* Job understands his experience as a question which can only be answered with more questions. His world is not a complete structure to which there can be only a passive response, nor is it a problem to which he, his consciousness, is the solution. It is a disordered flux within which he has to find a place; but this finding of a place . . . is also to adopt a "position," in every sense: to make an *option* about reality, to be committed to a "direction" (not an explanation . . .) of and in the world.[3]

This volume is precisely about making such a commitment—to explore what might be involved in making such an "*option* about reality"; what it is, in Gillian Rose's sense, to stake one's self in the anxiety and equivocation of the "broken middle"[4] and resist false and premature endeavors to heal or resolve or bring into harmony the sheer "brokenness" of the human situation, or to struggle toward a vision of the wholeness of a contradictory space, of a world which, the Christian community claims, is in need of repair, a world that is finally impotent at self-repair, but a world that is, all the same, the stage for "the most real of all events"[5]—the cruciform actuality upon which history hangs—the drama of love's ambition, amongst the contradictions of the world, to heal, a story toward which all human beings, precisely in their fragility and ambiguity, are called to bear witness.

And here we face a hurdle of which Bill Dyrness reminds us in this volume, and of which Flannery O'Connor also spoke; namely, that "there is a certain embarrassment about being a storyteller in these times when stories are considered not quite as satisfying as statements and statements not quite as satisfying as statistics." However, as O'Connor goes on to articulate, "in the long run, a people is known, not by its statements or its statistics, but by the stories it tells."[6] And so the dogged persistence of theologians and artists whose critical dialogue together in a mode of both deductive *and* inductive convergence (convergence not unlike that undertaken, for example, in Christoph Poppen's and The Hilliard Ensemble's extraordinary

3. Ibid., 178–79.

4. Rose, *The Broken Middle.*

5. Balthasar, "Church as Catholica," 244.

6. O'Connor, *Mystery and Manners*, 192.

performance of J. S. Bach's *Ciaccona for violin and four voices* [BWV 1004 ought to be concerned not with synthesis but with what Hans-Georg Ga damer famously refers to as an opening of "horizons" of meaning, the acquisition of such means that "one learns to look beyond what is close at hand—not in order to look away from it, but to see it better within a larger whole and in truer proportion."[8] So too T. S. Eliot: "To understand anything is to understand from a point of view."[9] In this sense, both artists and theologians are engaged in projects shot through with eschatology. By this I understand that both vocations are concerned with the opening up of "the new meaning which is to come to them in the future, and also in being 'seriously' open to the horizon which death gives to life."[10]

Paul Fiddes enucleates how this dialogue works in the interchanges that occur between creative writers (and the points made can be extended to all fields of human artistry) and systematic theologians, describing a "relationship of mutual influence without confusion, where the images and narratives of literature can help the theologian to make doctrinal state ments." Conversely, more intentionally doctrinal thinking is able to gift perspectives for the critical reading of literary texts. This is not to make obscure the fact that fundamental differences between these two voca tions remain—that poetic metaphor and narrative, for example, rejoice in "ambiguity and the opening up of multiple meaning," whereas the work of systematic theologians will tend, to various degrees, to concern itself with some reduction toward concepts of the images and stories upon which it draws.

> Literature emphasizes the playful freedom of imagination, while doctrine aims to create a consistent and coherent system of thought, putting into concepts the wholeness of reality that imagination is feeling after. Of course, doctrinal statements are bound to go on using symbol and metaphor since it is not possible to do without analogies in speaking of God as infinite and transcendent Reality . . . In short, literature tends to openness and doctrine to

7. Christoph Poppen and The Hilliard Ensemble, "Ciaccona für Violine."

8. Gadamer, *Truth and Method*, 272. Similarly, N. T. Wright, in thinking about some music, describes the opening up of "hermeneutic space"—a necessity, Wright suggests, "for people whose minds are so closed by secularism that they just literally cannot imag ine any other way of the world being." Wright, "Jesus, the Cross and the Power of God," n.p.

9. Eliot, "Imperfect Critics," 38.

10. Fiddes, *Promised End*, 6.

> closure. However, because no doctrine can be absolute or final, it needs to be constantly broken open by the impact of image and story in changing times and situations. Creative literature can also help the theologian in deciding between various options of interpretation; there are alternative ways in which the multiple meanings of the metaphors and stories of faith might be fenced around by concepts, and imaginative writing can enable the theologian to make judgements.[11]

Conversely, the Christian story can gift the reader and author of literary texts with a perspective for interpretation—"the innocent eye sees nothing."[12] While not imputing or second-guessing the religious intentions or otherwise of the artist, efforts by theologians to achieve a lucid understanding of the patterns and ranges of human experience can both heighten and deepen our sensitivity to aspects of experience within and beyond the work that one might otherwise fail to notice.

Certainly, this collection of essays was birthed upon the premise that artists and theologians can help us to see and hear better. As respondents to revelation, artists can draw attention to the order of things, and to their disorder. They can heighten our alertness to the world's beauty; they can present us with its simplicity, and confront us with its tragedy—this does not, of course, mean that such a dialogue is to be entered into for purely pragmatic reasons, to, in Iris Murdoch's words, be "seized and used" and "appropriated into the greedy organism of the self."[13] And certainly now and again the work of artists becomes something more. Like all human

11. Ibid., 7. Fiddes's use of the word "tends" is important here. Much recent work on Nicaea, for instance, would seem to suggest that any absolutizing of the claim that doctrine *per se* closes down the discourse of imagination is in danger of distorting the character of doctrinal statements. The *homoousion*, for example, is not in danger of closing down discourse, saved only by an appeal to "image and story in changing times and situations." See, for example, Williams, *Arius*; Ayres, *Nicaea and Its Legacy*; and Coakley, "What Does Chalcedon Solve," 143–63. Still, the tendency that Fiddes is highlighting here is real. Moreover, in some cases, the verbs employed here by Fiddes to draw the distinction between "literature" and "doctrine" are reversed; that is, literature may tend to closure, and doctrine to openness.

12. Gombrich, *Art and Illusion*, 271.

13. Murdoch, *The Sovereignty of Good*, 65; cf. Arendt, "The Crisis in Culture," 208: "That the arts must be functional, that cathedrals fulfill a religious need of society, that a picture is born from the need for self-expression in the individual painter and that it is looked at because of a desire for self-perfection in the spectator, all these notions are so unconnected with art and historically so new that one is tempted simply to dismiss them as modern prejudices."

gestures toward the truth of things, the work of artists can become an instrument through which God calls for our attention.

Attentiveness to God is also the business of Christian theology. Christian theologians are those who bear witness to, and who help us to be attentive to, the self-disclosure of God. They also strive to see things again in light of that self-disclosure. For Christian theology, it is argued, is justified only upon the claim that divine revelation has sought us out, and continues to do so, and that such revelation has reached us. And because of the indispensably fleshly shape of that revelation, Christian theology has inevitably to do with human lives and human concerns and human stories and human hopes. Of course, insofar as both theology and art are activities of human making and events of human truth telling, they are as vulnerable to the conditions and operations of death that pervade the human scene as any other human activity.

Essays

The essays compiled in this volume, each in their own way, seek to attend to the lives and burdens and hopes that characterize human life in a world broken but unforgotten, in travail but moving toward the freedom promised by a faithful Creator. Bill Dyrness's essay focuses on the way that the medieval preference for fiction over history has been exactly reversed in the modern period so that we moderns struggle to make a story out of the multitude of facts. Employing Augustine's notion of signs as those which move the affections, the chapter develops the notion of poetics as the spaces in peoples' lives that allow them to keep living and hoping, suggesting one critical role that art can play in imagining another world, a better world. For art offers to carry us to another place, one that doesn't yet exist, and in this way offers hope and sustenance to carry people through the darkest times. This is illustrated by the outpouring of Haiku after the recent tsunami in Japan, or in the spaces made available for poetry in Iraq. Most importantly, it is underwritten by the centrality of lament in the biblical materials wherein we are reminded that lament and prophecy provide aesthetic forms that carry believers toward the future that God has planned for the world.

The essay by Trevor Hart considers the place of human "creativity" (artistic and other sorts) and seeks to situate it in relation to God's unique role as the Creator of the cosmos. It draws on literary texts by Dorothy

Sayers and J. R. R. Tolkien, as well as theological currents from Jewish writers and Christian theologians, to offer a vision of human artistry as (in Tolkien's preferred phrase) "sub-creation," a responsible participation in a creative project divinely initiated, ordered, and underwritten, but left deliberately unfinished in order to solicit our active involvement and ownership of the outcomes.

Beauty, Hans Urs von Balthasar has suggested, is "a word from which religion, and theology in particular, have taken their leave and distanced themselves in modern times by a vigorous drawing of boundaries."[14] More recently, a number of theologians have addressed this distance and attempted to dismantle the boundaries widely assumed between certain Protestant theologies and the realm of the arts or aesthetics. In her essay, Carolyn Kelly seeks to contribute to that communal exploration by addressing the particularly imposing boundary line demarcating, on the one hand, Reformed affirmations of the beauty of *Truth* and, on the other, a Romantic commitment to the truth of *Beauty*. Kelly reflects on what Romantic and aesthetic "sensibility" might gain from its modern counterpart and, in turn, what Reformed theological "sense" might have to gain from a re-cognition of Beauty.

But what place is there for extravagant works of beauty in a world tarnished with the ugliness of poverty and injustice? This is a question taken up by Jonathan Ryan in his essay. Beginning with the recollection of the disciples' objection to an extravagant act of beauty retold in Mark 14:4, Ryan allows the "anointing at Bethany" narrative in Mark 14 to frame this question and to suggest the legitimacy—and necessity—of works of beauty and creativity for bearing witness to God's extravagant love for the world.

Libby Byrne's essay explores the premise that the artist's calling is to "live close to the wound." Locating this contention within the nexus that seems to exist between art, theology and philosophy, she argues that we are able to consider the prevailing conditions required for the artist to work toward the task of mending that which is broken, and, drawing on theory from Matthew Del Nevo and Rowan Williams, Byrne helps us understand the importance of melancholy and vulnerability in the sacramental work of human making. She provides examples of how this theory may work in practice with particular reference to the work of Anselm Kiefer and finally with her own studio practice, reminding us that it takes courage to choose to live and work close to our wounds, and also that by so doing the artist

14. Balthasar, *Glory of the Lord*, 17.

not only opens themselves to the possibility of transformation but also offers to others gifts that reverberate within the world and that call us to healing and wholeness.

New Zealand artists Allie Eagle and Joanna Osborne discuss the *den Imperative*, Eagle's art project that reframes much of the ideology she held as a feminist separatist during the 1970s. They also outline a reappraisal of direction and motivation in Eagle's thinking and highlight the theological and reconciliatory center of her current art practice.

Murray Rae takes up the question posed by Theodor Adorno following the Jewish Holocaust and considers whether art can have anything at all to say in the face of evil or whether some evils might, in fact, be unspeakable. Through a consideration of architecture and, in particular, the work of Daniel Libeskind at Ground Zero and in the Jewish Museum in Berlin, Rae contends that while architecture, along with the arts more generally, has no power to redeem us, much less to make amends, it can nevertheless give expression to our memories, our sorrow, and our penitence. He concludes that art may also reveal the extent to which the Spirit is at work within us, prompting us toward forgiveness and reconciliation and a true mending of the world.

In his essay on the Irish poet Seamus Heaney, John Dennison argues that one of the most notable—and least understood—aspects of Heaney's trust in the good of poetry and the arts in general is the way in which his account approximates religious faith. Some critics have been encouraged toward the conclusion that Heaney's poetics constitutes an active (if heterodox and often apophatic) extension of Christian theology through the arts. Most importantly here, John Desmond in his book *Gravity and Grace* argues that Heaney's writings assume certain fundamentals that mark his transcendental cultural poetics as Christian. Central to Heaney's thought, Desmond insists, is the doctrine of the Incarnation. Christian doctrine, and in particular the doctrine of the Incarnation, is indeed central to understanding the character of Heaney's public commitment to the restorative function of art. But, Dennison argues, if we attend to the development and structures of Heaney's thought, we can see how this influential account of the arts' world-mending powers is not so much extensive with Christian soteriology as finally delimited by the biblical and theological descriptions it knowingly appropriates. It allows us to see, also, the degree to which Heaney's trust in the adequacy of poetry turns on a refracted after-image of Christian doctrine, particularly that of the Incarnation.

Julanne Clarke-Morris's offering proposes that multimedia worship and worship installations would benefit from a more consistent approach to aesthetics and context than is often the norm. She suggests that new media art forms offer communities of faith a range of ready-made critical practices that could amiably be brought to bear in the case of liturgical installation art. Seeking to draw attention to the coherence and communicative power of multimedia liturgical installations in order to improve both their accessibility and artistic credibility, she investigates some significant insights from virtual reality art, immersion art, multimedia installation art, and site-specific art as resources for preparing worship installations and assessing their effectiveness.

The closing essay, penned by Steven Guthrie, bears witness to ways in which Christian scripture and the Christian theological tradition both testify to a natural world that has a voice; one that not only speaks, but *sings*. The Hebrew prophet Isaiah speaks of mountains and hills "bursting forth in *song*" (Isaiah 55), and St John exiled on the island of Patmos listens with astonishment to "every creature in heaven and on earth and under the earth" *singing* (Revelation 5). This idea is taken up in turn by Augustine, Boethius and many others in the tradition, where it is often joined to the Pythagorean idea of "the music of the spheres." According to this tradition, all of creation comprises a finely tuned symphony, the combined voices of which articulate the Creator's praise. This tradition of thought—conceiving of the world as a *singing* creation—is a valuable resource for all who hope to faithfully care for God's world. The musical creation described by Augustine and other theologians is a beautiful and profoundly interconnected cosmos, filled with an astonishing harmony of human and non-human voices. In this universal song, humans have a vital but circumscribed role. Silence, song and harmony have the capacity to make us more—or less—fully aware of, and more—or less—responsive to the world we inhabit. Music may act as a kind of aural armor by which we shut out the voices of the creation and others who inhabit it. It may also be a weapon by which we dominate the surrounding space. Or music may be a schoolmaster from whom we learn attentiveness and responsiveness, and with which we might join with all creation to participate in God's symphonic work of healing the creation.

Leitmotif

Carolyn Kelly's contribution, "Re-forming Beauty," draws attention to the tradition's deep indebtment to the three-fold notion of the good, the beautiful, and the true, a notion articulated in Plato and given significant mileage in Thomas Aquinas. Of course, one may well question whether Aquinas's presentation of this trilogy—like Kant's after him—is too divorced from the particular form that the divine life assumes in the world, recalling that God's beauty is not the infinite *serenity* of God's life so much as it is the infinite *drama* of God's life, a drama which, as Jonathan Edwards so wonderfully articulated, draws attention to God's intrinsic plurality. God is beautiful, argues Edwards, precisely *because* God is Triune.[15]

And so it is perhaps not entirely odd that the twentieth century that witnessed something of a renaissance of interest in the doctrine of the Trinity simultaneously witnessed a widescale broadening of the notion of beauty in the discourse of aesthetics. Beauty was no longer understood in the narrow terms outlined by Kant and others, and it became rightly recognized as having to do with "the experience and perception of reality that we associate with the imagination and creativity, with metaphor and symbol, with games, playfulness, and friendship. The arts, whether fine or popular in all their manifold forms are central to aesthetics because they embody and express this dimension of experience, they evoke memories and suggest possibilities, thereby enabling us to see reality differently."[16]

Where beauty has been banished from contemporary aesthetic discourse it has largely been in "reaction to the aestheticism of those who pursued beauty for its own sake, a Romantic escapism oblivious to the ugly realities of a world gripped by oppression."[17] But movements birthed by reaction alone are doomed to fail; and anyway, any account of aesthetics that claims the name "Christian" will have to deal with the fact that the very centre of divine unveiling divulges that the beautiful and the ugly are not so easy to disentangle as we might first expect. Indeed, a Christian account of beauty can neither ignore nor offer an easy escape from evil and tragedy. So Susan Sontag's reminder that we are not merely "spectators of calamities." We are also sometimes complicit, sometimes victims, sometimes survivors;

15. See Jenson, *America's Theologian*, 15–22.

16. De Gruchy, "Holy Beauty," 14.

17. Ibid.

18. Sontag, *Regarding the Pain of Others*, 19.

actualities that are powerfully sounded, for example, by the "Xenakisian cluster glissandos"[19] provided by fifty-two strings in Krzysztof Penderecki's "Threnody to the Victims of Hiroshima." What a Christian account of beauty is concerned with is a story of human reality bathed in the light of God, of beauty experienced now as both interruptive promise and anticipation of what is coming. But it is also a story, as this assortment of essays seeks to remind us, in which the capacity to seek the justice of which the kingdom speaks and the commitment to beauty to which the kingdom directs us are not unrelated.

It is not, therefore, improper—indeed, it may be incumbent upon Christian theologians and artists—to approach the question of beauty through a consideration of its opposite, namely, ugliness. Indeed, it is sometimes the case, as Theodor Adorno observes, that "Art must take up the cause of that which is branded ugly. In so doing, art should not try to integrate or mitigate ugliness, or seek to reconcile it with its existence by employing humour, which is more repulsive than all the ugliness there is. Instead, art has to make use of the ugly in order to denounce the world that creates and recreates ugliness in its own image."[20] And John de Gruchy suggests that it is precisely the "protest against unjust ugliness that reinforces the value and significance of beauty as something potentially redemptive. Indeed, if aesthetics were just about the beautiful we would never really understand 'the dynamic life inherent in the concept of beauty.'"[21] One of the nineteenth century's greatest theologians, Fyodor Dostoevsky, famously reminds us that if ugliness has the capacity to destroy life, "beauty will save the world."[22] Dostoevsky invites us not only toward suspicion of the uncomplicated sanguinity of the merely cheerful creeds, but also to see the invitation toward theological aesthetics as about faith seeking to understand reality—in its ugly forms too—from the vista of the beauty of God revealed *primarily* in the bloodied wounds of the cross where all that is ugly is transfigured by a profundity of beauty.[23] Such beauty, as Karl Barth insists, "embraces death as well as life, fear as well as joy, what we might call the ugly as well as what we might call the beautiful."[24] To speak most

19. Griffiths, *Modern Music and After*, 146.

20. Adorno, *Aesthetic Theory*, 72.

21. De Gruchy, "Holy Beauty," 14. De Gruchy cites from Adorno, *Aesthetic Theory*, 75.

22. Dostoevsky, *The Idiot*, 356.

23. See Goroncy, "Bitter Tonic for our Time," 105–18; Goroncy, "Fighting Troll-Demons," 61–85.

24. Barth, *CD 2/1*, 665.

responsibly of beauty in its deepest reality is, in other words, to speak not just of any beauty, but rather of a very specific beauty. Indeed, it is beauty so specific that it goes by a particular name, Jesus Christ. Jesus Christ—who he is and what God does in him—is the very beauty of God.

Jesus Christ—who he is and what God does in him—is also the centerpiece and compass of Christian vocation, however fulfilled. Consequently, both art and theology properly seek to speak about what our eyes have seen, about what our ears have heard, about what our lips have tasted, and about what our hands have touched. And both are equally concerned with the matter of hope—about what our eyes hope to see, our ears hope to hear, our lips hope to taste, and our hands hope to touch. And both are concerned too to be attentive to the immediate, to what is, to those realities contemporary to our senses. So art and theology are fixed on a triple vision, as it were—of attention to what is behind and what is immediately before us and what is over the horizon—a vision grounded (whether acknowledged or not) in the peculiar history of God's own past, future, and contemporaneity. And art and theology seek to respond to that triple awareness in ways that resist the temptation to dissect the trialogue, and they keep asking—each in its own particular way and with its own particular tongue—what are the foundational questions for all being. Another way of saying this is to say that all human making is a taking up of what we might call an ethic of responsibility, an ethic that is most properly rooted in divine kenosis, in God's love for and God's service of others, is orientated toward a particular end or series of ends, and is strengthened by human *conversation community*.

That such a *conversation* as this volume is concerned to contribute to is even possible recalls that "God is [not] to be understood as having 'made something' and then wondered what to do with it; rather . . . from the first the creative purpose was one of profound and secure relationship."[25]
such a relationship is to be truly characterized by that brand of love familiar to the divine life, then its prime instigator will also create room for creation to be itself. In other words, divine love achieves its end not through brute force but by patient regard for the otherness of the other. To be sure, God never retreats from creation into some kind of self-imposed impotence; God remains unswervingly faithful, interested, and involved in all that goes on. But this is not to suggest that all is in order. And so Christians, when they speak of creation, will want to speak, as many physicists choose to do,

25. Etchells, *Model of Making*, 50.

not only of creation's *order* but also of its *disorder*, not only about its *being* but also about its *becoming*, and about the significant space that God grants the world, space that implies some risk, and that can neither be ignored nor annihilated if all there is is to be repaired.

On the matter of *community*, Flannery O'Connor reminds us that "When the Catholic novelist closes his own eyes and tries to see with the eyes of the Church, the result is another addition to that large body of pious trash for which we have so long been famous."[26] In a field narrowed by such an ecclesiolatrous vision, the Christian artist, O'Connor believes, sacrifices reality birthed and fostered through extra-ecclesial but no-less graced experience in favor of a sole voice very likely to soon sing out of key. She properly calls for an end to what she understands to be a false dichotomy while drawing attention to a genuine tension that is neither false nor one typically handled with due care. O'Connor's concern, however, is not here to dissolve this tension between what "the church" sees and what "the artist" sees. Rather, she wishes to understand the nature of the Christian artist's responsibility to look with both eyes, as it were.[27] Such is the vision that undergirds this volume—that is, to enquire what it might look like when two particular human vocations are concerned to achieve and communicate a wholeness of vision (where wholeness is understood in ways not necessarily devoid of or resistant to contradiction, as we have already noted) and to take a stand on such. This can only be done through one's willingness to look at what is there to see—and further, to what is not yet seen. Either way, we are talking about activities of hope.

To press even further, or perhaps to press backwards, I would still want to insist (with Paul Ricœur and others) upon a more pronounced expression of and commitment to communal (*ecclesial* and other) existence; that the artist, like the theologian—whether a prophet or not—does not carve out their own story *ex nihilo*, but rather works *both* at different levels of consciousness in the streams and side pools of narratives—and of that most basic of all Narratives—into which their existence and vocation have been gathered up and formed, *and* in a network of relationality in which

26. O'Connor, *Mystery and Manners*, 180.

27. Maritain is trumpeting an analogous (though not the same) melody when he writes: "Do not make the absurd attempt to sever in yourself the artist and the Christian. They are one, if you really *are* a Christian, and if your art is not isolated from your soul by some æsthetic system. But apply only the artist in you to the work in hand; precisely because they are one, the work will be as wholly of the one as of the other." Maritain, *Art and Scholasticism*, 70.

their existence and vocation find the kind of meaning that is both healing and abiding. There is an acute distinction between disregarding one's own eyes in favor of those of others alone, and not altogether abandoning the cloud of witnesses. The former posture is a denial of our being-as-responsible and our being-as-gift. The latter is a performance (understood in its positive sense) of proper humility, hope and love, and an act of faith born of the conviction that whenever Jesus comes to us he always tends to bring his friends along with him as well. In like vein, there is no art without community.

Thus from its very inception, the desire behind this project was to bring together practicing artists and theologians with some mutual interests to explore the theme of *tikkun olam*, an exploration that is both a confession that things are not right with the world, and an act of hope that things might be bettered, or even made new. *Tikkun olam* (lit. "repairing" or "mending" or "welfare" or "perfection" or "healing" of "the world") is a phrase first found in the Mishnah (*mip'nei tikkun ha-olam*, "for the sake of *tikkun* of the world"), and which then found revived voice over a millennium later in the sixteenth-century Kabbalist, Rabbi Isaac Ben Solomon Luria (1534–72). Luria believed that the Creator of all things, in deciding to create a world, drew in—contracted—the divine breath in order to make room for the creation coming into being.[28] Into this enlarged space, the Creator then set vessels and poured into them the radiance of the divine light; but the light was too brilliant for the vessels, causing them to shatter and scatter widely. Since then, the vocation given to human persons has consisted of picking up and of trying to mend or refashion the shards of creation.[29] Of course, one may well argue that this is a vocation that we al

28. This notion is not altogether foreign to the Christian tradition either. See, for example, Moltmann, *God in Creation*, 86–93.

29. Many post-holocaust expressions of *tikkun olam* have tended to associate the idea with the "struggle against all forms of prejudice and racism, ranging from anti-Semitism to homophobia" (Berger, *Children of Job*, 4), commitments that found expression, for example, in writers Julie Salamon (*White Lies*), Lev Raphael (*Dancing on Tisha B'Av* *Winter Eyes*) and Carol Ascher (*The Flood*), and in filmmakers Pierre Sauvage (*Weapons of the Spirit*), Myriam Abramowicz and Esther Hoffenberg (*As If It Were Yesterday* Rubinek (*So Many Miracles*), and Debbie Goodstein (*Voices from the Attic*). Following this trajectory, more contemporary employment of the notion of *tikkun olam* tends to identify it with pursuits related to social justice and environmentalism. See, for example, Shatz et al., *Tikkun Olam*; Bayme, *Jewish Arguments and Counterarguments*, Jacobs, *There Shall Be No Needy*, 37–40; Rosenblum, "Is Gaia Jewish?," 183–205; Troster, "Tikkun Olam and Environmental Restoration." Among Jewish scholars, there is not a little criticism aimed at such contemporary and clichéd usage of the term in concert

ways fail at, and that it is important that we do fail. Indeed, the worse thing would be to succeed here. So George Mackay Brown, in *Beside the Ocean of Time*: "We never find what we set our hearts on. We ought to be glad of that."[30] And yet we must stay awake and gesture toward that location where such mending is indeed as fully comprehensive as it is wholly surprising.

And this, of course, recalls one great limitation that both art and theology share—namely, the impossibility of absolute innovation. "To add to the world, to extend the world and its possibilities, the artist [like the theologian] has no option but to take his material from the world as it is."[31] Even our best attempts at liberation from words, from the determinations of human language and imaginings, can only carry us so far, as we are brought to what Rowan Williams calls "a complete imaginative void, the dark night of an utter alienation from the 'available' world, 'the desert of the heart.'"[32]

Still, this volume is premised on the conviction that artists, theologians and others have things to learn from one another, things about the complex interrelationality of life, and about a coherence of things given and sustained by One who desires that the creation itself participate—in ways uniquely fitted for creatures—in God's own continuing creative movement with the world toward possibilities yet unveiled but that will be characterized, if anything is certain, by a reality made well. This book occupies the space—space, in Luria's thought that was created by the divine contraction or "tzimtzum"—to reflect on whether the world, wounded as it is by war, by

with reformist ideologies and political programmes far removed from the liturgical life and practices of the tradition. See Kanarek, "What Does *Tikkun Olam* Actually Mean?," 15–22. More recently, Melissa Raphael has discussed the notion in terms of humans as both the subject and object of ethical decision. On the question of whether one can view the Holocaust itself as art, she speaks of "the exercise of the Holocaust imagination," of the possibility of holocaust images functioning as "petitionary prayers," and of "the phenomenon of reverent looking; the spectacle of responsive spectation that is, in a supra-material sense, beautiful." She continues: "It is not the holocaustal suffering itself nor the material images of it that are holy, but the viewer's moral and spiritual reception of the images. Suffering is not itself redemptive; redemption or mending (*tikkun*) occurs in the moments of the viewer's will to redeem or take back the agonized moment into the care and sanctuary of his or her own moment. The holiness of still or moving images of the Holocaust, then, is primarily in the response of the viewer to the image, in the quasi-familial recognition that passes from one person made in the image of God to another: a re-call to and of love" (Raphael, *Judaism and the Visual Image*, 119, 130–33).

30. Brown, *Beside the Ocean of Time*, 217.

31. Williams, "Poetic and Religious Imagination," 180.

32. Ibid., 181.

hatred, by exploitation, by neglect, and, with Novalis, "by reason,"[33] we must add, by human imagination—can be healed. Can there be repair? And can art and theology tell the truth of the world's woundedness and still speak of its hope?

Not a few scholars, practitioners, and critics are now talking about the sense in which art is concerned to transform created things, to improve creation, to add value to creation, to, in Auden's words, "make a vineyard of the curse." J. R. R. Tolkien, more than most, understood this well. His fairy stories, and indeed his entire project of *mythopoesis*, attest his concern to ennoble, challenge, and inspire; indeed, more than that, to heighten reality itself so as to invite us to look again at familiar things and to see them, as if for the first time. Jacques Maritain, too, once suggested that "Things are not only what they are. They ceaselessly pass beyond themselves, and give more than they have."[34] In other words, it is claimed that there is absolutely nothing passive going on when a portraitist picks up a piece of charcoal, or a rapper preaches his lyric, or a dancer performs Swan Lake. So, while his vision of the arts may have fallen well short of what many would hope to articulate, Abraham Kuyper was right to insist that art "discover[s] in those natural forms the order of the beautiful, and . . . produce[s] a beauti ful world that *transcends* the beautiful of nature."[35] And others, too, have spoken of the way that the arts contribute to the transformation of disor der, bearing witness to the belief that creation is not indispensable to God's liberating purposes for all that God has made, purposes that point not to a return to a paradise lost but to a creation made new, a making new that apprehends the reality of human artistry and that proceeds in the hope that both the location and the vocation of the children of God is inseparable from creation itself.

Appropriately, then, each of the essays gathered here is concerned with the matter of hope, recalling that creation in its entirety leans forward,

33. "Poetry heals the wounds inflicted by reason"; cited in Austin, *Explorations in Art*, 67. I am not here encouraging slipping into some of those fashionable (at least in the 1980s!) attempts to play off rationality against, let's say, imagination. While reason is certainly a kind of wounding, it arises out of a prior, nameless, anguish. What the tradition (philosophical and religious) does, however, is provide one with the language with which to talk about that nameless anguish. When one is aggrieved by a friend, for example, one might give up on the friendship, or one might re-negotiate its terms. Here I am arguing for the latter. We do not turn to art because reason has wounded the world. That would simply be to exchange one kind of univocity for another.

34. Maritain, *Creative Intuition*, 127.

35. Kuyper, "Calvinism and Art," 154; italics mine.

and that human persons are made responsible to nurture an eschatological imagination. Indeed, as George Steiner writes in his masterful book *Real Presences*, "In root distinction from the leaf, from the animal, man alone can construct and parse the grammar of hope."[36] Christian faith, in other words, is entirely commensurate with being human, for Christian faith is, at core, concerned to give voice to creation's living in suspense. It has both an eschatological orientation and an eschatological horizon and, as such, is appropriately concerned with hope seeking understanding—*spes quaerens intellectum*. And this is precisely why faith, reality, and the human imagination are not at odds with one another, but most properly *belong* together.

The Christian claim too is that the faith of the Church is "constituted by the correspondence of its *credenda* with harsh, human reality, and with the divine reality that met that human reality and was broken by it, only in that breaking to achieve its healing." The claim here is that the keystone and healing of creation—like the vertebrae that run through its entire history—is wholly dependent, as Donald MacKinnon has noted, not upon "the delicate subtlety of our imaginative interpretations that is constitutive of this penetration of our human lot" but upon "a deed done, an incarnating of the eternal in the stuff of human history."[37] As MacKinnon noted elsewhere:

> At its heart there lies the recognition that historical self-consciousness belongs to the very stuff of human existence, that freedom in the sense of a true autonomy is at once the foundation of our every effort to make sense of our inheritance; but that it is a freedom menaced all the time by forces, many but not all of which lie outside our control, facing us by the pressure of their ugly insistence upon our purposings with a sense of overmastering futility, defeat, even besetting cruelty. The threat is of something much more profound than that of Cartesian *malin genie* [evil genius], it is the menace of a backlash somehow built into the heart of things that will lay our sanity itself in ruins. We are face to face not with a grisly theodicy that allows historical greatness to provide its own moral order (there are more than hints of this in Hegel) but with a cussedness which seems totally recalcitrant to the logos of any justification of the ways of God to man. And here the last word is with the cry of redemption.[38]

36. Steiner, *Real Presences*, 56.

37. MacKinnon, "Lenin and Theology," 21–22.

38. MacKinnon, "Finality in Metaphysics, Ethics and Theology," 105–6.

To be superintended by the movement of divinely given precursors which are themselves echoes of the eucatastrophic action that lies at the centre of all life is to take up that cry of redemption onto one's own lips, to live in the light that beams from an empty sepulchre, and to stay awake for the healing of the world's continuing bitterness and brokenness in the face and place of the divine endurance. "Jesus will be in agony until the end of the world. There must be no sleeping during that time."[39]

39. Pascal, *Pensées*, 289.

Bibliography

Adorno, Theodor W. *Aesthetic Theory*. Edited by Gretel Adorno and Rolf Tiedemann. Translated by C. Lenhardt. London: Routledge, 1984.

Arendt, Hannah. "The Crisis in Culture: Its Social and Its Political Significance." In *Between Past and Future: Six Exercises in Political Thought*, 197–226. London: Faber & Faber, 1961.

Auden, Wystan Hugh. "In Memory of W. B. Yeats." In *Selected Poems*, 82–83. London: Faber & Faber, 1979.

Austin, Michael. *Explorations in Art, Theology and Imagination*. London: Equinox, 2005.

Ayres, Lewis. *Nicaea and Its Legacy: An Approach to Fourth-Century Trinitarian Theology*. Oxford: Oxford University Press, 2004.

Balthasar, Hans Urs von. *The Glory of the Lord: A Theological Aesthetics. Vol. 1: Seeing the Form*. Edited by Joseph Fessio and John Riches. Translated by Erasmo Leiva-Merikakis. San Francisco: Ignatius, 1982.

———. "Church as Catholica (I): Demonstration of Its Catholicity to the Religions and World Views." In *The von Balthasar Reader*, edited by Medard Kehl and Werner Löser, 240–46. New York: Crossroad, 1982.

Barth, Karl. *Church Dogmatics 2/1: The Doctrine of God*. Edited by G. W. Bromiley and T. F. Torrance. Translated by T. H. L. Parker et al. Edinburgh: T. & T. Clark, 1957.

Bayme, Steven. *Jewish Arguments and Counterarguments: Essays and Addresses*. Hoboken: KTAV, 2002.

Berger, Alan L. *Children of Job: American Second-Generation Witnesses to the Holocaust*. Albany: State University of New York Press, 1997.

Brown, George Mackay. *Beside the Ocean of Time*. London: Murray, 1994.

Coakley, Sarah. "What Does Chalcedon Solve and What Does it Not? Some Reflections of the Status and Meaning of the Chalcedonian 'Definition.'" In *The Incarnation*, edited by Stephen T. Davis et al., 143–63. Oxford: Oxford University Press, 2002.

De Gruchy, John W. "Holy Beauty: A Reformed Perspective on Aesthetics within a World of Ugly Injustice." In *Reformed Theology for the Third Christian Millennium: The 2001 Sprunt Lectures*, edited by Brian Albert Gerrish, 13–25. Louisville: Westminster John Knox, 2003.

Dostoevsky, Fyodor. *The Idiot*. Ware: Wordsworth, 1996.

Eliot, T. S. "Imperfect Critics: The Local Flavour." In *The Sacred Wood: Essays on Poetry and Criticism*, 17–46. London: Routledge, 1950.

Etchells, Ruth. *A Model of Making: Literary Criticism and its Theology*. Basingstoke: Marshall, Morgan & Scott, 1983.

Fiddes, Paul S. *The Promised End: Eschatology in Theology and Literature*. Oxford: Blackwell, 2000.

Gadamer, Hans-Georg. *Truth and Method*. Translated by Garrett Barden and John Cumming. New York: Crossroad, 1982.

Gombrich, E. H. *Art and Illusion: A Study in the Psychology of Pictorial Representation*. 5th ed. Oxford: Oxford University Press, 1983.

Goroncy, Jason A. "Bitter Tonic for our Time—Why the Church Needs the World: Peter Taylor Forsyth on Henrik Ibsen." *European Journal of Theology* 15, no. 2 (2006) 105–18.

———. "Fighting Troll-Demons in Vaults of the Mind and Heart—Art, Tragedy and Sacramentality: Some Observations from Ibsen, Forsyth and Dostoevsky." *Princeton Theological Review* 13, no. 1 (2007) 61–85.

Griffiths, Paul. *Modern Music and After*. 3rd ed. Oxford: Oxford University Press,

Jacobs, Jill. *There Shall Be No Needy: Pursuing Social Justice through Jewish Law and Tradition*. Woodstock: Jewish Lights, 2009.

Jenson, Robert W. *America's Theologian: A Recommendation of Jonathan Edwards* York: Oxford University Press, 1988.

Kanarek, Jane. "What Does *Tikkun Olam* Actually Mean?" In *Righteous Indignation: A Jewish Call for Justice*, edited by Or N. Rose, Jo Ellen Green Kaiser, and Margie Klein, 15–22. Woodstock: Jewish Lights, 2008.

Kuyper, Abraham. "Calvinism and Art." In *Lectures on Calvinism*, 142–70. Grand Rapids: Eerdmans, 1983.

MacKinnon, Donald M. "Finality in Metaphysics, Ethics and Theology." In *Explorations in Theology* 5, 99–115. London: SCM, 1979.

———. "Lenin and Theology." In *Explorations in Theology* 5, 11–29. London: SCM Press, 1979.

Maritain, Jacques. *Art and Scholasticism, With Other Essays*. Translated by J. F. Scanlan. London: Sheed & Ward, 1939.

———. *Creative Intuition in Art and Poetry*. 3rd ed. Bollingen Series: The A. W. Mellon Lectures in the Fine Arts. New York: Pantheon, 1955.

Moltmann, Jürgen. *God in Creation: A New Theology of Creation and the Spirit of God* Translated by Margaret Kohl. Minneapolis: Fortress, 1993.

Murdoch, Iris. *The Sovereignty of Good*. London: Routledge, 1970.

O'Connor, Flannery. *Mystery and Manners: Occasional Prose*. Edited by Sally Fitzgerald and Robert Fitzgerald. New York: Farrar, Straus & Giroux, 1969.

Pascal, Blaise. *Pensées*. Translated by A. J. Krailsheimer. London: Penguin, 1995.

Poppen, Christoph, and The Hilliard Ensemble. "Track 21: Ciaccona für Violine solo und vier Stimmen nach einer Analyse von Helga Thoene." In *Morimur*. Recorded September 2000. ECM Records 289 461 895–2, 2001, compact disc.

Raphael, Melissa. *Judaism and the Visual Image: A Jewish Theology of Art*. London: Continuum, 2009.

Rose, Gillian. *The Broken Middle: Out of Our Ancient Society*. Oxford: Blackwell,

Rosenblum, Eric. "Is Gaia Jewish? Finding a Framework for Radical Ecology in Traditional Judaism." In *Judaism and Environmental Ethics: A Reader*, edited by Martin D. Yaffe, 183–205. Lanham, MD: Lexington, 2001.

Shatz, David, et al., editors. *Tikkun Olam: Social Responsibility in Jewish Thought and Law* Orthodox Forum Series. Northvale: Aronson, 1997.

Sontag, Susan. *Regarding the Pain of Others*. New York: Farrax, Giroux, & Strauss,

Steiner, George. *Real Presences*. Chicago: University of Chicago Press, 1991.

Troster, Lawrence. "*Tikkun Olam* and Environmental Restoration: A Jewish Eco-Theology of Redemption," *Jewish Education News*, Fall 2008. Online: http://www.bjpa.org/Publications/downloadPublication.cfm?PublicationID=4759.

Williams, Rowan. *Arius: Heresy and Tradition*. 2nd ed. London: SCM, 2001.

———. "Poetic and Religious Imagination." *Theology* 80, no. 675 (1977) 178–87.

Wright, N. T. "Jesus, the Cross and the Power of God." Paper presented at European Leaders' Conference, Warsaw, 2006.

1

"Prophesy to these Dry Bones"

The Artist's Role in Healing the Earth

William Dyrness

Introduction

This has been quite a time to be alive: earthquakes, tsunamis, the Arab Spring, and nuclear meltdown, all played out against the background of long term climate change and increasing food shortages—mending the world appears more of a challenge than ever before. One might be tempted to think that art is the last thing we need to encourage. This is not the time to brew some coffee and write a poem; it's time for us to roll up our sleeves and get to work. I happen to think, however, that the theme chosen for this volume, long before all the tragedies of recent years, was providential and timely, and I think the theme provides ample leverage to fight off this defensive posture, and that is what I will try to do in this essay.

When our children were little there was one book that was a favorite: It was about Frederick, a mouse who loved colors and shapes. The other mice tolerated Frederick with condescending smiles, as he mussed about in colors and shapes while they were busy planting harvesting and preparing for winter. What good was he, they wondered? But Frederick was not discouraged; he found plenty to occupy his attention, he was busy with his colors and the textures he loved. All the other mice smiled: poor little Frederick. Perhaps you know the story, it is a good place for us to start.

What Really Matters?

This story raises for me a central question: What is it that really matters to people? To get at this let me turn to a more serious guide: Dante, the famous medieval theologian and poet. In his journey through the Inferno, Dante often encounters people he knows from Florence, right alongside mythical figures he has read about in classical poetry. There they are side by side in hell—my students and I have often puzzled over this. In climbing down to the seventh circle in the Inferno Canto XII, for example, Dante finds centaurs firing arrows at those who seek to escape their punishment. One of them, the mythical Nessus, who carried Deianira across a river and was shot by Heracles’s poisoned arrow, calls Dante and Virgil’s attention to Guy de Montfort, who avenged his father Simon’s death by murdering Henry, son of the Earl of Cornwall, in church. Dante describes these centaurs running around as “in the world above, they used to hunt” (*Inferno* 12.57), though he knows as well as anybody they never did run around in the world above.

Guy’s murderous deed, however, was, as we say, historical, and it earned him his place in hell. Yet, with a touch of irony, Dante has the centaur point out Guy to Dante and Virgil—the fictional fingers the historical.

What is going on here? How can myth occupy the same space as history, let alone illumine the historical? One source of this endorsement of fiction over history is Aristotle’s famous treatment of poetry. There the Philosopher differentiates between the poet and the historian in this way: “The one [historian] relates what has happened, the other [poet] what may happen. Poetry, therefore, is more philosophical and a higher thing than history: for poetry tends to express the universal, history the particular.”

You see: the poet describes what is universal, while the historian merely describes contingent events. If you put it this way, which one is superior?

We moderns are put off by this apparent confusion over truth and history—as if, during our journey through the afterlife, Raskolnikov appeared and pointed out Osama bin Laden to us! But what if, in fact, Raskolnikov might illumine bin Laden? You see what is implied: the universal truths, what I call poetic truth, might illumine our particular history. Dante and his contemporaries understood intuitively that a universal story, that is a narrative that encompasses the whole of humanity and its history, should guide our reading of the events of history. And for Dante there was no

1. Aristotle, *Poetics*, 17.

question that the story of God's actions in Israel and Christ, especially as these were mediated through the liturgical life of the Church, was the controlling universal story. But they were also convinced that other smaller stories could also embody universal truths; they could help fill in the details of God's universal saga. The incorporation of ancient mythology, Dante believed, could contribute to his spiritual aim, which was "to remove those living in this life from a state of misery, and to bring them to a state of happiness."[2] Along with the frequent citations of Scripture, and interpreted by that Scripture, this cultural wisdom, for Dante, could play a role in the pilgrim's journey to God.

But what I want us to notice is what has happened to us: for the modern reader, especially the Protestant Christian reader, this order has been exactly reversed—the historical has *supplanted* the poetic. I won't belabor all the steps in this process, nor suggest it is entirely mistaken. But what I want us to see is what has been lost in this development. The story has been lost—we struggle to fit all the facts, what we call data, into a meaningful narrative. My argument here is that we must retrieve the impulse behind Dante's construal of things: that the story, or what I prefer to call the poetics of life, is essential not only to bring the historical and literal to life, but also to arouse people to live that life. But why fiction? Why Poetry? Because art carries us in a way that history, by itself, cannot. The story, poetics, is what matters to people. As Paul Ricœur says, the world for him "is a set of references opened by every set of descriptive or poetic text I have ever read, interpreted or loved."[3] I still remember, for example, my first encounter with a great piece of literature. Someone recommended I read *Jude the Obscure* by Thomas Hardy. The next weekend was spent immersed in this story, and I cried as Jude lay dying while the graduation celebration that he had tried to become part of passed outside his house. I was shaped by the poetic.

This means that we cannot only look to the scientists to help us heal the earth, but also, and perhaps primarily, to artists. Indeed scientists themselves are increasingly recognizing the role of metaphor in their understanding. In a recent article on the interaction of genetic and environmental factors, Richard Lewontin, Professor of Zoology and Biology at Harvard University, noted how in the last twenty-five years, scientists "have considered how language, models and metaphors have had a determinative

2. Dante, "Epistola X," 202.

3. Ricœur, *Time and Narrative,* 1:80.

role in the construction of scientific explanation in biology."[4] So even the scientists have come to understand Aristotle's point: the ability of metaphor to illumine fact.

Enter the Artist

Here is where the role of the artist comes in. Artists deal with poetics—with language, models and metaphors; they dress the literal in colors, shapes and sounds so that it becomes attractive, engrossing. Let me develop a bit what I am calling "poetics." Another major source for Dante was St. Augustine who insisted that people are defined not by what they know or accomplish—things that promote pride—but by what (and who) they love. In his handbook for helping young monks interpret Scripture, *On Christian Teaching,* Augustine describes our life as a journey of the affections that is meant to bring us to our true homeland, found only in God. He argued that Scripture is full of signs that move us along in our journey. Then he expanded on this and argued that any sign that attracts our affections and moves us forward in our journey may be loved. But only for the sake of God—as he says all things are to be loved in God and God is to be loved in all things. So that we love signs (or what we call today "symbols") for how they move us. As he put it: "We love the means of transport only because of our destination."[5]

Artists traffic in signs—things that people love—and these can pro vide the means of transport of peoples' journey. Poetics describe all the parts of life that people love—the walks on the beach, the loving gesture of a friend, a Bach sonata, the things that carry us along in life, things we live for—and all the things the artist celebrates. Philip Sidney, in his famous de fense of poetry written in 1595, argued that the poet "ever sets virtue so out in her best colors . . . that one must be enamored of her."[6] But, in defending poetic practice, Sidney points out something that I want to emphasize: that Scripture itself is filled with poetry that figures forth to teach and delight. David's psalms are divine poems that "give a face to God," enabling readers

4. Lewontin, "It's even less in your genes," 23.
5. Augustine, *On Christian Teaching*, 27.
6. Sidney, *Miscellaneous Prose of Philip Sidney,* 90.
7. Ibid., 79.

to "see" God coming in majesty, or riding on the waves of the sea.[8] The images, moreover, go beyond teaching, Sidney thinks, to "entice" one to enter into the way of virtue.[9] Beside the Psalms, the Bible engages readers' imaginations in the parables of Jesus and in the elaborate visions of the Apostles and Prophets. The great events of Scripture are invariably clothed in color and light, from the growing light of creation through the cloud of fire in the wilderness, to the darkness of the cross and the tongues of fire at Pentecost, suggesting that these intend, not just to teach, but to spark delight or fear. These biblical precedents, especially in what is known as the wisdom tradition, suggest that poetic theology was part of God's intention all along.

As Sidney put it, some people do things with nature, the poet "doth grow in effect another nature." He makes things better or new, "freely ranging within the Zodiac of his own wit."[10] The artist can heal by growing another nature—but always by starting with the materials of this one, transforming them with the alchemy of art.

Where Does the Artist Start?

Artists start by paying attention, by loving what they find. Georges Rouault, the Catholic painter, on vacation exasperated his companions by taking hours on his walks, stopping to peer engrossed into a shop window, picking up something from the ground to examine it. As a friend put it, "Rouault thought with his hands and in the material, pondering with his eyes."[11] Thinking in the material! This means that artists pay special attention to God's creation, and find there inexhaustible riches. I think all great art starts with a great love—a love for the materials, the sounds, words, shapes, loving these by noticing, by paying attention. In Matthew 6, in urging his disciples not to worry, Jesus tells his disciples: "Consider the lilies, see how they grow." This is what Jesus means: Pay attention to how they grow. This takes time; it is not the work of one day or even a week (this is why artists and creative writers always look to outsiders like they are wasting a lot of time!). But it takes not only time, but a deep love for what is there. For

8. Ibid., 77.

9. Ibid., 92.

10. Ibid., 78.

11. See Dyrness, *Rouault*, 167–69.

in growing another nature, the poet has to love what is worth making—imagining, coloring and shaping. Jesus loved these things, which is why he could say: "I tell you, even Solomon in all his glory was not clothed like one of these lilies" (v. 29), and how much more will he care for you? Jesus wanted to do something special in the disciples' lives, and with our lives, that was akin to what he did making lilies!

Artists in my experience intuitively contrive to make something spe cial out of what they find, to make things special, to "redeem them"—even when they would deny the existence of some transcendent world, they want to create experiences beyond ordinary life. Indeed, a good example is to be seen in an incident from one of David Malouf's novels, *Harland's Half Acre*. The leading character, Frank Harland, grows up in the home of a poor farmer in Australia—his mother had died before he knew her. Inspired by his father's incredible ability to create real worlds in the stories he tells, Frank becomes an artist, drawing everything he saw and things he dreamed about.

As he learns the elements of drawing from a local artist who takes him under his wing, Malouf notes: "[Frank] was freed into discipline, then freed again into his old happy state of dreamlike self-discovery, but with a sure ness of touch in which the adventuring mind moved out into uncharted spaces, over horizons that were merely notional . . . with nothing to guide you at last but a firm hand, and the assured, all-risking, ever watchful and untiring spirit."[12]

Later when his work was becoming known, Frank comes to live with a musician named Knack. Knack likes Frank's work and would stand for long periods before it with hands behind his back as though looking out a window. Once while looking at a scene Frank had painted, he said:

> "I like this country you have painted, Frank. This *bit* of it. It is splendid. A place, I think for whole men and women, or so I see it—for the full man, even if there are no inhabitants as yet. Perhaps it is there I should have migrated."
>
> He gave a dark chuckle. It was one of his jests.
>
> "But it is *this* country," Frank said . . .
>
> Knack looked.
>
> "No, Frank, I don't think it is. Not yet anyway. It has not been discovered, this place. The people for it have not yet come into

12. Malouf, *Harland's Half Acre*, 39.

> existence, I think, or seen they could go there—that there is space and light enough—in *themselves*. And darkness. Only you have been there. You are the first."[13]

Frank had created another world—and yet it was this world. Notice the artist never leaves things the way she finds them; she wants to do something special with everything she touches. The musician does not just want to make a nice melody but, as Jeremy Begbie puts it, frame a melody that we didn't know to listen for! Or show us colors and shapes that we didn't know to look for, or language that shocks and delights. In other words, artists push us to see and hear what doesn't yet exist, but should.

But should! It is precisely here where the imagination—the dreaming of the artist—is indispensable. Bill Shore, in a new book on ending malaria around the world, argues that the most important tool that has been deployed in the fight against malaria is the ability to imagine its eradication. In fact the title of the book is *The Imagination of Unreasonable Men*. In the book, he credits Bill and Melinda Gates in the fight against malaria. What they have done that the NGO community has not done, he says, is to "fill the imagination gap . . . [A] vitally important space between the impractical and the impossible."[14] Melinda Gates had the courage to propose that we can end malaria; not believing this, Shore says, is, in part at least, a failure of the imagination.

Bill and Melinda Gates may or may not be motivated by specifically Christian motives, but historically there is only one source for such an audacious imagination: the Christian hope for the future. What gave them the moral energy to propose that we can end malaria is God's promise that one day there will be no life threatening diseases—the fact that God, like the artist, did not leave the world as he made it. As God says through the prophet Isaiah:

> I am about to create Jerusalem as a joy, and its people as a delight.
> I will rejoice in Jerusalem and delight in my people;
> No more shall the sound of weeping be heard in it,
> or the cry of distress . . .
> They shall not labor in vain or bear children for calamity;
> For they shall be offspring blessed by the Lord—
> and their descendants as well . . .
> The wolf and the lamb shall feed together,

13. Ibid., 116.

14. Shore, *The Imagination of Unreasonable Men*, 122.

> The lion shall eat straw like the ox;
> They shall not hurt or destroy on all my holy mountain,
> says the Lord. (Isa 65:19, 23–25)

Here is a world for the whole person. Not one artists discover in themselves, but one coming from God, this world, remade. The Christian imagination is shaped by this particular future—not some golden age in the past or some utopia that never existed and never will. But this detailed vision of a future God has planned for this world—for us and our world, not some other world. This vision allows us to doubt whatever everyone else believes and imagine what no one else has seen. It is into this vision of the future that we fit our understanding of art's ability to heal the earth.

I have been struck by the way the western tradition of art has been haunted by this vision of a better world and the role artists ought to play in its realization. There is a recurring belief that artists should play a key role in remaking society. In the early nineteenth century Saint-Simon and Proudhon in France argued that art can be the engine of a new social order, and that artists should be seen as the new priests. Pierre-Joseph Proudhon foresaw creative activity as gradually entering the world and creatively remaking it. The critic Charles Baudelaire believed this so strongly that he was convinced that if art was useless, so was life—all was blackness without art. In the twentieth century, Kasimir Malevich shouted: "Let us seize the world from [the] hands of nature and build a new world belonging to man himself." And Piet Mondrian, speaking from his Dutch reformed background, believed that "one day the time will come when we shall be able to do without all the arts, as we know them now; beauty will have ripened into palpable reality. Humanity will not lose much by missing art."[15]

The question is where does such audacious hope come from? What led these artists to believe the world could be remade? In our tradition there is only one place. The fact is these are all working in the aftershocks of what G. K. Chesterton called the great blow against the backbone of history: the life, death and resurrection of Jesus the Christ.

Because Christians believe God has given us the preview, the down payment, of this new order in the resurrection of Jesus from the dead, we can have the audacity to imagine another world. I have been struck recently by Jesus' response to the death of Lazarus his friend as John remembers it in John 11. When Jesus hears the news of Lazarus's death, in the midst of his own grief, he tells Martha, "Your brother will rise again" (John

15. Quotations from Clark, *Image of the People*, 20.

25, 26). "Oh yes I suppose," Martha answers vaguely, "in the last day." Oh yes, in some other world. Then Jesus says, in effect, it is not some other world; it is this world that is being transformed. He says to Martha, "I am the resurrection and the life. Those who believe on me though they die, will live, and everyone who lives and believes in me will never die." This is the promise that echoes over every Christian grave, but Jesus does not end here. He turns to Martha (as he does to us) and asks: "Do you believe this?" Can you imagine resurrection?

As the poet Julia Esquivel writes:

> What keeps us from sleeping
> is that
> they have threatened us with resurrection
>
> Accompany us, then
> on this vigil
> and you will know
> how marvelous it is
> to live
> threatened with resurrection.[16]

This is why a Melinda Gates can imagine a day when malaria will be gone, because God says there will be such a day; Jesus says to us "I am the resurrection and the life." Can we imagine such a day?

Well, to be honest, not on most days. More often the artist feels like Ezekiel set down in the middle of the valley filled with dry bones. Carried to this barren valley full of bones by the spirit and asked to prophesy to the bones, Ezekiel writes: "[God] led me all around them. There were very many lying in the valley and they were very dry" (Ezek 37:2). Then God says to Ezekiel, as Jesus would to Martha, "Mortal, can these bones live?" Ezekiel says, "O Lord you know." So God says to Ezekiel, "Prophesy to these bones . . . thus says the Lord God to these bones: I will cause breath to enter you and you shall live" (vv. 4, 5). Notice, God will do it but Ezekiel bears the message: Prophesy to these dry bones. Ezekiel might have said: Come again? God, I have prophesied to all Israel by the river, they did not listen, now will these bones hear? Yes, prophesy to them. Say to them, "breath shall enter you and you shall live" (v. 5). They say, "Our bones are dried up and our hope is lost . . . therefore prophesy say to them: I am going to open your graves and bring you up from your graves" (vv. 11, 12). How can this

16. Esquivel, "They Have Threatened Us With Resurrection," 59–61.

be, Ezekiel surely wondered? "You will know that I, the Lord have spoken and acted" (v. 14).

Imagining that day animates our life and our art, it is wagering on resurrection, it is working with the grain of creation.

I know what you are thinking. We may be threatened by resurrection but we are also tormented by the face of suffering and the fact of death. Artists, like everyone, work in the shadow of earthquakes and violence, of the horrors of nature turning against us, of bodies that betray us and the valley of the shadow of death. How might artists respond to such challenges? How can art contribute to healing?

One way, the dominant way we see today, is to dispose of hope and let melancholy do its work. After all, nostalgia has its artistic uses. Melancholy and irony are everywhere in the arts today. A good example is the work of Colin Thubron who writes movingly about his secular pilgrimages along the Silk Road in North Asia. In his most recent book, *To a Mountain in Tibet*, he returns to the Tibetan sacred mountain (Mt Kailas) and writes about his journey. Though he has lost all faith, it is still the sacred that attracts him. He had recently watched his mother struggle for her last breath, and had not long before lost his twenty-one year old sister in an avalanche. In the book, an imaginary old merchant on the silk road questions Thubron: Why even in your sixties do you take these hard journeys? "What is this fascination with foreign religions? Is it because you've lost your own?" Thubron answers: "Now there are too many dead. Those you love take away part of you, the self you were with them. So the Pure Land seems beautiful in its way, but was lost."[17]

Beautiful but lost—still Thubron's travels and his creative work gives him space to carry on. It is in its own way a means of transport for him, though for him it is a journey without a homeland. Something similar happened in Japan after the recent tragedies. Quietly, two weeks after the disaster, while the horror still unfolded, there appeared in the mass circulation *Asahi Daily*, on page 14, in the spot that the paper devoted to poetry, something amazing, even healing. It was a haiku by Yoshikatzu Kurota:

> About the nuclear power plant
> too much detail I hear
> such unhappiness.

17. Cited in Iyer, "On the Sacred Mountain," 67.

Then there were more, soon a virtual torrent: Yasuharu You, 78, a Buddhist monk had written one commemorating his experience in the 2004 earthquake:

> It's cold and wet
> camping outdoors
> Aftershocks multiplying
> the misery.

He then followed up with this poem:

> Days of disaster
> I can never forget
> the cold and wet.

Murasaki Sagano submitted this tribute to her mother who died five days after the 2011 tsunami:

> Mother's pain
> into the spring sea
> her last sleep.

At the end of the article in our metropolitan paper with these haiku was the headline of another article: "Japan's government urges more residents near the damaged Fukushima to leave their homes."

The poetic gives space for us to go on living; we survive by making aesthetic sense of things. This becomes our mode of transport, it carries us through. But the Christian wants to go further, stubbornly looking through the darkness toward a particular future, often straining to make it out. And the question of Jesus rings in our ears: Do you believe this? About a month after the Japan tsunami, the Bach Collegium Japan, under the leadership of Masaaki Suzuki, performed the B Minor Mass at Carnegie Hall in New York City. Before the concert, Clive Gillinson, the Hall's director, when introducing the Collegium, recalled the earthquake, though no one needed a reminder; it was at the front of everyone's mind. But what did Bach have to say to such a disaster? Alex Ross, the music critic of the *New Yorker*, says in his review: "From the first colossally churning chords it was clear that Bach had heard the news in advance."[18] What was the news? Darkness, but also the ethereal chorus above the churning chords: "Christ, have mercy; Lord have mercy; Christ have mercy." And behind these there were echoes of other words: "I am the resurrection and the life."

18. Ross, "The Book of Bach," 86.

But Where Is God?

But there is something more specific that the Christian faith provides the artist besides hope and a future, which at times may contribute more than anything else: that is the Lament. The Lament is a liturgical form of prayer that takes God's promises seriously and asks why they are not visible. They make up a substantial portion of the psalms that were used in Israel's worship: most famously, Psalm 22, which Christ repeated in the cross:

> My God, My God why has thou forsaken me?
> Why are you so far from helping, from the words of my groaning?
> O my God, I cry by day, but you do not answer;
> And by night, but find no rest. (Ps 22:1–2)

What a strange form of worship. Why should our complaint about God's apparent indifference be a part of our prayer? And, in fact, these laments play little or no role in our contemporary worship. Kathleen Billman and Dan Migliore in their book on lament studied a range of modern liturgies and found that the Psalms of lament were consistently omitted in the Scripture readings, even when they formed part of the day's lectionary. But the lament, as a prominent part of Israel's worship, suggests that our cries for help are a necessary and appropriate part of our life with God. Without this, Billman and Migliore say, "there is no recognition of the real bondage and alienation of present reality . . . no genuine cry for deliverance, and no openness for new acts of God's grace."[19]

But for our purposes, here is the important point: At the end of the day, lament is a poetic category. Lament gives aesthetic form to both our dismay over suffering and our hope in God. As beauty is meant to move us toward God, so the lament shapes our prayers in a way that moves us toward connecting tragedy with God. It shapes our desperate cries into prayers for deliverance. I am always struck by the tendency people have to ask when tragedy strikes, "Where is God?" Many even want to blame God: "If God were good and all-powerful as people say, why can't these disasters be stopped? Why must the children die?" This complaint comes naturally to our lips. It is often made both by Christians and by people who have stopped believing in God (and given as the reason for a loss of faith). I believe there is something sound in this impulse, sometimes there are things so earthshaking, so incomprehensible, that only God can help. These

19. Billman and Migliore, *Rachel's Cry*, 126.

events seem somehow to direct our attention toward God. This is why the lament must become more a part of our active Christian imagination and our artists' vocabulary, for it is to God that we must direct our anguished cries. God does not only listen, but he has himself taken up these cries on the cross.

There is a beautiful passage near the end of Bo Caldwell's book *City of Tranquil Light*, which is the fictionalized story of her Mennonite grandparents who were missionaries to China. After twenty-five years of struggle and suffering, during which they lose an infant daughter Lily, Will and Katherine are forced to return to Southern California because of Katherine's declining health. With great sadness they leave their beloved city, filled with gratitude to God for the great joy they had known. Will becomes pastor of a Chinese church in Glendale, California, and watches as Katherine weakens and dies. Not long after, Will finds some words written in the bible Katherine read from each morning: "We often wait for God with hope. But sometimes we must wait for hope. When we don't feel hope we wait for it and it always comes." The date on the inscription was six months after their daughter's death. Will writes:

> From that night on I yielded to my sadness. I began to speak to God more forthrightly than I ever had in my life before, unburdening myself to Him, confiding in Him, questioning Him, even railing against Him. Doing so often made me ill at ease; a part of me feared my outbursts might cause God to distance Himself. But I continued to reveal myself to Him, and His presence became imbued with a fierceness I had never known, as though He were clinging to me as much as I was to Him. When the pain was great, I thanked Him for it. Not always sincerely, but I said the words and trusted that was enough.[20]

For Will, lament became a means of healing—"From that time on I began to heal," he says later. And Bo Caldwell's image of Will and Katherine carries us along so we feel we can join Will in his morning prayers, and "rise to meet the day and to praise my dear Lord, and to finish my course with joy."[21]

20. Caldwell, *City of Tranquil Life*, 274.

21. Ibid., 283.

Conclusion: The role of art in our healing

Lament is a sign that we are pursued both by the suffering of this world and by the hope of something better. It is one of the surest indications that these worlds—that of suffering and that of hope—belong together; one cannot be exchanged for the other. Modern artists are often homeless, adrift, holding on to whatever flotsam comes to hand. They struggle to make sense of their journey, unable to tell a proper story, and yet unable to resist the impulse to do so. They cannot give up the urge to see through the world to something beyond or beneath. And they embody their hope in poetic form, so though their rhythms carry us along, they do not heal.

You may remember the story of Frederick the artist mouse. It does not have a happy ending. Because dark days come to the community of mice, winter and famine set in, and they have to stay inside during the long cold days. But now, strangely, all Frederick's projects they thought a waste of time come into their own. For it is the colors and shapes that he stored away that gives them hope and brings joy into their lives. It becomes their means of transport, allowing them to make it through the long cold winter.

Meanwhile creation itself suggests there is more, St Paul says. It yearns for the revelation of this new country for which we all long, and which, as Malouf has Knack say, is a "place for whole men and women." But Scripture also insists, like Frank, it is *this* country. And this after all is the final secret of poetic theology—to have eyes to see through this painful country to the place where there is space and light enough, where we will live in God.

Artists cannot heal the earth, at least not on their own. But they can join with others in believing that communities can be restored, ecosystems renewed, and diseases can be fought. Their role is to provide the means of transport for these projects. But here is my final point: They can do this because God gives them hope, because the Spirit of the resurrected Jesus has been poured out on all flesh, all communities, all cultures. This gift is the key that unlocks our Christian poetics. For St Peter promises: "In the last days it will be, God declares, that I will pour out my Spirit on all flesh, and your sons and your daughters shall prophesy, and your young men shall see visions and your old men shall dream dreams" (Acts 2:17–
artists of faith endowed with the poetics of hope, and the poetics of lament, can carry us along, get us through, give us hope and a reason to believe in ourselves and the future—indeed with the touch of the Spirit they can be a means of healing.

Especially then in the darkness of our violent and hungry world the poetics is essential to our healing. Recently I heard an interview with a veteran of the Iraq war, Brian Turner, on National Public Radio.[22] Turner is poet and a veteran suffering from post traumatic stress, who has struggled for years to readjust to civilian life—watching for people walking behind him or crouching on overpasses. Finally, toward the end of the program, the interviewer said, "There is something that I have been wanting to ask: was it [the war in Iraq] worth it?" Turner answers: "No, I don't think so, and many Iraqis have told me this." Then he told another story. In the 1920s, during the British rule of Iraq, the government called on a British civilian to open a bookstore in Baghdad (which, by the way, is still open to this day). In this space, over the years, in special readings, modern poets—T. S. Eliot, Ezra Pound—were introduced. Because of this place, Turner found, the rich centuries old tradition of Arab verse in Iraq had been transformed and renewed. Today, Turner said, we have left behind scars of war, and spent shells, but where is the cultural conversation? Where, I am asking, is the poetics?

Here then is the artist's role in healing the earth: Prophesy to these dry bones.

22. "Morning Edition," KPCC, July 15, 2011, 8am, PDT.

Bibliography

Aristotle. *Poetics*. Translated by S. H. Butcher, Mineola: Dove, 1997.

Augustine. *On Christian Teaching*. Translated by R. P. H. Green, Oxford: Oxford University Press, 1997.

Billman, Kathleen D., and Daniel L. Migliore. *Rachel's Cry: Prayer of Lament and Rebirth of Hope*. Cleveland: United Church, 1999.

Caldwell, Bo. *City of Tranquil Life: A Novel*. New York: Holt, 2010.

Clark. T. J. *Image of the People*. Berkeley: University of California, 1999.

Dante. "Epistola X ('Inclyta vestrae Magnificentiae laus'): Letter to Can Grande della Scala." In *Dantis Alagherii Epistolae: The Letters of Dante*, translated and edited by Paget Toynbee, 160–211. Oxford: Clarendon, 1920.

Dyrness, William. *Rouault: A Vision of Suffering and Salvation*. Grand Rapids: Wm. B. Eerdmans, 1971.

Esquivel, Julia. "They Have Threatened Us With Resurrection." In *Threatened with Resurrection: Prayers and Poems from an Exiled Guatemalan*, 59–61. Elgin: Brethren, 1982.

Iyer, Pico. "On the Sacred Mountain." *NYRB*, April 7, 2011, 67.

Lewontin, Richard C. "It's even less in your genes." *NYRB*, May 26, 2011, 23.

Malouf, David. *Harland's Half Acre*. New York: Vintage, 1997.

Ricœur, Paul. *Time and Narrative*. Vol. 1. Translated by Kathleen McLaughlin and David Pellauer. Chicago: University of Chicago Press, 1984.

Ross, Alex. "The Book of Bach." *New Yorker*, April 11, 2011, 86.

Shore, Bill. *The Imagination of Unreasonable Men: Inspiration, Vision and Purpose in the Quest to End Malaria*. New York: Public Affairs, 2011.

Sidney, Philip. *Miscellaneous Prose of Philip Sidney*. Edited by K. Duncan-Jones and Jan van Dorsten. Oxford: Clarendon, 1973.

2

Cosmos, Kenosis, and Creativity

Trevor Hart

Unfinished Business

On 7 October 1936, Dorothy L. Sayers, a writer as yet acknowledged primarily for a string of successful murder mysteries, had received a letter from the organizers of the Canterbury Festival inviting her to write a play for their forthcoming 1937 event.[1] The invitation came both as a surprise and an honor. A surprise because, although she was in fact just about to take her first dramatic production to the stage (*Busman's Honeymoon*, co-written with Muriel St Clare Byrne, was cast and rehearsed in that same month, and had its opening night in mid-November[2]), this venture was not widely known about and Sayers's talent as a playwright was still effectively untried. An honor, because her immediate predecessors in writing for the Festival were anything but up-and-coming, let alone unknown and untested. In 1935 the event had been graced by T. S. Eliot's *Murder in the Cathedral*, and in 1936 by Charles Williams's *Thomas Cranmer of Canterbury*.[3]

1. A version of this essay also appears in Hart, *Between the Image and the Word*.

2. See Reynolds, *The Letters of Dorothy L. Sayers*, 1:401 (10 October 1936, to L. C. Kempson), 405 (14 November 1936, to Margaret Babington).

3. Williams appears to have suggested Sayers's name as his successor. According to

No wonder her response expressed initial caution on the grounds that the project was "rather out of my usual line."[4] Notwithstanding this fact, Sayers accepted the challenge.

In accordance with the Festival's theme that year (the celebration of artists and craftsmen), but wishing also to maintain its focus on the history of the Cathedral, Sayers selected for the plot of her drama events surrounding the rebuilding of the church's choir in the late twelfth century. protagonist was William of Sens, the French architect duly chosen by the Cathedral Chapter to undertake this work. Four years into an expensive but thus far successful renovation project, the historical William was seriously injured, falling from a cradle he himself had designed to facilitate installation of the keystone to the great arch. His body broken, the master craftsman was compelled to resign his commission, leaving his work unfinished, to be completed by others. Sayers locates the circumstances of this accident at the heart of her play, using it to explore some fundamental questions about the place of human "making" in God's scheme of things. Picking up on fragments of evidence provided by the contemporary chronicler, she characterizes William at first as a man whose spiritual qualifications for building the Lord's house are at best questionable. If, as the Cathedral Prior suggests, William's avarice, promiscuity and generous disregard for truth are at least offset by his evident skill and his passion to use it well, it is nonetheless *this* that is the occasion of his quite literal downfall. Immediately before the ascent that will maim him, Sayers places the following words on William's lips:

> We are the master-craftsmen, God and I—
> We understand one another. None, as I can,
> Can creep under the ribs of God, and feel
> His heart beat through those Six Days of Creation . . .
>
> . . . since all Heaven was not enough
> To share that triumph, He made His masterpiece,

Reynolds's biography, the two had certainly been in contact since 1935, and possibly earlier. As Reynolds notes earlier in her work, Sayers had in fact tried her hand at drama before, incorporating a short mystery play ("The Mocking of Christ") in her collection *Catholic Tales and Christian Songs*, and a letter written to *The New Witness* in January 1919 reveals that Williams had read this. See Reynolds, *Dorothy L. Sayers*, 98–101

4. Reynolds, *The Letters of Dorothy L. Sayers*, 1:401 (7 October 1936, to Margaret Babington).

5. The original choir had burned down in 1174. For the history see Mair, "The Choir Capitals of Canterbury Cathedral 1174–84," 56–66.

Man, that like God can call beauty from dust,
Order from chaos, and create new worlds
To praise their maker. Oh, but in making man
God over-reached Himself and gave away
His Godhead. He must now depend on man
For what man's brain, creative and divine
Can give Him. Man stands equal with Him now,
Partner and rival.[6]

In theological terms, this is a convenient summary of Promethean excess at its worst, and William compounds the tragic hubris further when, to the warning that such blasphemous sentiments may tempt God to strike him down, he responds: "He will not dare;/He knows that I am indispensable/To His work here."[7] This is, of course, a misplaced confidence, and only moments later the sword of the Archangel Michael cuts the rope on which William dangles precariously above the flagstones of the Cathedral floor, sending him plunging to his physical ruin, but (as it turns out) his spiritual redemption.

Having depicted the folly and outrage of William's theologically informed "aesthetic" and the nature of its outcomes, though, the drama does not proceed, as we might reasonably expect, to eschew the analogy and proposed correlation between divine and human modes of creativity that lies at the heart of it. Instead, it suggests provocatively that God, the great Master Architect of the cosmos (and so William's divine exemplar), has indeed placed himself in a circumstance where he needs human agents to complete the work begun in creation, albeit not quite in the manner that William self-importantly supposes. This, indeed, is the spiritual lesson that William is to learn through his fall and his subsequent inability to complete the masterwork he has begun. His initial proud refusal to relinquish a micro-managing, hands-on oversight of the precise shape "his" work will now take is redeemed when he finally grasps a theological truth lying at the heart of the doctrine of the incarnation—in becoming one of his own creatures, God himself has embraced humiliation, suffering, failure and death, leaving others behind to pick up his work and carry it forward.[8] Though it is not articulated in the dialogue, close at hand lies the idea that, far from

6. Sayers, *The Zeal of Thy House*, 69–70.

7. Ibid., 70. On William's "blasphemy," see Reynolds, *The Letters of Dorothy L. Sayers*, 2:14 (26 February 1937, to Laurence Irving).

8. See Sayers, *The Zeal of Thy House*, 99–100: "Not God Himself was indispensable,/ For lo! God died—and still His work goes on."

being the first moment of *kenosis* identifiable in God's dealings with the world, the incarnation should be understood as the most acute instance of a wider pattern beginning with the divine decision to create as such.[9] himself does not jealously exclude but actively conscripts the agency of others in the realization and redemption of his creative project, the drama enquires, how can any human maker be prepared to do less?

There is, of course, another story to be told about the incarnation, and one that it would be very dangerous to lose sight of. According to a soteriological tradition stretching from Irenæus of Lyons to Karl Barth and beyond, God has, precisely by taking flesh (thereby simultaneously earthing the Trinitarian dynamics of the life of God within the patterns of human history and drawing our humanity redemptively within the penumbra of his own existence), reversed the impact of sin and alienation upon our nature and so established a place within the creaturely sphere where already he dwells together with us in fellowship, so fulfilling by way of prolepsis the purpose of creation itself.[10] Put differently, in Christ God substitutes his own humanity for ours, and thus himself provides the free creaturely response in which creation comes to its intended goal and fulfillment. Nonetheless, the logic of this divine self-substitution is not to displace creaturely action altogether, but precisely to create a context in which, understood as a participation in Christ's own action through the Spirit, it may be undertaken freely and without fear of failure or falling short; in the peculiar "already-not yet" modality of human existence situated in between the incarnation and the eschatological consummation of all things, what has been achieved by God for us remains as yet to be worked out in, and with, and through us, and within this context there is much for us still to do, and no compromising of the integrity of our actions in doing it.

While, therefore, in William's hubris Sayers shows us the worst and most problematic aspects of the Humanism that emerged from the Renaissance, as Nicholas Wolterstorff notes, she does so finally not to damn the

9. The notion of creation entailing a voluntary self-limitation on God's part is especially prominent in forms of Kabbalistic mysticism influenced by Isaac Luria (1534 especially in the distinctive doctrine of *Tsimtsum* or divine concentration/contraction. See Scholem, *Major Trends in Jewish Mysticism*, 260–64. The idea also finds emphasis in strands of the Christian tradition, most recently in the work of Jürgen Moltmann. See Moltmann, *God in Creation*, 72–93.

10. This is the central idea of Barth's twofold insistence that the covenant between God and Israel fulfilled once for all in Jesus Christ is the internal basis of creation, and creation the external basis of the covenant. See Barth, *CD 3/1*, 94–329.

project but to seek its redemption by re-situating elements of it within a quite different religious and theological perspective.[11] In place of autonomous man, struggling nobly for artistic liberation amidst a rivalry with God, Sayers offers an alternative vision, of human artistry and craftsmanship—understood now in explicitly Christian theological terms—as at the very least a "spiritual" vocation equivalent to others ("William's devoted craftsmanship," she tells a correspondent, has "more of the true spirit of prayer than . . . self-righteous litanies"[12]), and at best as something much more besides. The play closes with a speech to the audience by the Archangel Michael, and in his words we find the first inkling of a theme to which Sayers would return and which she would work out more fully in her own mind over the next several years. Human making and craftsmanship, it suggests, is not a breach of divine copyright or set in deliberate counterpoise to God's own creative activity; rather, the basic structure of our human ways of engaging with the world "creatively" should be identified as a concrete vestige of and participation in God's own triune being, and as such the proper locus of that "image and likeness" of God in which our humanity is itself made: "For every work of creation is threefold, an earthly trinity/to match the heavenly."[13]

Grammars of Creation

Putative analogies between divine and human modes of making are all well and good, but, it might reasonably be objected, in Christian theology across the centuries the doctrine of creation has more typically been linked to the apprehension of God's radical ontological *otherness* from the world, and appealed to, indeed, in a manner taken as definitive of this vital gap. What differentiates "the heavens and the earth" or "all things, visible and invisible" from God most sharply in other words is precisely the fact of their *creatureliness*. God alone is "uncreated"; nothing else is or ever could be. Thus we find the categories of the doctrine of creation cross-fertilizing

11. See Wolterstorff, *Art in Action*, 67–69.

12. See Reynolds, *The Letters of Dorothy L. Sayers*, 2:47 (4 October 1937, to Father Herbert Kelly).

13. Sayers, *The Zeal of Thy House*, 110. The play closes with this speech which, although cut from the 1937 production to meet the strictures of prescribed length, was restored in subsequent performances and can be seen in retrospect to be pregnant with the seed that would grow into *The Mind of the Maker*.

naturally and properly with those of Trinitarian and incarnational theology in biblical and patristic thought. For those whose theological understanding was shaped by Second Temple Jewish monotheism, Richard Bauckham has recently argued, to speak of Christ in Pauline or Johannine fashion as participating directly in the creation of the cosmos (e.g., Col 1:15–John 1:3) was without further ado to include him scandalously within the "unique identity of the God of Israel."[14] Meanwhile, in the fourth century dispute over the precise status of the person of the Son of God, the creedal identification of Christ as the one by whom "all things were made" and the concomitant insistence that, being of one substance with the Father, he himself is "begotten, not made," was taken to be a clinching argument against the Arians. In each case, the relevant theological premise taken for granted is that God alone is uncreated, and God alone creates in the relevant sense.

What, then, is the relevant sense? What is it that only God has done and is capable of doing? Most fundamentally, in this context the term refers to the divine donation of existence as such where otherwise there was neither scope nor possibility for it, an act of absolute origination necessarily unparalleled within the creaturely order itself. Thus, for Aquinas, "God's proper effect in creating is . . . existence *tout court*."[15] Here, the philosopher's "interrogation of the ontological"[16]—"Why is there not nothing?—finds a response reaching beyond the categories of philosophical ontology alone and drawing explicitly on the resources of a theology of grace. There is "not nothing" because God freely grants something *esse* alongside himself and invites it to "be with him"; in doing so, furthermore, God establishes a "primordial plenitude"[17] of meaning and possibility, an orderly habitation fit for human (and other sentient creaturely) indwelling and flourishing. All this, of course, bespeaks the radical transcendence of God with respect to the cosmos, and its concomitant dependence on him not just for its inception but for its continuing moment-to-moment existence. Furthermore, what distinguishes "creation proper," Colin Gunton argues, is its status as something done and dusted "in the beginning," the necessary presupposition of historical existence rather than a feature of it. What remains, he

14. Bauckham, *Jesus and the God of Israel*, 18; cf. p. 26f.

15. Aquinas, *ST*, 1a.45, 4.

16. Steiner, *Grammars of Creation*, 32.

17. I owe this phrase to Michael Northcott.

insists, is not "more creation, but simply what creator and creature alike and together make of what has been made."[18]

All this being so, it is unsurprising that the linguistic trespass whereby Renaissance humanists transplanted *creare*, *creator* and *creatio* from the hallowed ground of Christian liturgy and doctrine (which hitherto had been their sole preserve) onto the soils of art historical and art theoretical description in the sixteenth century—to refer now not to divine but to fully human activities and accomplishments—occasioned considerable nervousness at the time, and has ever since aroused protest in some theological quarters. The semantic fields of "creation," George Steiner notes, overlap and interfere,[19] and those who borrow and try the term on for size in whatever human context situate themselves and their actions of "making," whether knowingly or not, in relation to divine precedent. Even in the past fifty years or so, when the metaphor has spread well beyond the reach of aesthetics into fields as varied as hairstyling, pedagogy, economics, technology and the media,[20] and fully aware that the lexical genie cannot now be put back in the bottle, some Christian authors have advocated a strategy of counter-cultural resistance, refusing in principle to sanction use of the term "creation" for anything other than a particular sort of "act of God" and its outputs, or at least interjecting whenever occasion permits (and we remember to do so) that, in the strict and proper sense, "finite agents do not create"[21] (they merely "make," or "invent," or whatever).

While such theological concerns and emphases are important, though, there is more yet to be said about "creating" and the "presumption of affinity"[22] involved in wider uses of the relevant vocabulary. As Gunton himself admits, if divine creating is indeed an action situated properly within the grammar of the perfect tense (God always *has* created), there is nonetheless a vital sense in which "creation" itself (the output of that action)[23] remains incomplete and a work very much still in progress.[24] In

18. Gunton, *The Triune Creator*, 89. Gunton draws directly here on the account provided in O'Donovan, *Resurrection and Moral Order*, chapters 2–3.

19. Steiner, *Grammars of Creation*, 17.

20. See, e.g., Florida, *The Rise of the Creative Class*.

21. Gunton, *The Triune Creator*, 1n2.

22. Steiner, *Grammars of Creation*, 18.

23. Gunton reminds us that the term "creation," whether applied to God or human agents, tends to be used in a dual sense, to refer both to the action of "creating" and the thing duly "created." Gunton, *The Triune Creator*, 1.

24. Ibid., 88–89.

the Genesis narrative the advent of the seventh day marks a fire-break in the characterization of the divine action, a point in time by which certain things are already established and "given," and beyond which they need not be repeated or modified. The world is now "finished" (Gen 2 asmuch as it is ready for immediate occupation, and after this, Pannen berg suggests, in a fundamental sense, God "does not bring forth any new creatures."[25] Wherever in pre-history we imagine this point in time to have arisen, though (in the text it is only with the appearance on the scene of hu man beings), it is clear that in another equally fundamental sense all this is as yet only the beginning of "God's project,"[26] not its divinely intended end. The fulfillment of God's "creative" labors, shaping and reshaping a world fit for human and divine cohabitation (see, e.g., Rev 21:3–5), must therefore be traced not in protology, but in an eschatology christologically and sote riologically determined and orientated.[27] While we may still wish to insist upon reserving talk of "creation proper" for a particular set of precise and technical theological uses, therefore, it is nonetheless clear that the term has a penumbra already gesturing toward the possibility of a wider and extended set of uses, even within the grammar of theology itself.

The shape of the biblical witness to creation is entirely consonant with this semantic overspill. Hebrew possesses no single term covering the range of meanings of the English "creation," and while the Hebrew poets certainly take trouble to demarcate some lexical holy ground that must never be trespassed upon (the singular verb *bārā'* being set apart from the wider imaginative field to name a unique and non-transferable activity of "cre ation proper"[28]), their witness to God's primordial performance equally re sists reduction to any "single or simple articulation" of the matter.[29] Instead, the writers deploy a string of different verbal images to describe some, at least, of what occurs "creatively" during the first six days (shaping, making, forming, commanding, etc.), these being by definition suggestive of human

25. Pannenberg, *Systematic Theology, Vol.* 2, 36. Cf. Barth, *CD 3/1*, 182.

26. Gunton, *The Triune Creator*, 202.

27. It is on these grounds that Barth interprets the divine judgment in Gen as a valediction but as an ordination. All that God has made is pronounced "very good" for the accomplishment of creation's intended goal in the fulfillment of the covenant in Christ. See Barth, *CD 3/1*, 212–13.

28. So Brueggemann, *Theology of the Old Testament*, 148–49. For instances see Ber nhardt, "bārā,'" 246; Koehler and Baumgartner, *The Hebrew and Aramaic Lexicon of the Old Testament*, 153–54.

29. Brueggemann, *Theology of the Old Testament*, 149.

or other creaturely analogy. Moreover, recent work by Brown, Fretheim, Levenson and Welker has urged that, if we would be faithful to the imaginative logic of the biblical text here and elsewhere, we must recognize arising within it quite naturally the suggestion that aspects of God's fashioning of the cosmos are not only analogous to but actually conscript and demand the participation of creaturely forces and agencies as such.[30] The God of Scripture, Brown suggests provocatively, is no jealous guardian of his own "creative" prerogatives, but one whose work as Creator is—by virtue of his own choosing and self-limiting—ultimately achieved *per collaborationi*.[31]

Such poetic suggestion concurs, of course, with what we now understand of the shaping of the material cosmos, an understanding no longer tolerating imaginative confinement of it to a single working week situated "in the beginning." Whatever we may suppose about the temporal status of the primal act of incipience granting *esse* charged with meaning and potential to all things (including, Augustine reminds us, the structuring function of creaturely time itself[32]), several centuries of learning in physics, geology and biology serve to assure us that the work of forming a physical cosmos fit for human indwelling is one which, precisely insofar as it harnesses and involves the created capacities embedded within the cosmos itself, cannot be hurried but takes a long time. Again, wherever we locate the advent of creation's seventh day, to the best of our knowledge those same creaturely forces and processes are ones that rumble on beyond it, possessed of an abiding remit, a temporal future as well as a murky pre-historic past. Correspondingly, many of the biblical images used to picture God's ancient forming of the cosmos are extended perfectly naturally to picture his hand still at work, shaping the world's history and moving it toward its promised future.[33]

30. See, e.g., Brown, *The Ethos of the Cosmos*, 36–52; Fretheim, *God and World in the Old Testament*; Welker, *Creation and Reality*, 6–20. Brueggemann, too, refers to a "transactional" quality in the OT's description of the relationship between Creator and creation. See Brueggemann, *Theology of the Old Testament*, 528.

31. Brown, *The Ethos of the Cosmos*, 41.

32. Augustine, *City of God*, 11.6.

33. Thus, for instance, the image of God as a *yotser* (potter) fashioning humanity from the clay is deployed quite naturally both in the narrative account of Gen 2:7–8 and in Jeremiah's poetic engagement with Israel's political history, fortunes and prospects (Jer 18:1–11; cf. Isa 29:16, Wis 15:7), and Paul's imaginative redescription of all this in the light of Christ (Rom 9:14–26; cf. 1 Tim 2:13, where the only other NT use of the Gk verb *plassein* refers back to God's fashioning of Adam from the earth, thus completing the exegetical circle). Cf. Cranfield, *Epistle to the Romans*; Dunn, *Romans 9–16*; McKane, *Jeremiah*.

If Brown's further argument, that in the "creation traditions" of Scripture itself, God's activity of generating and ordering a physical *cosmos* understood to be of a piece with—and not properly separable from—his calling forth an accompanying *ethos* to render an integral material-spiritual-social "world,"[34] then acknowledgment of the *enhypostatic* inclusion of creaturely agency in the relevant processes by which this same world is "made" becomes inevitable (there can be no cultivation or culture without human activity), as does the concomitant insistence that its making continues beyond the threshold of the day of divine rest. Of course Adam's divinely mandated naming of the animals must be situated on a wholly different plane from God's own earlier "creative" speech acts; but, if Brown's appeal to a biblical "cosmopolis"[35] is correct, as a symbol of the birth and flowering of human "culture" Adam's act of linguistic *poiesis* is nonetheless part and parcel of God's project to *establish* a world (which in this sense comes "unfinished" from his hand), and not merely concerned with preserving or yet (since it arises in the narrative prior to sin's appearance) with redeeming one. Currents in the psychology of perception ever since Kant, and others in contemporary cultural theory point to the likelihood that categories such as "object" and "subject," "nature" and "culture" (cosmos and ethos) themselves are more closely entangled than we typically suppose, the boundaries between them permeable rather than absolute; however much may stand authoritatively over against us as something already divinely "given," therefore, it seems that the reality of the "human world" (the world as experienced humanly[36]) is in any case always one mediated by some relevant human activity of making—whether individual or social, explicit or occult. "The world," Iris Murdoch insists, "is not given to us 'on a plate,' it is given to us as a creative task . . . We *work*, . . . and 'make something of it.' We help it to be."[37] If so, Steiner avers, the hermeneutics of "reception theory" offers us a vital aesthetic analogue for the creation of a "world" that comes to us thus, deliberately (and wonderfully) "incomplete" and full of promise, implicating us directly and dynamically in the processes by which the "work" takes shape, realizing (and doing so only gradually) some if not all of the plenitude of potential meaning invested in it by the divine artist.

34. Brown, *The Ethos of the Cosmos*, 1–33.

35. See ibid., 13–14.

36. Cf. O'Hear, *The Element of Fire*.

37. Murdoch, *Metaphysics as a Guide to Morals*, 215.

38. Steiner, *Grammars of Creation*, 53.

Again, therefore, while for perfectly good theological reasons we may still wish to reserve talk of "creation proper" for something that God and God alone does, and does during creation's first "six days" alone, it seems artificial and perhaps even theologically unhelpful to draw the relevant lines with too thick a pencil. The biblical texts associated naturally with a doctrine of "creation," it seems, flag continuities as well as discontinuities both between patterns of divine and creaturely action and between what precedes and follows the divine "Sabbath" on the seventh day. Taken together with other considerations drawn from theological and "non-theological" sources, this suggests that "what creator and creature alike and together make of what has been made"[39] might even yet helpfully be viewed under the aegis of a "creation theology," rather than being subsumed rigorously and without further ado instead under the alternative rubrics afforded by doctrines of "preservation," "providence," or "redemption."

Making Good

The idea that God grants humankind a responsible participation in his own creative project is central to the Jewish notion of *tikkun olam*, the mending or perfecting of the world. As Jonathan Sacks notes, this notion has very ancient roots in strands of biblical and Mishnaic teaching, but receives its definitive synthesis in the kabbalism of the sixteenth-century mystical rabbi Isaac Luria.[40] The central theme of the doctrine in its various forms is that the world that we inhabit as God's creatures is as yet imperfect (and in this sense God's creative vision remains unfulfilled or incomplete), and that every Jew, in the radical particularity of his or her circumstance, is called to share actively in the process of "mending," "perfecting," or completing the harmonious whole that God intends his creation to become and to be.[41] In its Lurianic version, as Sacks is at pains to point out, this participation is understood to be through particular concrete acts of piety and spirituality

39. Gunton, *The Triune Creator*, 89.

40. See Sacks, *To Heal a Fractured World*, 72–78. For a more extended discussion of the idea see Scholem, *Major Trends in Jewish Mysticism*, 244–86, and Scholem, *The Messianic Idea in Judaism*, 78–141, 203–27.

41. De Lange notes that in Lurianic kabbalism the despoiling of the world occurs not in a prehistoric fall contingent on human freedom, but before or during the act of creation itself. The world is thus always a fractured, imperfect, or incomplete project within which humans are called to act to secure the good. See De Lange, *An Introduction to Judaism*, 206; cf. Sacks, *To Heal a Fractured World*, 74–75.

(and thus chiefly a matter of the soul) rather than by engagement in politi cal initiatives for social justice or efforts to adjust the human impact on our created environment; but in the last hundred years or so the phrase has acquired a more inclusive connotation, all acts designed to avoid evil and do good, specifically religious or otherwise, being understood as a manifes tation of *tikkun*.[42] The gist of this participatory vision is summed up neatly by Rabbi Joseph Soloveitchik:

> When God created the world, He provided an opportunity for the work of his hands—man—to participate in His creation. The Creator, as it were, impaired reality in order that mortal man could repair its flaws and perfect it.[43]

Christians are likely to have some legitimate theological concerns and questions about elements of this religious narrative, and its linking of divine and human agency so directly in an account of the completion and redemption of the created order. Two concerns in particular stand out and demand some response. First, there is the suggestion that the world was from its inception already flawed or fractured, and received from God's hand, therefore, in a state needful of repair by (among other things) the work of human hands. Any such suggestion compromises the doctrine of creation's primal goodness, and flirts dangerously with gnostic notions of a world created not by God himself, but by an incompetent demiurge. Christian orthodoxy has always resisted such ideas, insisting that the world is from first to last the work of a Creator the hallmarks of whose character are infinite goodness, wisdom and love, and accounting for the brokenness and alienation of historical existence by appealing to the radical misuse of freedom and a consequent "fall" of humankind into a condition of sin and death.[44] As Paul Fiddes observes, however, the theological notion of "fall" is not inexorably wedded to a U-shaped narrative in which primal perfection is compromised and lost, to be restored again in due course by a divine salvage operation.[45] The primal goodness of creation can be understood otherwise than this. So, for example, Karl Barth interprets the

42. See Sacks, *To Heal a Fractured World*, 78; cf. De Lange, *An Introduction to Juda ism*, 206–8.

43. Soloveitchik, *Halakhic Man*, 101, cited in Sacks, *To Heal a Fractured World*

44. See, among patristic rejoinders to the idea, Irenæus, *Against Heresies*, and Augus tine, *City of God* 11.17; 11.23; 13.1–3. For discussion, see Hick, *Evil and the God of Love*

45. Fiddes, *Freedom and Limit*, chapter 3.

divine pronouncement in Genesis 1:31 not as a valediction, but instead as an ordination, proleptic and eschatological in its vision: all that God has made is indeed "very good," given its promised end in the fulfillment of the eternal covenant.[46] And it is true, surely, that the goodness with which Christian faith is finally concerned is not one speculatively posited in a remote prehistoric past, but one as yet to come, anticipated decisively in history's midst in the humanity of Jesus, but realized only in the promised future of God when all things shall be made new, and God himself will dwell amongst us as "all in all." Thus Fiddes outlines an understanding of fall not as a temporally situated once for all departure from an original perfection, but rather as the continual outcome of a human creatureliness as yet incomplete and imperfect, and therefore caught up in a dialectic between the possibilities of freedom and the limits of finitude, a dialectic constantly resolving itself either in trust and obedience or (more typically) anxiety and idolatry.[47] Such a view does not, of course, view creatureliness and fallenness as the same thing, or ascribe the origination of evil and death to the Creator himself. Sin, and its consequences, remain the result of the creature's free choices. But this sort of view does face squarely the fact that sin arises due to a vulnerability and weakness built into the structure of our finite existence, at least potentially. Doctrines of the fall of the Augustinian sort, which prefer to posit an original human perfection, face a number of significant difficulties of their own. They are, of course, entirely remote from anything in our experience of what it is to be human, and find it notoriously difficult to account for how or why it was that creatures enjoying unalloyed felicitude and imperturbability should choose to set it aside at all.[48] And such doctrines do not finally succeed in their aim of exonerating God of all responsibility for the presence of sin and evil in his world. To the extent that they ascribe ultimate sovereignty to God in creation and in redemption, they are at least compelled to acknowledge that he called into being a world that was, in Milton's phrase, "free to fall"[49] and perhaps even bound finally to do so. Neither understanding of fallenness involves predicating sin and evil as functions of creation itself, or as necessary components of human

46. Barth, *CD* 3/1, 212–13.

47. That is, seeking security in finite objects and goals, and granting these a worth properly due only to God.

48. See the discussion of this same problem as it arises in Milton's *Paradise Lost* in Hart, "Poetry and Theology in Milton's *Paradise Lost*," 129–39.

49. See Milton, *The Paradise Lost* 3.99.

existence as such; but each in its way finally admits that the *possibility* sin and evil is given in the nature of the world as it comes to us from God's hand. The difference between them, finally, is that one seeks to "justify the ways of God to men" by directing our imaginative gaze backwards to a primordial creaturely perfection, whereas the other (granting that the creation itself comes to us as yet incomplete and empirically "imperfect") prefers to direct us to Christ, and to the fulfilment of God's promise in the future of Christ.

The other theological concern likely to trouble Christians in the notion of *tikkun olam* outlined above is the ascription of what is apparently too high a premium to the significance of human actions vis-à-vis the completion or perfection of the world, putting at risk an adequate account of divine transcendence and a theology of grace as the sole source of both our creation and redemption. That this is indeed a problematic inference of the Lurianic doctrine is suggested by Gershom Scholem, who notes the way in which an organic unity and continuity "between the state of redemption and the state preceding it" tends to characterize some kabbalistic visions, so that redemption "now appears . . . as the logical consequence of the historical process,"[50] with God and humankind functioning effectively as partners (albeit unequal partners) in the enterprise. The specious wedding of process and progress that haunts our culture courtesy of the remaining vestiges of modernity grants such ideas a seductive allure even at the outset of the twenty-first century, and makes it all the more urgent that theologians speak clearly and unashamedly of the transcendent nature of Christian hope, vested as it is in God's sovereign otherness and Lordship, and not in any possibilities or potentialities latent within the creaturely (and fallen) order as such.[51] Any indication that the world's redemption might be contingent in some way upon the nature of the actions we perform in the eschatological interim may well seem to compromise this transcendent commitment, and to constitute a pernicious form of "works righteousness" inimical to the logic of the Christian Evangel.

As Sacks observes, in Judaism itself there is an unresolved tension at this point, *tikkun olam* functioning both as a principle for ordering human action in the midst of history and as an object of daily prayer and

50. Scholem, *The Messianic Idea in Judaism*, 47–48.

51. See the critical rejoinder to the so-called "myth of progress" in Bauckham and Hart, *Hope Against Hope*.

eschatological expectation.[52] It is, paradoxically, *both* something that God will do and must be implored to do (since we cannot), *and* something that we must do in the here and now and in the nitty-gritty of everyday decisions and actions. The achievement of cosmic harmony thus comes both "from above" and "from below"—from the side of the creature in faithful response to the Creator's calling and approach. Within the religious vision of Judaism, this dual insistence is bound either to remain an unresolved dialectic or else resolve itself in some form of religious and ethical synergism likely to place a crushing burden of responsibility on human shoulders. As we have already had occasion to notice, though, Christianity has a different framework to offer respectfully for consideration, one within which such seemingly contradictory claims may legitimately be situated and made sense of, without any confusion arising between them or any loss of integrity or force attaching to either as a result. In the messianic, priestly humanity of Christ, the Church discerns and proclaims a fully human action of *tikkun* corresponding directly to the creative and redemptive purposes and activity of God the Father and energised from first to last by the activity of the Holy Spirit. Furthermore—and decisively—this same human action is that undertaken by God himself, substituting his own humanity for ours at the heart of the covenant he has made with creation, not in such a manner as to exclude our due response, but rather to provide a context within which the partial and faltering nature of that response no longer has the power to crush us, being relativized in significance (though not rendered wholly insignificant) by the response of Christ made on our behalf.

Within a Trinitarian and incarnational account of atonement, and a corresponding understanding of human action as a participation in the priestly human action of Christ, in other words, the "from above" and "from below" dimensions of *tikkun olam* are able to be correlated and held together, and their whole dynamic situated within the overall triune pattern of God's activity and life. Only God can finally heal the world and bring it to completion. But he has chosen to do so not *without* a corresponding human action, but precisely in, with and through such action, concluded once and for all in the humanity of his own Son, but participated in and replicated ever and again in the Spirit-filled lives of others until the time when God will be all in all. Only God can bring about the "new creation" to which the apostles and prophets bear poetic witness; but in the meanwhile, we are

52. It arises at the heart of *Alenu*, the closing prayer of each daily liturgy. See Sacks, *To Heal a Fractured World*, 75–76.

called already to live in ways that declare this new creation to be a hidden reality, performing parables of it in the midst of history, and so conforming historical existence, piece by piece, more fully to its promised destiny in God's hands. It is this emphasis upon the significance of the piecemeal and the seemingly inconsequential that is one of the attractions of the notion of *tikkun olam*. Too often Christians are driven by a utilitarian ethic that supposes things worth doing only if some return can be identified on the investment, rather than understanding that good actions are worth doing precisely and only because it is good to do them, and that the world is in some sense made better thereby, even when no grand strategy is advanced or outcome accomplished in the process. At one level, indeed, acknowledgment of the self-substitution of God's humanity for ours in Christ renders *every* other human action inconsequential; and yet, paradoxically, it simultaneously charges every action with a new significance by situating it within the sphere of action undertaken in union with Christ, and thus rendering it either a witness to or a denial of its reality as such. That the healing and completion of the world will not depend finally on my actions or yours is a vital inference of this theological vision; but that we are called, commanded even, to immerse ourselves fully in our own small part of the world and to do all that we can in every sphere of it to "make good" the peculiar claims of faith concerning the world's origin and promised end, is an equally vital entailment. And it is, we should recall, precisely *this* world, and not some other, that will be taken up and made new by God in the fullness of time. And in that sense, nothing that we do, no choice that we make or action that we undertake in life, is wholly without eschatological consequence. For it is itself the object of God's redemptive promise.

The Liturgy of the Arts

One of the gains of an adequate theology of the priesthood of Christ is that it liberates us to acknowledge the potential liturgical significance of parts of our identity and action we have hitherto held back or supposed relatively "secular" and lacking in religious merit. The news that the Son of God has laid hold of our humanity in its entirety and offered it back, crucified and risen, to his Father in the power of the Spirit for our sakes, compels us in our turn now to offer back to God in joyful thanks nothing less than all that we personally are, and have and may yet become. As Jonathan Sacks notes, in biblical thought *homo sapiens* is the one creature that is itself identifiably "creative," capable not just of adapting to its created environment, but of making more of that environment than is initially given in it;[53] enhancing, or adding value to it. Indeed, in as much as the world is apprehended as meaningful, it constitutes a distinctly human environment, shot through with significance that transcends its materiality alone, a union of material being and semiotic excess in which "a thing is not just what it is," and its reality takes time to unfold.[54] A distinctly human engagement with or indwelling of the world is thus inevitably and always one in which we "make something of" the world rather than functioning as mere passive observers or consumers of it. To live responsibly in this sense, Rowan Williams suggests, is to draw out what is not yet seen or heard in the material environment itself, to "uncover what is generative in the world,"[55] and so, working with the grain of the cosmos, to aid and assist in the imaginative effoliation by which the world approaches more fully what it is capable of being and becoming. In offering our humanity back to God, therefore, we offer back too the world in which we are embedded bodily and culturally, and what we have made of it for good or ill.

The sort of creative imagination involved in human artistry, Williams submits, is thus not an eccentric or exclusive sort, but precisely an acute form of our wider human engagement with the world, with its distinctive dialectic of imaginative give and take.[56] The premise of artistry is that perception is always incomplete, that truthfulness unfolds as we continue to explore it, that there is always an excess of meaning in what is given to us for consideration.[57] Yet artistry, considered thus, is no mere cataloguing of the world's given forms, no "mimetic" inventory of the extant. Art brings new things into existence, and, precisely in doing so, discovers that which it makes. Precisely because significance has no purchase apart from the actions and responses of those who indwell the order of signs, because human acts of signification and sense-making are already factored into our apprehension of an orderly and value-laden world (one in which "cosmos" and "ethos" are, as it were, perichoretically related), every act of discovery, of the uncovering or disclosure of new meaning, necessarily entails acts of making too, and every act of making lays bare some latent but hitherto

53. Sacks, *To Heal a Fractured World*, 79.

54. Williams, *Grace and Necessity*, 26.

55. Ibid., 162.

56. Ibid., 140.

57. Ibid., 135–39.

unrecognized semiotic possibility. In art, as in life more generally, our calling is thus, paradoxically, to "change the world into itself,"[58] but we can do so precisely and only by means of imaginative responses that help to make of it more and other than it is as yet. Again, the necessary supposition is that world is in fact not yet "itself," but in some sense unfinished, with much more still to be drawn out of its primordial plenitude and fashioned in accordance with the "generative pulsions" divinely invested and humanly intuited in it.[59] This is not "creativity" of a sort that craves trespass on the soil of divine prerogatives, but it is nonetheless a participation in the unfolding of "creation," and in God's making of new things and making all things new. It is precisely by means of our imaginative and "creative" responses to the given world in the arts and elsewhere, therefore, that the world approaches that fullness of which it is capable (or, conversely, is held back from it).[60]

Having opened this chapter with a discussion of the work of Dorothy L. Sayers, it seems fitting to draw it to a close by referring to the thought of her direct contemporary and compeer, J. R. R. Tolkien.[61] Looking back over his already lengthy career in 1954, Tolkien suggested to a correspondent that the whole of his literary output, imaginative and critical, had from the first really been concerned with exploring a single question, namely, the relationship between divine Creation and acts of human making or "sub-creation" as he preferred to call it.[62] Two poetic texts in particular tackle the issue head-on, and in a manner that points to single abiding insight present

58. Ibid., 18.

59. Ibid., 27. Williams borrows the word "pulsions" from Maritain. See Maritain, *Creative Intuition in Art and Poetry*, 302–06.

60. Williams, *Grace and Necessity*, 154.

61. They were hardly colleagues, despite the popular association of Sayers's name with those of Lewis, Tolkien, Williams and others. In a letter to his son Christopher, Tolkien professed a "loathing" for Lord Peter Wimsey and his creatrix! See Tolkien, *Letters of J. R. R. Tolkien*, 82 [71, to Christopher Tolkien, 25 May 1944]. Doubtless the hyperbole can be taken precisely as such; but while they shared some common theological and aesthetic concerns, and despite the identifiable kinship between some of their ideas, Tolkien thought Sayers's detective fiction vulgar.

62. Ibid., 188 [153, draft, to Peter Hastings]. The letter was seemingly never sent. A related suggestion is contained in an earlier letter to Milton Waldman written in "all this stuff," Tolkien writes (alluding to his entire mythological enterprise), "is mainly concerned with Fall, Mortality, and the Machine" (Ibid., 145 [131, undated, to Milton Waldman]). A footnote to the text reads "It is, I suppose, fundamentally concerned with the problem of the relation of Art (and Sub-creation) and Primary Reality."

from his very earliest ruminations on the subject: Primary and Secondary Reality, the world received from God's hand and "what we make of it" in various acts of human *ars* are not to be too sharply distinguished, since they are both "ultimately of the same stuff,"[63] and our creaturely participation in each demands of us further acts of imaginative response and making. Creation, in other words, always solicits and enables further acts of a "creative" sort rather than jealously guarding its own prerogatives.

The Elvish creation myth "Ainulindalë" was cast in its final form in the 1950s and published only after Tolkien's death more than twenty years later, but its earliest version belongs to the imaginative genesis of Middle-earth itself in the years immediately following the First World War.[64] It concerns Eru, or Ilúvatar, and his creation of the cosmos, not by solo virtuoso performance, but by calling into existence creatures themselves capable of sharing in the joyful task of bringing a world to completion. The metaphor in terms of which the myth pictures this creative interplay is itself, appropriately, an artistic one. Ilúvatar propounds a great musical theme, and invites the Ainur or Valar (the angelic first-created) to join in the music-making, each adorning the main theme with his own, to the end of a great and glorious harmony sounding forth. The creativity of the Ainur, therefore, is at once wholly unlike Ilúvatar's own creative act, while yet constituting an extension, development of and participation in it. While each of the angelic creatures is free to fashion his own individual melody, the skill or "art" of the matter lies not in any sheer creativity *ex nihilo*, but precisely in the harmonious development of a theme that Ilúvatar himself has already propounded and that determines, as it were, the form of the overall work. The core image, then, is that of harmonizing by free and spontaneous ornamentation. For his part, we are told, Ilúvatar will "sit and hearken, and be glad that through you great beauty has been wakened into song."[65] Creaturely acts of subcreation, therefore, are here contingent on a divine self-limitation which, paradoxically, creates the conditions for that which pleases God's heart and

63. Tolkien, *Tree and Leaf*, 30. The citation is from the essay "On Fairy Stories" first published in 1947. Given the consonance of the idea with those expressed in earlier works, and its place in the argument of the essay as a whole, it seems likely that it dates back to the lost original (presumably much shorter) text of the lecture "Fairy Stories" delivered in the University of St Andrews on 8 March 1939. On the history see Hart, "Tolkien, St Andrews, and Dragons," 1–11.

64. See Tolkien, *The Silmarillion*, 15–22. On the different rescensions of the myth see Hart, "Tolkien, Creation and Creativity," 39–53.

65. Tolkien, *The Silmarillion*, 15.

satisfies his desire the most—reciprocal acts of a "creative" sort, taking what God has given and offering it back enriched and enhanced in accordance with its original God-given store of possibility. Of course, such kenotic shar ing of responsibility opens the emergent cosmos to malign influence, and Tolkien's myth, while hardly a *calque* on its biblical equivalent, has its own Miltonic Satan figure in Melkor, the most gifted angel of all, in whom sub-creative desire falls away from its proper orientation and manifests itself in the reality-denying wish "to be Lord and God of his own private creation." Melkor's capacity for weaving discord and ruin amidst the primal harmony of the divine design is considerable, and it calls forth from Ilúvatar a deeper and superior artistry in order to redeem it, not (unlike the God of at least one Christian hymn) drowning out "all music but his own,"[67] but rather taking the offending and destructive noise up skillfully into the pattern of his own music-making in such a way that its significance is finally transfig ured and made good. The bringing of the creative vision to fulfillment and completion, therefore, is by no means automatic or straightforward; but it contingent on creaturely as well as divine action and response and, in God's hands, it is finally secure rather than uncertain. In earlier versions of the myth, Tolkien was much more bold in his suggestion of a world given by God only in what amounts to outline form, with empty spaces deliberately left unfilled and adornments unrealized, looking to the "eucharistic" art istry of the Ainur for their due enrichment and completion. Later editions tone this down slightly, as Tolkien perhaps increasingly realized the danger of theological misunderstanding, and felt the need to indicate more clearly the distinction he believed must indeed be drawn between that creating that God alone does and is capable of doing, and creaturely "sub-creating" as he had by now dubbed it. For, while the myth is first and foremost a work of the literary imagination, making no obvious claim as such to a truth beyond its own borders, it is also an exploration and daring sketch of the contours of a theological aesthetic—an account not of primordial angelic sub-creating, but that "artistry" to which human beings find themselves called in the very midst of Primary Reality.

The poem "Mythopoeia" had its origins in a now legendary after-din ner conversation between Tolkien, C. S. Lewis, and Hugo Dyson conducted

66. Tolkien, *The Letters of J. R. R. Tolkien*, 145 [131, undated (1951), to Milton Waldman].

67. "Crown Him with Many Crowns" by Matthew Bridges (1800–94) and Godfrey Thring (1823–1903). The full text may be found in *The Methodist Hymn Book*, No.

in the grounds of Magdalen College on the evening of 19 September 1931.[68] Among other things, the substance of the conversation touched upon the capacity of myth (and by extension other imaginative and poetic forms) to deal in the stuff of reality and truth, rather than being (in the reported words of Lewis,[69] the "Misomythus" of the poem's cryptic inscription) lies "breathed through silver." In his verse Tolkien playfully drives home his polemical point, that poetry may indeed be a sharp instrument in the hands of truth, helping us to cut the world at its joints, and he decries by comparison the sort of arid rationalism and literalism for which everything is exactly what its label says it is, and nothing is ever found to be more or other than it is. The poetic eye, the poem itself suggests, is thus the one best fitted to explore a world believed to be chock full of deep connections and hidden meanings, rather than exhausted in our measured consideration of its mere surface appearances. Furthermore, such acts of *poesis* are fundamental to the roots of human language and perception themselves ("trees are not 'trees,' until so named and seen—/and never were so named till those had been/who speech's involuted breath unfurled . . ."[70]), and whatever world of meanings and significances we apprehend around us is therefore already in part a product of prior poetic responses to what is divinely given from beyond ourselves—a "refracted light" that has been splintered from its pure white into a glorious array of colors only by being passed first through the prism of our humanity. We experience the world in accordance with the capacities invested in our nature, and far from being essentially passive and receptive, those capacities turn out to involve us necessarily in acts of construction, interpretation and "sense making" from the very first. There is, of course, a distinction to be drawn between Primary and Secondary Reality, but it must not be drawn with too thick a pencil, since both are bound up with our peculiar poetic disposition toward things, and the boundaries between them are flexible and permeable:[71] we make, as

68. See Carpenter, *J. R. R. Tolkien*, 196–99.

69. The occasion was prior to Lewis's return to Christian faith from the atheism of his early adult years, and a significant moment in the narrative of that return. See Carpenter, *J. R. R. Tolkien*, 197–98.

70. Tolkien, *Tree and Leaf*, 86.

71. Thus, artistic imagination may grant us "Recovery . . . a re-gaining—regaining of a clear view. I do not say 'seeing things as they are' and involve myself with the philosophers, though I might venture to say 'seeing things as we are (or were) meant to see them'" (ibid., 57–58). The concession, albeit made in passing, is significant, both including human response already within any accounting of the "real," and suggesting the latter's susceptibility to modification by poetic redescription.

Tolkien puts it "in our measure and in our derivative mode," by the law in which we're made—"and not only made, but made in the image and likeness of a Maker."[72] To be participant "in our measure and . . . derivative mode" in God's own continuing creative engagement with the world and its possibilities of meaning, drawing it closer by constant small scale acts of "guerrilla theatre"[73] to what, in God's creative vision, it was always intended to be, and what, through the work of his own hands, it will yet become and be, this, Tolkien suggests, is not just our right, but our distinctive creaturely calling and charge, whether used or misused.[74] And it is for acts of imagina tive sub-creating that God looks and longs in his human creatures, crav ing nothing more than the glimpse of his own creative heart having found purchase and offered back in joyful thanks from the side of the creature. If, as Williams suggests, artistry is indeed but an acute and paradigmatic case of our wider human disposition to the world, then here the arts, holiness and worship promise to fuse in a manner as yet to be fully reckoned with in most of our churches, and with some potentially fruitful implications, perhaps, for a newly cast Christology. "Dis-graced" we may well be, Tolkien avers; but neither the right nor the responsibility has decayed. "We make still by the law in which we're made."[75]

72. Ibid., 56; cf. ibid., 87.

73. Wilder, *Theopoetic*.

74. Tolkien, *Tree and Leaf*, 87.

75. Ibid.

Bibliography

Aquinas, Thomas. *The "Summa Theologica" of St. Thomas Aquinas*. Translated by Fathers of the English Dominican Province. 2nd ed. 22 vols. London: Burns Oates & Washbourne, 1920–1925.

Barth, Karl. *Church Dogmatics 3/1: The Doctrine of Creation*. Edited by Geoffrey W. Bromiley and Thomas F. Torrance. Translated by J. W. Edwards, O. Bussey, and H. Knight. Edinburgh: T. & T. Clark, 1958.

Bauckham, Richard. *Jesus and the God of Israel*. Grand Rapids: Eerdmans, 2008.

Bauckham, Richard, and Trevor Hart. *Hope Against Hope: Christian Eschatology at the Turn of the Millennium*. Grand Rapids: Eerdmans, 1999.

Bernhardt, Karl-Heinz. "bārā.'" In *Theological Dictionary of the Old Testament*, edited by G. Johannes Botterweck and Helmer Ringgren, translated by John T. Willis, 242–49. Grand Rapids: Eerdmans, 1990.

Brown, William P. *The Ethos of the Cosmos: The Genesis of Moral Imagination in the Bible*. Grand Rapids: Eerdmans, 1999.

Brueggemann, Walter. *Theology of the Old Testament: Testimony, Dispute, Advocacy*. Minneapolis: Fortress, 1997.

Carpenter, Humphrey. *J. R. R. Tolkien: A Biography*. London: HarperCollins, 2002.

Cranfield, Charles E. B. *A Critical and Exegetical Commentary on the Epistle to the Romans*. Vol. 2. Edinburgh: T. & T. Clark, 1979.

De Lange, Nicholas. *An Introduction to Judaism*. Cambridge: Cambridge University Press, 2000.

Dunn, James. *Romans 9–16*. Word Biblical Commentary. Dallas: Word, 1988.

Fiddes, Paul. *Freedom and Limit: A Dialogue Between Literature and Christian Doctrine*. Basingstoke: Macmillan, 1991.

Florida, Richard. *The Rise of the Creative Class*. New York: Basic, 2002.

Fretheim, Terence E. *God and World in the Old Testament: A Relational Theology of Creation*. Nashville: Abingdon, 2005.

Gunton, Colin. *The Triune Creator: A Historical and Systematic Study*. Grand Rapids: Eerdmans, 1998.

Hart, Rachel. "Tolkien, St Andrews, and Dragons." In *Tree of Tales: Tolkien, Literature and Theology*, edited by Trevor Hart and Ivan Khovacs, 1–11. Waco: Baylor University Press, 2007.

Hart, Trevor A. *Between the Image and the Word: Theological Engagements with Imagination, Literature and Language*. Farnham: Ashgate, 2013.

———. "Poetry and Theology in Milton's *Paradise Lost*." In *Genesis and Christian Theology*, edited by Nathan MacDonald et al., 129–39. Grand Rapids: Eerdmans, 2012.

———. "Tolkien, Creation, and Creativity." In *Tree of Tales: Tolkien, Literature and Theology*, edited by Trevor Hart and Ivan Khovacs, 39–53. Waco: Baylor University Press, 2007.

Hick, John. *Evil and the God of Love*. London: Macmillan, 1966.

Koehler, Ludwig, and Walter Baumgartner, editors. *The Hebrew and Aramaic Lexicon of the Old Testament*. Translated by M. E. J. Richardson et al. Rev. ed. Leiden: Brill, 1994.

Mair, Roslin. "The Choir Capitals of Canterbury Cathedral 1174–84." In *The British Archaeological Association Conference Transactions for the year 1979*, 5:56 London: British Archaeological Association and Kent Archaeological Society,

Maritain, Jacques. *Creative Intuition in Art and Poetry*. London: Harvill, 1953.

McKane, William. *A Critical and Exegetical Commentary on Jeremiah*. Vol. 1. Edinburgh: T. & T. Clark, 1986.

The Methodist Hymn Book. London: Methodist Conference Office, 1933.

Milton, John. *The Paradise Lost*. Edited by James Robert Boyd. New York: Barnes,

Moltmann, Jürgen. *God in Creation: A New Theology of Creation and the Spirit of God* Translated by Margaret Kohl. London: SCM, 1985.

Murdoch, Iris. *Metaphysics as a Guide to Morals*. London: Vintage, 2003.

O'Donovan, Oliver. *Resurrection and Moral Order. An Outline for Evangelical Ethics* Leicester: IVP, 1986.

O'Hear, Anthony. *The Element of Fire: Science, Art and the Human World*. London: Routledge, 1988.

Pannenberg, Wolfhart. *Systematic Theology*. Vol. 2. Translated by Geoffrey W. Bromiley. Edinburgh: T. & T. Clark, 1994.

Reynolds, Barbara. *Dorothy L. Sayers: Her Life and Soul*. London: Hodder & Stoughton, 1993.

Reynolds, Barbara, editor. *The Letters of Dorothy L. Sayers*. Vol. 1, *1899–1936, The Making of a Detective Novelist*. New York: St Martin's, 1995.

———. *The Letters of Dorothy L. Sayers*. Vol. 2, *1937–1943: From Novelist to Playwright* New York: St Martin's, 1998.

Sacks, Jonathan. *To Heal a Fractured World: The Ethics of Responsibility*. London: Continuum, 2005.

Sayers, Dorothy L. *Catholic Tales and Christian Songs*. Oxford: Blackwell, 1918.

———. *The Mind of the Maker*. London: Methuen., 1941.

———. *The Zeal of Thy House*. London: Gollancz, 1937.

Scholem, Gershom. *Major Trends in Jewish Mysticism*. New York: Schocken, 1941

———. *The Messianic Idea in Judaism: And Other Essays on Jewish Spirituality*. New York: Schocken, 1995.

Soloveitchik, Joseph B. *Halakhic Man*. Translated by Lawrence Kaplan. Philadelphia: Jewish Publication Society of America, 1983.

Steiner, George. *Grammars of Creation*. London: Faber & Faber, 2001.

Tolkien, J. R. R. *The Letters of J. R. R. Tolkien*. Edited by Humphrey Carpenter. Boston: Houghton Mifflin, 1981.

———. *The Silmarillion*. Edited by Christopher Tolkien. London: Allen & Unwin,

———. *Tree and Leaf, including the poem Mythopoeia & The Homecoming of Beorhtnoth* London: HarperCollins, 2001.

Welker, Michael. *Creation and Reality*. Minneapolis: Fortress, 1999.

Wilder, Amos. *Theopoetic: Theology and the Religious Imagination*. Philadelphia: Fortress, 1976.

Williams, Rowan. *Grace and Necessity: Reflections on Art and Love*. Harrisburg, PA: Morehouse, 2005.

Wolterstorff, Nicholas. *Art in Action*. Carlisle: Solway, 1997.

3

Re-forming Beauty

Can Theological Sense Accommodate Aesthetic Sensibility?

Carolyn Kelly

Tikkun Olam echoes two great themes of the Christian faith: the reality of human brokenness or alienation, and the reality of God's redemptive involvement in human history. Firstly, it draws attention to the fact that our world, or creation, is "out of joint"; aspects of it are wrongfully and sorrowfully separated. Secondly, it reiterates the call for human beings to participate in God's re-creating or "mending" of that world. In this essay, we will explore the relationship between the arts and theology in the Western Church over the last two centuries or so, and the ways in which they have become alienated from one another. We will then reflect on what resources are to be reclaimed from our tradition in order to imagine and "re-form" a theological aesthetic.

In earlier times, "theology" and "aesthetics"—what we have become accustomed to regard as discreet disciplines—were more naturally intertwined in the life and practices of the church. With the rise of the secular academy and various religious and cultural changes in the West in the modern era, however, these increasingly inhabited separate spheres. Now, the arts and theology have become identified with quite different communities and ways of seeing the world. In part, this separation reflected the aligning of theology with the *understanding* or cognitive functions and "knowing" (the realm of truth claims), whilst the "creative" realm of the arts, metaphor and symbol were identified with the workings of *imagination* (the realm of "myth"). Hans Urs von Balthasar, the twentieth-century Catholic theologian, observed this alienation in Western Christianity and charted its development through several volumes of *The Glory of the Lord: A Theological Aesthetics,* published in English in 1982.

Balthasar's vision of a "theological aesthetics" has since persuaded a number of Catholic and Protestant theologians to re-examine this dissociation within modern Christianity. More recently this has generated discussion in both theological and arts communities, and has indirectly inspired conversations such as those that the essays in this collection are concerned with. However, such enterprises are valuable not so much because they provide an opportunity to discuss theology and aesthetics as discreet disciplines that occasionally relate, but because—or *if*—they genuinely make room for each to inform the other, for each to present or disclose a different side of the same diamond. Such a process allows for active engagement between artists and academic theologians in concrete opportunities for collaborative practice. This echoes Balthasar, whose theological aesthetics formed the first part of a trilogy of Christian theology in which beauty, goodness and truth were integrated and invited the readers' participation: beginning with the disclosure of the glory of Jesus Christ; unfolding the drama of God's salvation history; and setting out the logic of the truth of God and the incarnate Word.[1]

Balthasar's aesthetic was thus theo-centric; it was *about* "the Glory of the Lord." Whilst this attended closely to the workings of the human mind, faith and culture, it reflected the belief that all facets of human life, "all things," owe their existence to and have meaning through Christ (Col
Balthasar reminds us that human making and being only ever exist within that doxological framework, whether it is acknowledged or not. So as much as it is human dialogue, our conversation may also be an act of worship in that it proclaims God as the divine Artist who anticipates and enables human creativity. This transcendent reality confronts and redirects our imagined futures; the immediate situation of our work together is transformed by that other presence. Our meeting face-to-face, however imperfectly, also "images" the holy, triune community as we are caught up within the drama of God's life in and for the world. So beyond the sum of the parts we play here and now, we find ourselves drawn into a greater narrative. To shift metaphors, we see the possibility of embodying a "poem" (in the sense of

1. Nichols, *The Word Has Been Abroad*, xiii.

Greek *poeisis*), a new thing being made from disparate parts. But, in coming together we accept this implies a loss: neither the arts nor theology can be part of a restored entity without some diminishment of its own identity or form, although such independence might have become customary. Some practitioners in either realm might even question whether such an accommodation is desirable or necessary.

In response, we might first acknowledge that "sense" and "sensibility" share an etymological root, that there is something of their meaning in common even though their recent estrangement would suggest otherwise. This dynamic was captured in *Sense and Sensibility* (published in 1811), Jane Austen's memorable portrayal of the Dashwood sisters. Austen keenly observed and wittily recounted a tension evident in her culture and readily understood by her early nineteenth-century readers, for recent cultural developments had magnified the differences between them as ways of experiencing the world. "Sense" was highly valued in the literature of the previous Augustan age and referred to the ability to observe carefully, to reflect and exercise measured judgment. "Sensibility" described the more affective and impulsive tendencies characteristic of the new romanticism. In the first chapter we read of Elinor's good sense: she had "strength of understanding and coolness of judgment . . . her feelings were strong, but she knew how to govern them." Her younger sister Marianne, had an "excess of . . . sensibility," "she was sensible and clever, but eager in everything: her sorrows, her joys, could have no moderation . . . she was everything but prudent." Marianne was encouraged "in the violence of . . . afflictions" by her indulgent mother, whilst Elinor, although equally affected by the family's misfortunes, could exercise self-control and "struggle": "she could exert herself."[2] Elinor's forbearance highlighted Marianne's lack of prudence and impulsiveness, and whereas Elinor reigned in her feelings and considered their social implications, Marianne, encouraged by her reading of Romantic poets, was prone to abandon herself to empathy and improper behavior with an unsuitable lover.[3] Austen's own strength of understanding and cool judgment, her abundance of "sense," informed her brilliant character contrast. But Austen also shows how both sisters acquire wisdom by a counter-balancing of the two tendencies; both grow through affliction and association with the other (and both get their man in the end). This mutual influence seems to have been echoed in Austen's writing: her classicism reflected the sane, clear-

2. Austen, *Sense and Sensibility*, chapter 1.

3. Ward, "The Persistence of Romanticism," 165.

sightedness of the Augustan age but also exhibited a vitality characteristic of, perhaps even *enhanced* by, the influence of Romanticism.[4]

In applying Austen's categories to theology and aesthetics I am taking some liberties (which those who prefer exact definitions will have to tolerate) in the hope that they evoke a tension I have observed and continue to negotiate. This essay seeks to address that tension and pose it as a question with several layers: *Can* "theological sense" (that robust Protestant orthodoxy that affirms God's revelation, the testimony of scripture and human reasoning) possibly accommodate "aesthetic sensibility" (a "Romantic" reading of the world in which the human subject participates in creation, which allows for sense experience and the imagination as a means of knowing)?

To begin, we must consider beauty. Historically, beauty has shaped theology and aesthetics, yet it now has an ambivalent position with respect to both. Balthasar, writing fifty years ago, went as far as to suggest that religion had *taken leave of beauty*. Most particularly, he suggested, Christian theology had distanced itself by "a rigorous re-drawing of boundaries":

> Beauty is the last thing which the thinking intellect dares to approach, since only it dances as an uncontained splendour around the true and the good and their inseparable relation to one another. Beauty is the disinterested one, without which the ancient world refused to understand itself (but) . . . which . . . has bid farewell to our new world, a world of interests, leaving it to its own avarice and sadness. No longer loved or fostered by religion, beauty is lifted from its face as a mask, and its absence exposes features on that face which threaten to become incomprehensible to man. We no longer dare to believe in beauty and we make of it a mere appearance in order the more easily to dispose of it.[5]

These observations remain pertinent, for "beauty" is still problematic. In more ancient times it referred to something transcendental with its origins and definitions in the realm of the ideal. Today, in ordinary language, "beautiful" is extolled simply as "a gladness to the senses,"[6] and people refer to it in this way with comparative ease. But in recent centuries, particularly in the West, the idea of beauty has also been subjected to multiple applications and considerable "conceptual tinkering and transposing," which

4. Wynne-Davies, *Bloomsbury Guide to English Literature*, 382.

5. Balthasar, *The Glory of the Lord*, 18.

6. Sontag, "An Argument About Beauty," 21.

have rendered it virtually unusable as a communal notion.[7] A theological aesthetic might attempt to refer to beauty in a way that acknowledges this complex history of meanings, but also allows that it is, quite simply, what brings gladness to the human heart. Both will be framed in relation to the triune God and the beauty of the "form" of Christ.

Perhaps, if we gather in the name of that beautiful One, we act in faith that beauty and the "thinking intellect" *can* meet face to face, a hope shared by a number of contemporary theologians and artists. Yet many remain cautious, and acknowledge the significant challenges posed by any meaningful interaction between the two. Edward Farley, for example, has recently described the odd tension or "lack of relation" he observed in his own comprehensive interpretation of the Christian faith. Farley noted that although since childhood he had experienced the world through his senses and feelings and seen it as in some way enchanted, that fascination with "the sights, colours, occurrences and sounds of everyday life" was almost totally ignored in his theological writing. There, the "powerful aesthetic dimension" of life was strangely absent, even though it had been extremely important to him: "It was as if the most concrete way in which human beings experience their world—namely, their emotional participation in surprising, interesting and attractive events—had no place in the world of faith. Faith, it would seem, is simply about "something else": church doctrines, the after-life, Jesus, the Bible, liberation."[8]

Farley had observed this odd lack of relation—the disconnection between faith and the aesthetic dimension of human life—in the work of a number of his peers.[9] In a similar vein, Balthasar had suggested both Protestant and Catholic theologians of his time deliberately distanced themselves from the word "aesthetic" because it described a "frivolous, merely curious and self-indulgent" attitude.[10] So, whether such distancing has been deliberate or by default, systematic treatments of the Christian faith rarely acknowledge or incorporate aesthetic experience.

Some reserve is understandable, for romantic "sensibilities" have spawned aesthetic*ism*, and to accommodate this in any significant way would undermine the integrity of reasoned expressions of Christianity. As Karl Barth argued persuasively, Romantic values and their offspring

7. Ibid., 21.

8. Farley, *Faith and Beauty*, vii.

9. Ibid., vii.

10. Balthasar, *The Glory of the Lord*, 51.

are already pervasive in the West, with significant results for human self-understanding and flourishing. A certain degree of clear-headedness is required for today's secular academic milieu. Unlike Marianne Dashwood, whose excess of sensibility was tempered by real experience and who ultimately acknowledged the sage advice of the elder sister and the faithful attentions of the true-hearted lover, aesthetic movements during the last two centuries have not always been receptive to theological insights. A mutual suspicion has been observed.

This means that the multiple identities attributed to "the beautiful" have largely developed independently from Christian formulations, whether of beauty, truth, or goodness. Thus, beauty has been deployed by specific communities in quite distinct ways.[11] From the late eighteenth century, aesthetic judgments of beauty related to human sensual experiences of the world. Initially, when still an unquestioned criterion of value in the arts, beauty referred to a general sense of what was excellent or desirable, such as the idea of harmony[12] or an experience of the sublime. Then, from the early 1800s as beauty was increasingly identified with the sensual and with "feeling," it had more personal associations and was drawn into the individual psyche and identified with emotions. Reduced to the immanent realm, it became less and less a consideration in theological treatments. No longer a transcendental value, beauty lost the power to express even *self*-transcendence.[13]

Later, for groups like the bohemian pre-Raphaelites, beauty became its own justification. At the end of the century, the culture of *décadence*
the aesthetic tastes of a privileged minority came to define the art world. Balthasar suggested that for nineteenth-century champions of an aesthetic worldview, the "right" attitude to life was antagonistic to religious ethics in general, and particularly opposed to what was positively Christian.[15]

In yet another twist, early twentieth-century modernists aligned beauty with conservative standards and so rejected the pervasive idealized notions of beauty that had been applied to the natural world or to the female form.[16] For Gertrude Stein, calling a work of art "beautiful"

11. Sontag, "An Argument About Beauty," 22.
12. Ibid.
13. Farley, *Faith and Beauty*, 39.
14. Verdun, "Broken Beauty, Shattered Heart," 39.
15. Balthasar, *The Glory of the Lord*, 51.
16. Fuglie, "Beauty Lost, Beauty Found," 59.

was tantamount to saying it was dead.[17] Later, in post-war consumerism, beauty became identified with clichéd sentimental forms and harnessed for mass-marketing. Other reactions, some Christian forms of which were influenced by pietism, spurned a variety of alternative interpretations that rejected the association of beauty with "high" arts, or with extravagance and materialism. Most recently, in post-modern secular culture, beauty has taken a new identity as the marginalized one, a *persona non grata*. Ironically, this significant twentieth-century move occurred within arts communities; considerations of beauty were often seen as restrictive, or as an elitist preoccupation. Sontag suggests beauty continues to take a battering in our culture wars: "In the cultural climate favouring the more user-friendly art of recent years, the beautiful seems, if not obvious, then pretentious . . . That beauty applied to some things and not to others, that it was a principle of *discrimination*, was once its strength and appeal. Beauty belonged to the family of notions that established rank . . . and the right to exclude. What had been a virtue of the concept became its liability. Beauty . . . was revealed as . . . excluding too much."[18]

So in the modern era, beauty has been identified with various aesthetic excesses and counterfeit forms; it has been extolled, and marginalized. The antagonism toward traditional understandings of beauty has been perplexing for some within the Christian community. For those shaped by church cultures reflecting ideals of beauty celebrated in "classical" Western art and literature, contemporary art (particularly the more extreme and controversial forms) can be mystifying and unedifying. A desire to preserve some communal idea of "the beautiful" has also produced counter-reactions from communities concerned to preserve theological orthodoxy and certain standards of ethical conduct.

But theological reflection need not demonize modern articulations of beauty, nor be hasty in rejecting even awkward attempts to re-formulate it. To "re-form" a theological aesthetic will require us attending to the different ways beauty is actually perceived and expressed in real communities and in the arts. These particularities occur within the broader canvas of modern culture, but also within the much bigger picture of human history suggested by the biblical narrative. In the Judeo-Christian tradition, Hebrew descriptions of beautiful aspects of creation were not featured or enjoyed in

17. Cited in Sontag, "An Argument About Beauty," 22.

18. Sontag, "An Argument About Beauty," 23.

their own right.[19] In the New Testament, the Greek word *kalon* (translated as "beautiful") depicted what was visually lovely, but also what was true, fitting and good; "*kalon*" reflected who God is and what God does. theological aesthetic will thus frame beauty in relation to the good, true and beautiful God, *as well as* to the rich diversities of cultural expression. In the modern era, allowing for both these realities has presented a challenge.

Is a second naïvety possible? With all that we know of modern life and thought, can the simple understanding that beauty "gladdens the senses" be restored? At this point we will address two important strands of thought.

Protestant thinking about the arts has been significantly influenced by Søren Kierkegaard and Karl Barth. In the mid-nineteenth century Kierkegaard confronted the resurgent aesthetic element that had begun earlier with Romantics, and would later flower in the work of Friedrich Nietzsche. Kierkegaard rightly saw that aesthetics, separated from logic and ethics (or the arts separated from considerations of truth and morality), was given a particular value of its own: "many were to proclaim aesthetics, so understood, to be the supreme value of any world-view."[21] This development had infected liberal Protestant theology. In his earlier polemical writing, Barth would develop Kierkegaard's line of thought suggesting one only has to "scratch" a modern person to discover the Romantic.[22] And for the Romantic, Barth suggested, the creative human subject reigned supreme. In his survey of the nineteenth century, Barth saw Romanticism as the defining weakness Protestant theology could not shake off.[23]

In a detailed discussion of the philosopher-poet Friedrich von Hardenberg or Novalis (1772–1801), Barth explored the implications of romantic aesthetics. Although he praised the young man's insight and brilliance, Barth lamented the exalted claims Novalis made for human creativity, expressed in such philosophical *Fragments* (1, 875) as "poesy is the key to philosophy."[24] Barth acknowledged Novalis's personal piety, but found too much in his writings that suggested religious knowledge could be gained by means other than God's revelation: "The secret path leads inwards. Eternity

19. Dyrness, *Senses of the Soul*, 81.

20. Ibid., 80.

21. Balthasar, *The Glory of the Lord*, 50.

22. Barth, *Protestant Thought*, 225.

23. Ibid., 226.

24. Cited in Barth, *Protestant Thought*, 238.

. . . is within us, or nowhere."[25] And, "through absolute will love can be transformed into religion."[26] Barth continued:

> The extreme is reached now on the one side and now on the other—philosophy seems to be merged and to disappear in art, art in philosophy, love in religion and religion in love . . . The creative subject plays and dances, on a high wire in peril of its life, to be true, but it dances well, and for this reason will not fall in spite of everything. It achieves infinite rejoicing and infinite sadness. But that is all it does achieve . . . Its beauty surely cannot be in dispute. It is surely a God at least, this dancer . . . a God whom to serve as God might make a human life truly rich enough, and in view of whom it might seem folly to begin to look out for another. Who needs yet more if he has that, having himself as a premise of the whole? . . . Does not Romanticism truly seem to wish to raise itself to a denial of this other God?[27]

For Barth, Novalis's religion was "without doubt in the first place a work of man, something to do with Romantic civilisation" and his *Sacred Songs* represented the *hubris* of the Enlightenment in new guise, the "magic religious teaching of pure Romanticism."[28] This "teaching of love" would become "the esoteric secret" of nineteenth-century religious thought.[29] In his early work Barth defined this characteristic Romantic belief in the creative human subject as the critical flaw in subsequent Christian theology.

Barth thus clarified the implications of Romantic aesthetics and its excesses, reiterating how any account of human creativity *must begin with reference to God as Creator*. This biblically-informed reading of humanity's relation to the world reminds us that Adam and Eve's mistake was to enjoy creation's splendor in an idolatrous way. The first sin of humankind was to act on a distortion of truth and a mistaken desire, a kind of unfettered aesthetic experience in denial of its Maker; a bid for freedom that has been replayed in various forms ever since. The relegation of beauty in modernity has at least something to do with this fundamental effect of sin: the

25. *Fragments* 593, cited in Barth, *Protestant Thought*, 239.

26. *Fragments*, 47, cited in Barth, *Protestant Thought*, 245.

27. Barth, *Protestant Thought*, 248.

28. Ibid., 245.

29. Ibid., 247.

beautiful *imago*, the human being, has lost its self-transcendent capacity and became ugly.[30]

Theological sense, then, rightly scoffs at the idolizing of human de sire and the reduction of the "good" to what feels right, now. It reaffirms that *God is Creator*, reminding us of our creaturely status. It recalls the oft-forgotten fact that we relate to God *because God relates to us*. It proclaims God's sovereignty over the created order, God's freedom in relating to it, and the primacy of God's self-revelation. In short, it counters a human readiness to see reality primarily on its own terms and that experienced by the senses. But neither will it cease to celebrate God's loving kindness toward humanity and creation; that God the creator notices even the hairs on our head and the tiny bird that falls. Barth rightly clarified the centre of Christianity as being the gospel's insistence on the radical *agape* of Christ. So if we are to speak of desire, we are reminded that its deepest expression and realization can only be in light of God's "desire" toward humanity, a divine self-revealing that is beautiful, joyful and pleasurable for human be ings; therefore, *it attracts us*. This Christian understanding of beauty begins and ends with God; it is oriented toward God's glory, and not toward the *imago dei*.[31] Such voices that counter the modern tendency to glorify the human are still needed within arts and faith communities.

However, that is not the only problematic tendency with which we must grapple in our theological reflection. Within Barth's early polemic lay the potential for a theological antagonism to romantic thought and its reading of the human element and "creativity." This development was noted by Balthasar who deeply admired Barth but who saw in the dialectic at the heart of Protestantism, which Barth represented, the danger of its being separated from the "mystery of love" that generates it. This allowed for the fostering of a tendency toward negation.[32] Balthasar suggested that Barth's contemplation of objective revelation did not adequately trans Protestant theology; it did not sufficiently show how the beauty of belief might find concrete expression. As a result, it did not effectively deal with the beautiful as a theological category.[33] This omission also flowed from Kierkegaard's reaction and his opposing of the "martyr of truth" and the creative "genius": "The determining factor in those who follow Kierkegaard

30. Farley, *Faith and Beauty*, 91.

31. Ibid., 73.

32. Balthasar, *The Glory of the Lord*, 56.

33. Ibid.

consciously or unconsciously is the opposition they sense between the two realms (aesthetic and religious)."[34]

This meant that later, Barth's reaction to Novalis and his dialectical reading of other nineteenth-century writings spawned interpretations that magnified the distance between the aesthetic and the religious (and creation and revelation) to such an extent as to imply they were antagonistic and competitive.

In response, we could ask whether a robust theology after Barth *must* be dialectically opposed to modern expressions of human *eros*: can human desire have a place in serious theological discussion? How might "objective revelation" be subjectively experienced and concretely expressed? What particular forms, or gifts of beauty, might these be? Need "aesthetic sensibility," shaped as it has been by various permutations of romanticism, remain marginal and exiled on the basis of its excesses? We have briefly explored how this alienation has impoverished the arts, how aesthetics and the human element have suffered beauty's loss or been corrupted when goodness and truth no longer shape and inform them. Now we must turn to the implications for theology when the aesthetic dimension of human life is diminished.

Barth highlighted the imperative for modern theology to counter certain romantic excesses. But this may have contributed to certain other emphases, such as a tendency to negate the sensual and to reject the imagination. This reserve has perhaps filtered through to practical theology, affecting Christians' readiness to engage prophetically in art and culture. As Edward Farley has noted, this can mean theological reflection about "faith" occurs at a distance from the concrete ways in which people experience the world; it is always about "something else."[35]

This gulf is not only a recent phenomenon. In the mid-nineteenth century, the Scottish writer George MacDonald grappled with the incompatibility of the Calvinist faith he inherited and his aesthetic inclinations (informed by his reading of Romantic poets). In 1855 MacDonald wrote in a letter to his father about his "deepest conviction . . . that in Scotland especially, and indeed in all dissenting modes of teaching in England, a thousand times too much is said about faith": "I would never speak about faith, but speak about the Lord himself—not theologically, as to the why and wherefore of his death—but as he showed himself in his life on earth,

34. Ibid., 51–52.

35. Farley, *Faith and Beauty*, vii.

full of grace, love, beauty, tenderness and truth. Then the needy heart can not help hoping and trusting in him, and having faith, without ever thinking about faith. How a human heart with human feelings and necessities is ever to put confidence in the theological phantom which is commonly called Christ in our pulpits, I do not know."[36]

A century later, Balthasar echoed this concern in the suggestion that joy would be the first casualty when all traces of an aesthetic attitude are removed from theology.[37] He also identified the particular challenges facing the Protestant church because of the absence of a Marian spirituality, writing that when the image of woman has vanished from the theological realm, "an exclusively masculine, imageless conceptuality . . . takes over," and faith finds itself banished from the world.[38]

More recently, Farley has also observed a skewed emphasis and the risk of a form of "philistinism" attending a preoccupation with safeguarding truth: "The human being's need to manage, control, organise and fend off whatever threatens its idols replaces its engagement with what is consistently new, real and beautiful. The Philistine does not seek beauty but control and a managed life; the useful is the Philistine's primary concern . . . (They are) too insistent on managing the world to take risks with what is really different, autonomously other or mysteriously beautiful."[39]

An aversion to risk and a preoccupation with "managing" the world itself may undermine theological orthodoxy. Mary Warnock, admittedly an observer of theology rather than a practitioner, echoes Balthasar's suggestion that the insistence, in the name of theological caution, that each thing in the world "is what it is and . . . suggests nothing else" diminishes the ability to see *through* objects in the natural world *to* what might lie beyond them. This resistance compromises the capacity for joy.[40] Historically, the Christian tradition has affirmed that God's freedom in creation and redemption is not contrary to the fact of God's care for, and sustaining of, all creatures: God *may* be known in and through the world *because it is created through Christ, in whom all things live, move and have their being* 17). This loss of meaning (or "enchantment") attributed to the created order is perhaps the haunting absence Farley observed, the loss of a precognitive,

36. MacDonald, *George MacDonald and his Wife*, 222.

37. Balthasar, *The Glory of the Lord*, 50.

38. Ibid., 423.

39. Farley, *Faith and Beauty*, 91.

40. Warnock, "Religious Imagination," 147.

childhood capacity to be moved by its mysterious attractions.[41] Inevitably this diminishes as people grow older and their cognitive faculties develop, but need it be entirely forsaken? Is there is a kind of *re*-cognition, what Farley calls "a lifelong relation to *things*" that is essential to being human? And, if human beings can aesthetically respond to what is attractive and engaging about the world, surely such participation has a central place in theological reflection and practice? What constitutes the realm of the "sacred" with which we, as theologians, are to be concerned?

Rowan Williams offers some interesting and helpful insights on this dilemma. Citing Jacques Maritain's dictum about "things being more than they are,"[42] Williams suggests this idea has several implications, all of which lead toward the frontiers of theology: "If there is *always*, that to which things are related irrespective of what I can . . . make of them, that awareness of a depth in the observable world beyond what is at any moment observable is close to what seems to be meant by 'the sacred.'"[43]

This depth, what Balthasar calls the "gratuitous energy" in the world's life, has a surplus dynamic, a generative capacity.[44] If theology is concerned with the proper human response to that world, then theological reflection will also go beyond the merely functional. The human (aesthetic) response to this reality will itself overflow in acts of re-creation, or re-making through art.[45] Of course, the theologian will go further and affirm that whilst this response might be in some way common to humanity, underlying it is the prior reality of God's freedom in creation and the particularity of God's self-revelation. Furthermore, an adequate aesthetic response recognizes the "freedom of the object": things are there because God made them so and in *that* sense they exist for their own sake.[46] So, each finite phenomenon "reveals the non-necessity of creaturely existence and thus the creator's freedom."[47] This recognition was echoed in G. M. Hopkins's poem *Pied Beauty*: "all things counter, original, spare, strange" are given life by God, and this fact evokes the human response of worship and praise, to the one "*whose beauty is past change*." When beauty is understood in this way, hu-

41. Farley, *Faith and Beauty*, vii.
42. Williams, *Grace and Necessity*, 153.
43. Ibid., 154; original emphasis.
44. Ibid., 155.
45. Ibid.
46. Balthasar, cited in Williams, *Grace and Necessity*, 154.
47. Williams, *Grace and Necessity*, 156.

man creativity *is* limited; yet it is also enhanced. The theologian will say God is always "making other," and that this creative capacity is intrinsic to God's being. The theologian will also affirm that divine creativity is not capable of imitation but is uniquely itself.[48] But the theologian might also affirm that God's freedom in making and self-giving realizes in human be ings *a desire for life and joy*.[49] Art *is* a human pursuit; it exists within the realm of the creaturely. Yet, it also "images" or echoes a divine creativity. Perhaps this was Coleridge's meaning in his discussion in the "Biographia Literaria," and Imagination as being both Primary and Secondary.[50]

A theological aesthetic holds these realities together in the recogniz ing of Christ as the "form" of God's beauty. Although God's generative love in the world is universal in scope, it is particular in form, and uniquely expressed: "The most profoundly free action human beings can take in relation to their identity, the action that most fully realises the image of God, in theological terms, is to elect to discover and mould what they are in the process of "remaking" the world in a love that is both immeasurably different from God's . . . and yet endowed with some share in it . . . Human making seeks to echo, necessarily imperfectly, the character of God's love as shown in making and becoming incarnate."[51]

This is how we mend the world, and how we hold in tension sense and sensibility. Barth saw the implications of an excess of romantic sensibility in "modern man" and his theology, and we would do well to recall Barth's caution. However, for the poet Allan Tate, who wrote at a similar time, ra tionalism, with its counterpart of the uneducated heart, allowed the intel lect a disproportionate role—"man is a dull critter with enormous head."

In light of this mutual suspicion, Mary Warnock has suggested rea sons for the church's ambivalence to the Romantics and the imagination, observing that the "pleasures" extolled by Romantics have often been con trasted with the more practical response demanded by "the true reading of the Gospel story which changes people lives": "For it has often seemed that no one's life was ever changed, except perhaps for the worse, by the beautiful, even by the sublime. Wordsworth's testimony is discounted. He was not, after all, a theologian. And so there have been repeated efforts

48. Ibid.

49. Ibid., 164.

50. Coleridge, "Biographia Literaria," chapter 13.

51. Williams, *Grace and Necessity*, 165.

52. Cited in Wilder, "Protestant Orientation in Contemporary Poetry," 252.

to cut out the aesthetic from the centre of worship; to return to the facts. Christianity must be rendered intelligible and plain, poetry and music must be banished, unless they are somehow shown to be the only vehicle for the historic truth."[53]

What would it mean for the aesthetic to be *restored* to the centre of worship? Can *eros* be reclaimed by the *agape* of Christ? Can beauty be redeemed *and* redeeming? Before considering a passage of scripture, we will briefly touch on some features of Romanticism, that supremely aesthetic attitude that has had such a chequered history in relation to theology. The Romantics, however misguided and self-absorbed some of their claims about nature and imagination proved to be, did attend to beauty.

English Romanticism is generally thought to have begun with the publication of Wordsworth and Coleridge's *Lyrical Ballads* in 1798. It ended around the time of Shelley and Byron's death in the early 1820s, although its influence clearly extended well beyond. Initially, these poets were motivated to counter the reductive empiricism of the eighteenth century in which only the measurable world was "real" and human knowing through sights, sounds, emotions, was illusory.[54] Such imaginative identification came at some cost, not least because it too readily became its own justification. The Romantic imagination thus took upon itself the capacity to judge not only what was beautiful, but also what was true and good. As evident from Barth's comments on Novalis, it was precisely this claim that led to difficulties because it was framed independent of a theology of revelation.

Nevertheless, however discredited, Romantic poets did have an astounding capacity to reflect on human experience and closely attend to the particularities in the natural world and their surplus "meaning." For William Blake, one could "see a world in a grain of sand/And a heaven in a wild flower" ("Auguries of Innocence"). Subsequently, in Western thought, this mystic contemplation of the world would either be uncritically appropriated or, as in reformed theology, be rejected outright. But still, its influence is profound; these poets were indeed experts on "the way the world looks, feels, tastes, smells, sounds."[55]

For these poets, aesthetic experience was not an idle delusion, but *part of reality*. The Romantics, especially Coleridge, sought to abolish the opposition between the "imaginary" and the "real" and allow for the imagination

53. Warnock, "Religious Imagination," 154.

54. Nuttall, "Adam's Dream and Madeline's," 127.

55. Ibid.

as an organ of perception.[56] In this regard, John Keats was an important figure in English romanticism. Keats died of tuberculosis in 1821 at the age of twenty-five, although he had already won the admiration of Shelley and other writers. Keats saw the imagination as creative and its products and insights as truth-bearing, that it provides the primary material of knowledge. Keats's thought was not informed by philosophy as Coleridge's was, but he affirmed a similar belief that science, facts and rationality were not the only meaningful ways of "knowing," or of experiencing the world, and that mere chains of deductive reasoning of themselves tell us nothing.

often-quoted line, "O for a life of sensation rather than thoughts!," in a letter to John Bailey,[58] represented a significant departure from the reduced empiricism of earlier writers. But it would also open the way for the "excess of sensibility" Austen would portray in the young Marianne.

In this vein, Keats is often quoted for lines such as "Beauty is truth, truth beauty"—that is all/Ye know on earth, and all ye need to know," from *Ode on a Grecian Urn*. Just as Novalis implied human love and creativity were divine, Keats's writing suggested the human apprehension of beauty had religious weight: "I am certain of nothing but of the holiness of the Heart's affections and the Truth of Imagination."[59] His first major poem, *Endymion*, began with the assertion "A thing of beauty is a joy forever," and continued to extol the wonders of imagination. The daring implication in Keats's work, although it is debated how much he recognized and qualified it himself, is that beauty was transcendent, irreducible and self-authenticating.[60]

Nevertheless, Keats did acknowledge that even the most intense and profound poetic intuitions of beauty are still evanescent. Notably, his enigmatic affirmation about truth *being* beauty (and beauty truth), was stated within quotation marks. At the very least, this suggests a provisional tone in Keats's identification of beauty with truth. But it was this combination of evanescence and transcendence that pushed his thought toward making claims that were religious in character: the imperative for the artist or poet to continuously re-create beauty encouraged the idea of their work being

56. Ibid., 129.

57. Ibid., 126.

58. Cited in Nuttall, "Adam's Dream and Madeline's," 126.

59. Cited in Nuttall, "Adam's Dream and Madeline's," 125.

60. Nuttall, "Adam's Dream and Madeline's," 131.

creative in some primary way.[61] Together with their readiness to attribute divine qualities to nature, this aesthetic further distanced Romantics from an orthodox Christian understanding of revelation, and if there is to be any meaningful discussion on theology and the imagination this incompatibility must be negotiated.

Bearing in mind these excesses and the nature of Barth's critique, how is it possible that theology would be enhanced by this kind of poetic engagement, for certainly there is much at stake if theology does not keep its head? But, we might ask, what could be lost if it does not come to its senses? Warnock is unequivocal about the imaginative impoverishment of modern religious life, and refers to an essay by Dennis Nineham: "Men seem to need help . . . at the level of the *imagination*; they need some way of envisaging realities such as God, creation and providence imaginatively, in a way which does no violence to the rest of what they know to be true. They need to be able to mesh in their religious symbols with the rest of their sensibility."[62]

If Farley and others are right, then theological reflection aims to reconnect faith with the concrete ways human beings experience their world; it must *aid* their emotional participation in the surprising, attractive and interesting events that faith declares to be real.[63] An aesthetic sensibility signals this capacity, the readiness to sensually engage with what is beautiful and interesting in the world, to perceive its "meaning" and not be afraid to rejoice in it, to take risks in abandoning oneself. That much we can relearn from the romantic. But, theological steadiness is also necessary to free our romantic selves from the kind of imaginative empathy that becomes self-authenticating, from naïve pantheism and from making exalted claims for human knowing and creating. Religious orthodoxy must affirm what is true and trustworthy; what people *can* know and experience, that God's love is mending the world. This is good sense, and it undergirds aesthetic flourishing. It shapes the poetic imagination in a way that is receptive to transcendent presence; it informs human perceptions of beauty and desires so they are attuned to true goodness and beautiful truth.

Finally, even if some remain ambivalent about integrating this aesthetic dimension into reflection about faith (and whether the poet may help or hinder that), there are ample resources to rediscover and reclaim

61. Ibid., 134.

62. Warnock, "Religious Imagination," 156.

63. Farley, *Faith and Beauty*, vii.

within the theological and biblical traditions themselves. So in conclusion, we reflect on the Gospel accounts of a woman washing or anointing Jesus, particularly that recorded in Mark 14:3–9, a scene in which the true, the good, and the beautiful interact and inform one another. In this encounter, the full range of senses is engaged: it is a moment of startling beauty and vulnerability; it recounts a right action of prodigious generosity to the end of true testimony or witness. But it is also a sensually-charged encounter replete with possibilities of misinterpretation and at risk of emotional excess in which Jesus' true identity and destiny is "known" by a woman who sees with her heart, and who speaks with her body. This meeting between the human Jesus and the unnamed woman enacts that of the creative divine Subject meeting and blessing the human subject and her offering; it replays that dynamic interplay, the mirroring of divine grace and human initiative. It then shows how each gifts the other in concrete offerings of the most precious material. It exemplifies how theological truth might be apprehended and enacted through sensual experience; it proves that an "aesthetic sensibility" *might get things right.*

The account in Mark's Gospel closely resembles that in Matthew's (chapter 26), and bears some similarity to the anointing of Jesus by Mary of Bethany in John chapter 12. It is also echoed in Luke's account of the anointing of Jesus' feet by "a woman of the city, a sinner" in the home of Simon the Pharisee.[64] In chapter eight of the Gospel of Mark, "an unnamed woman" anoints Jesus on the head whilst at Bethany in the home of Simon the leper. There, no tears or hair are mentioned but, as in the other Gospels, "expensive perfume" is used and there is an air of intimate contact—at the centre of the action in a gathering of religious men, a lone woman touches, or anoints, Jesus. There is much to be said about this passage, but three particular features of the woman's testimony—which hereafter is expected to accompany "the good news" and "be told in remembrance of her" (v. 9)—pertain to our discussion and suggest how we might construe the relationship between theology and the arts.

First, her action is *prodigious*. The woman uses perfume to anoint Jesus, when presumably water and oil would do. What is more, she uses expensive perfume to the value of "three hundred *denarii*," the equivalent of a laborer's annual wage. This generosity is interpreted by the onlookers as irresponsible and excessive because such money might have been given

64. Unless otherwise indicated, quotations of Scripture are from the New Revised Standard Version (NRSV).

to the poor: "Why was the ointment wasted in this way?" (v. 4). The Greek word for waste (*apoleia*) has the same root as that used by Jesus just after Peter's confession earlier, in Mark 8:35: "whoever loses (or wastes) their life for my sake (*apolessay*) will find (or gain) it."[65]

The author draws the reader's attention to several contrasts. The passage develops the nature of discipleship in light of Peter's confession and sheds light on the call to "lose" one's life for Jesus' sake.[66] In addition, it provides a stark contrast with Judas' betrayal: by encircling this passage with details about the plot to kill Jesus, the writer compares the woman's action to that act of staggering ugliness and mean-spiritedness. A less extreme but no less significant contrast is also posed between this unnamed woman who has no specified social status, and the disciples or invited guests who observe and pass judgment on her. One almost imagines them likening her to the modern aesthete, the "frivolous and self-indulgent."[67] Their reactions also recall Farley's suggestion that the "philistine" is one for whom the beautiful is reduced to considerations of usefulness or monetary value, as something that pays off. However, despite its excessive nature, Jesus calls hers a "*good* service" (v. 6), a "*beautiful* work" (Gk =*kalon*), and the strength of the Greek seems to be "she has wrought a good work in me." So it is precisely this act of wastefulness that enables true worship.

Secondly, the woman's action is *prophetic*: "she has anointed my body beforehand for its burial" (v. 8).[68] This demonstrates her insight, *her* answer to the question posed in 8:29: "Who do you say I am?" It seems almost implied that her physical response is sufficient evidence for Jesus who says that she, alone of the gathered observers, correctly acknowledges his identity and acts appropriately. Furthermore, the woman seems to have been one of the few to have connected Jesus' identity with his suffering and death. Thus, her prodigious act echoes and foreshadows *his* excessive offering, his "pouring out." In contrast to Peter's misunderstanding, the Bethany woman anoints Jesus' head and she knows what this means.

But even if her cognitive assessment of the situation could be shown to be in some way incomplete, by exercising this concrete act of generosity she is *acting into more than she knows and can articulate*. Her prophetic testimony is completed by the act itself; her right theological judgment is

65. Grassi, *The Hidden Heroes of the Gospels*, 35–39.

66. Ibid., 36.

67. Balthasar, *The Glory of the Lord*, 52.

68. Grassi, *The Hidden Heroes of the Gospels*, 36.

conveyed without saying a word, not through rational expression. By thus witnessing to Jesus' death, she identifies with it and shows herself to be a true disciple: she *participates* in his suffering and mission.[69]

In doing so, she took an enormous risk, making herself vulnerable in a way that echoed the risk of the incarnation itself. Her readiness to sacrifice also foreshadowed the drama and uncertainty of Jesus' coming sacrifice. But by doing so, she helps to en-flesh the reality of God-with-us: God, in the vulnerable form of a human foetus, entered the very world declared "very good" at creation, but nevertheless one in which "something could happen . . . that would make its splendor more splendid . . . *or* . . . could happen to injure this coherence and destroy its beauty."[70]

The costly participation of the woman's action is reiterated in the thrice-mentioned ointment (*to Myron*), underscoring this as the nature of true discipleship.[71] It is further connected to Jesus' death by a careful play on words, for the ointment allows her to anoint him for burial. And, like the widow in the preceding passage (Mark 13:24), there is a "pouring out": both women give everything; their gestures are financially and socially costly. This is the most effective *martyrion*.[72] This story also recalls the risks attached to poetic, imaginative identification, as prone to judgment and charged with amoral latitude.[73]

So at the very least, contemplating this passage may cause us to exam ine our own reading of scripture and response to Jesus Christ, for it declares an expression of emotive, bodily and "indulgent" worship to be exemplary behavior and prophetic witness. That very sensual response formed a stark contrast with the self-righteous anger and evaluations of the onlookers (along the lines of stewardship and propriety) that invited Jesus' harshest criticism. How would we respond to such a display, and how might we censure its eruption into an orderly church service or academic discussion of Christology? Inasmuch as we, later readers and onlookers, are told to remember her, perhaps we are called to echo such generous excess, to be prepared to "waste" and pour out our life and to risk such vulnerability and censure. Indeed, this is how discipleship seems to be advocated in the New Testament; death is the costly means by which new life is generated.

69. Ibid., 37.

70. Dyrness, *Visual Faith*, 75.

71. Grassi, *The Hidden Heroes of the Gospels*, 37.

72. Ibid., 39.

73. Nuttall, "Adam's Dream and Madeline's," 125.

In addition, this passage challenges the binary oppositions of sense and sensibility, passion and right judgment, beauty and truth. This woman's action perhaps looked more like an expression of romantic "ecstasy" than good theological sense, but along with her generosity of spirit it also demonstrated a truthful and prophetic apprehension of Jesus. And surely, as a "creative" act, this images, or mirrors, the Creator's own self-giving and freedom—the redeemer's laying down his life for his friends. If there is a generative love at the centre of holiness—"a dearest freshness deep down things" (Hopkins, "God's Grandeur")—then this, generous to the core, will bestow life itself.[74] But we need each other—romantics and women who love too much, and children, and theologians—to help reveal the aspects of it we have become inured to. So we gather in faith that beauty and the thinking intellect *can* meet face to face; and in our self-giving, through our art and thought, help to mend the world.

74. Williams, *Grace and Necessity*, 167.

Bibliography

Austen, Jane. *Sense and Sensibility*. London: Penguin, 2003.

Balthasar, Hans Urs von. *The Glory of the Lord: A Theological Aesthetics*. Vol. 1 *the Form*. Edited by Joseph Fessio and John Riches. Translated by Erasmo Leiva-Merikakis. San Francisco: Ignatius, 1982.

Barth, Karl. *Protestant Thought: From Rousseau to Ritschl, being the translation of eleven chapters of Die protestantische Theologie im 19. Jahrhundert*. Translated by H. H. Hartwell. London: SCM, 1959.

Coleridge, Samuel Taylor. "Biographia Literaria." In *The Selected Poetry and Prose of Samuel Taylor Coleridge*, edited by Donald A. Stauffer, 109–428. New York: Random House, 1951.

Dyrness, William. *Senses of the Soul: Art and the Visual in Christian Worship*. Eugene, OR: Cascade, 2008.

———. *Visual Faith: Art, Theology, and Worship in Dialogue*. Grand Rapids: Baker Academic, 2001.

Farley, Edward. *Faith and Beauty: A Theological Aesthetic*. Aldershot: Ashgate, 2001

Fuglie, Gordon. "Beauty Lost, Beauty Found: One Hundred Years of Attitudes." In *Broken Beauty*, edited by Theodore L. Prescott, 59–76. Grand Rapids: Eerdmans, 2005.

Grassi, Joseph A. *The Hidden Heroes of the Gospels: Female Counterparts of Jesus*. Victoria: Collins Dove, 1989.

Keats, John. *Selected Poetry*. Oxford: Oxford University Press, 1998.

MacDonald, Greville. *George MacDonald and his Wife*. London: Allen & Unwin,

Nichols, Aidan. *The Word Has Been Abroad: A Guide Through Balthasar's Aesthetics* Edinburgh: T. & T. Clark, 1998.

Nuttall, A. D. "Adam's Dream and Madeline's." In *Religious Imagination*, edited by James P. Mackey, 125–41. Edinburgh: Edinburgh University Press, 1986.

Sontag, Susan. "An Argument About Beauty." *Daedalus* 131, no. 4 (2002) 21–26.

Verdun, T. "Broken Beauty, Shattered Heart." In *A Broken Beauty*, edited by Theodore L. Prescott, 25–42. Grand Rapids: Eerdmans, 2005.

Ward, Geoff. "The Persistence of Romanticism." In *The Bloomsbury Guide to English Literature*, edited by Marion Wynne-Davies, 147–67. London: Bloomsbury,

Warnock, Mary. "Religious Imagination." In *Religious Imagination*, edited by James P. Mackey, 142–60. Edinburgh: Edinburgh University Press, 1986.

Williams, Rowan. *Grace and Necessity: Reflections on Art and Love*. London: Continuum, 2005.

Wilder, Amos N. "Protestant Orientation in Contemporary Poetry." In *Spiritual Problems in Contemporary Literature*, edited by Stanley R. Hopper, 243–60. New York: Harper, 1957.

Wynne-Davies, Marion, editor. *The Bloomsbury Guide to English Literature*. London: Bloomsbury, 1995.

4

Questioning the Extravagance of Beauty in a World of Poverty

Jonathan Ryan

It is not an original question, but a challenge posed by many—ancient and modern, artists and theologians, followers of Jesus and of Plato and of Marx: What place is there for extravagant works of beauty in a world tarnished with the ugliness of poverty and injustice? Reports of famine in Somalia have recently dominated global news, with photographs of hopeless families gathering at refugee camps, and yet here, we devote our attention toward more beautiful images. If we are asked to "spend ourselves in behalf of the hungry" (Isa 58:10), how can we justify the expenditure of artistic creativity, the time and resources invested into the creation of beauty?[1]

It is not an original question, and I find it even in the mouths of the disciples who, confronted by an act of extravagant beauty, pose the question of Jesus: "Why this waste?" (Matt 26:8; Mark 14:4). Though the anointing of Jesus at Bethany may not initially strike us as an artistic or aesthetic act, it has commonly been referred to in discussions of beauty in the Christian tradition. For amongst the Gospel narratives, the anointing action of this woman is conspicuous in its vivid imagery and creativity, engaging the senses and the imagination, with Jesus himself drawing our attention to the inherent beauty of the action. Accordingly, it is within this scene that I wish to locate this discussion, particularly as it is presented in Mark's

1. Unless otherwise indicated, quotations of Scripture are from the New International Version (NIV).

Gospel (Mark 14:3–9), allowing our questioning of extravagant beauty to be framed by this narrative. I do so without pretending that the questions of the disciples are identical to those we wrestle with in our time, but simply in the hope that entering into this scene might offer a gospel perspective on these issues.

Mark tells the story as follows:

> While [Jesus] was in Bethany, reclining at the table in the home of a man known as Simon the Leper, a woman came with an alabaster jar of very expensive perfume, made of pure nard. She broke the jar and poured the perfume on his head.
>
> Some of those present were saying indignantly to one another, "Why this waste of perfume? It could have been sold for more than a year's wages and the money given to the poor." And they rebuked her harshly.
>
> "Leave her alone," said Jesus. "Why are you bothering her? She has done a beautiful thing to me. The poor you will always have with you, and you can help them any time you want. But you will not always have me. She did what she could. She poured perfume on my body beforehand to prepare for my burial. I tell you the truth, wherever the gospel is preached throughout the world, what she has done will also be told, in memory of her."

As is often the case, the disciples don't come off particularly well in this Gospel account. However, I would like to contend, at risk of unpopularity, that when the disciples respond to the woman's outpouring of perfume by asking, "Why this waste?," they have a point. Certainly, they have had a bad sense of timing at Bethany, their tact is appalling, and I find them a little "bloke-ish" here; however, I believe their question is both legitimate and appropriate, particularly when considered in the wider context of their call to discipleship.

Let us recall, for example, that their life as disciples has begun with the call to leave everything, and follow Jesus.[2] In doing so, they have quickly noted the attention Jesus has consistently paid to the poor, and his compas sion toward them. Similarly, they have heard his words of judgment on the extravagance of wealth. When Jesus says here, "The poor you will always have with you," (v. 7) they are unlikely to hear these as words of resignation on Jesus' part (as is sometimes suggested), but rather as words of challenge. And in Matthew's Gospel, the disciples encounter this lavish anointing at Bethany, having only just been instructed that their welcome into God's

2. Miller, *Women in Mark's Gospel*, 131.

kingdom will be determined, at least in part, by their response to the poor, the hungry, and the thirsty (Matt 25:31–46).

And yet here, gathered in the home of a social outcast, they have been confronted by an act of extravagance that appears to fly in the face of all of this. A woman, apparently unknown to them and their movement, has arrived uninvited, carrying an alabaster jar. An expensive gift, they wonder, or a contribution to the cause? However, unlike Joanna and Susanna, and the other women of means who had "provided for [Jesus and the disciples] out of their resources" (Luke 8:3, NRSV), this woman breaks open this costly vessel, and empties its opulent contents—all of it—over the head of Jesus.

"Why this waste of perfume?" they object. "It could have been sold for more than a year's wages [NRSV: "three hundred denarii"] and the money given to the poor" (vv. 4–5). Again, additional context may help us appreciate their indignation. Let us recall, for example, that with only two denarii, the Good Samaritan was able to provide for the needs of the Jericho road victim; with two hundred denarii, the disciples estimated they could feed a crowd of five thousand men, plus women and children (Luke 10:35; Mark 6:37). The expense involved in this anointing act, then, is extravagant indeed, and understandably a cause of scandal and offence to those committed to the wellbeing of the poor. So while our tendency is to immediately write off the disciples as uncultured and pastorally insensitive men, forever ignorant of who Jesus is and what he is trying to achieve, here I would like to give them a little more credit.

The disciples, of course, are not alone in expressing such an objection. They are preceded by a tradition of Hebrew prophets, who displayed a low tolerance for lavish acts of worship that disregarded the needs of the poor. And the history of the church has seen many periods of reform in which followers of Jesus have opposed excessive adornment—or indeed, any adornment—in worship and in churches, insisting that this was an injustice toward the poor.[3]

Whatever we might make of these examples, it is clear that Christians have always wrestled with the question of how our commitment to beauty and art relates to other commitments we have as followers of Jesus, not least our commitment to the poor, and to the justice-making work of God's kingdom. Though at times, the consequences have been regrettable, I believe

3. For example, de Gruchy draws attention to the Cistercian and Carthusian reforms of the twelfth century, and the later concerns of John Calvin. See de Gruchy, *Christianity, Art and Transformation*, 32, 42–43.

that this "wrestling" is unavoidable for Christians. We cannot readily adopt the belief that art cannot be questioned, that art is somehow beyond the realm of good and evil.

But nor can we adopt the impulsive objection of the disciples, because for all that we might say to justify their question, clearly there is something fundamentally missing in the disciples' vision. Despite the vivid visuality of this scene, they cannot "see" what is going on, and how it relates to the rest of the Jesus picture. "The house was filled with the fragrance of the per fume," John records (John 12:3), but they seem oblivious to the sweetness of the woman's devotional act. It takes Jesus himself to correct them, saying: "Leave her alone. Why are you bothering her? She has done a beautiful thing to me." (v. 6). Surely, his response will catch the disciples off guard, not least because Jesus endorses this woman's offering on the basis of its beauty. Accordingly, their questioning of her extravagant gift must be re-evaluated, and it is in the midst of this exchange of question and response, that some of our contemporary questions can be re-evaluated also.

One of the reasons that we might question the place of extravagant acts of beauty is because art and the aesthetic realm is often perceived to have little relevance to other dimensions of life. While the philosophers of antiquity distinguished between the true, the good and the beautiful, the interrelatedness of these properties was well understood. Not so in the late modernity of Western culture, however, where human existence has been increasingly fragmented and compartmentalized. One of the legacies of our philosophical forebears has been a clear demarcation between the realms of aesthetics and ethics. It was Kant's view, for example, that the true, the good, and the beautiful each pertained to "a separate realm of human experience," and that consequently, "aesthetic judgments . . . concern neither truth nor moral goodness."[4] This suggested a divorce between the aesthetic and the ethical, and the consequence for the arts, Jeremy Begbie argues, has been isolation and alienation: "of art from knowledge, of art from action, of artist from the physical world, of artist from fellow artist, of artist from society."

Such views have profoundly shaped the way we think about aesthetics in Western culture, and accordingly, it can be difficult to appreciate what relevance, if any, art and the pursuit of beauty has to the reality of global poverty. Rather than thinking in terms of the whole person, we commonly

4. Vanhoozer, "Praising in Song: Beauty and the Arts," 112.

5. Begbie, *Voicing Creation's Praise*, 199.

categorize poverty as an economic issue, or a political issue, or an issue of power imbalance; rarely is poverty perceived to be an aesthetic issue.

However, the biblical worldview was not familiar with such dichotomies. "[T]he Hebrews had no special language for art and beauty," William Dyrness observes, "precisely because beauty was not something that occupied a separate part of their lives."[6] Furthermore, he notes that in the prophetic writings, "the absence of beauty is sometimes associated with the oppression of the poor."[7] Conversely, where Israel encountered God's beauty, be it in the tabernacle and temple, or through prophetic vision, they were invariably drawn to once again live rightly before God and neighbor.[8]

A second, and closely related reason why extravagant acts of beauty may prompt indignation is because they may not appear to have any pragmatic purpose. In response to the woman's lavish outpouring of perfume, the disciples' immediate reaction is to consider the opportunity cost, which they estimate in measurable terms. Perhaps the disciples describe this beautiful act as a waste, not because it lacked aesthetic merit, but practical function. Would they have reacted differently, we wonder, if this anonymous woman had employed her resources and creativity to present Jesus with a decorative banner to accompany his triumphal entry into Jerusalem, or a set of screen-printed cloaks for the disciples, promoting their cause?

We conventionally use the word "philistine" to describe those who oppose any artistic expression that does not also display a practical or didactic function. While disciples of Jesus have often espoused this view, it is problematic for Christians for a number of reasons. It presupposes, as we earlier reflected, that the aesthetic dimension is not in itself inherently related to the other dimensions of human existence. It devalues God's gift of beauty, often assuming, in Platonic fashion, that material things of beauty are of only passing significance, and it is only the spiritual realm that is truly important. Furthermore, this insistence on art's pragmatic function opens us up to the dangerous possibilities of ideological art—or, in softer form, commercial advertising—where artistic expression becomes appropriated for underwriting and propagating certain political views, or marketing certain agendas.

6. Dyrness, *Visual Faith*, 70.

7. Ibid., 78.

8. See, for example, Walter Brueggemann's discussion of Israel's "tradition of seeing," in his *Theology of the Old Testament*, 425.

As we have observed, beauty is, in fact, intrinsically related to the "practical" concerns of the disciples regarding poverty and injustice. Political theorists and theologians have amply demonstrated the way in which artistic vision is a powerful mobilizing force for the work of liberation. However, the value of works of beauty cannot be reduced to pragmatic outcomes. As de Gruchy observes, "The transformative power of art does not lie in any overt political content or didactic intention but precisely in its aesthetic form and creative character. Art exercises its critical power by being art, by simply being there."[10]

Thirdly, the value of such acts of beauty may be questioned because they are perceived to be incapable of conveying anything of real meaning. Begbie relates how the Western mind came to associate art and aesthetics with sensual perception, noting that "the senses were generally regarded as unreliable for getting at the truth of things."[11] Beauty may excite us, or give us pleasure, but such experience is subjective; matters of universal truth were believed to be the domain of rational thought and empirical investigation, not artistic expression.

The woman's anointing action could well be perceived in such terms: emotionally moving, engaging the senses, yet she does not *say* anything; there is no verbal confession or creed associated with her action. And yet, as Jesus acknowledges, in her wordless gesture that anticipates his death, she has conveyed a truth where words would falter.

When it comes to the commitment to justice or poverty, it may be perceived that it is only practical acts of compassion, or words of justice, that "count," as if the redemptive work of God is outworked primarily in rational and ethical, but not aesthetic terms. De Gruchy summarizes this problem well when he observes that "The heirs of modernity . . . have lost faith in the redemptive power of beauty. Ugliness has become far more prevalent and potent while beauty has become subjective taste, not a power beyond ourselves that has the capacity to transform."[12]

As an aside, I find it interesting that many scholarly commentaries on this anointing scene appear to disregard the aesthetic in their pursuit for the "symbolic meaning" of the scene. While they may provide exegetical comment about the syntax of "alabaster," or the uses of nard in first-century

9. Brueggemann's *The Prophetic Imagination* is a classic example.

10. De Gruchy, "Holy Beauty," 24.

11. Begbie, *Voicing Creation's Praise*, 187.

12. De Gruchy, *Christianity, Art and Transformation*, 101.

Palestine, few linger long enough to consider the beauty of this woman's gesture, moving quickly instead toward interpreting the text. But where is the contemplation of this evocative action itself, of its aesthetic appeal?

Of course, I do not mean to suggest that contemplating works of art, and acts of beauty, should not lead us to interpretation. Indeed, Jesus himself offers an interpretation of this woman's action, explaining that "She poured perfume on my body beforehand to prepare for my burial" (v. 8). But before he does so, he first draws attention to the "beautiful thing" that she has done.

In our encounter with beauty, David Bentley Hart identifies our misguided eagerness to "discover something more fundamental than whatever merely 'accidental' form might manifest it."[13] However, beauty "resists reduction to the 'symbolic,'" he insists.[14] "In the moment of the beautiful, one need attend only to the glory that it openly proclaims, and resist the temptation to seek out some gnosis secretly imparted."[15]

To summarize our discussion so far: the disciples have questioned the extravagance of this beautiful act, indignantly asking, "Why this waste?" Such an objection is just as likely to be voiced in our own contemporary setting, and I've suggested a few reasons why such a question might be posed. Firstly, because of the isolation of the aesthetic realm from other spheres of human life. Secondly, because such acts of beauty are perceived to lack any pragmatic purpose. And thirdly, because it is often believed that the realm of beauty is incapable of expressing anything truly meaningful or substantial. Of course, in giving all this airtime to the disciples, we have been altogether distracted from the woman and her beautiful offering; to these we now turn.

The beautiful act of this anonymous woman is generally described as "an anointing," which could imply that her action was simply another typical instance of the anointing ritual. But of course, there is nothing typical or routine about this scene at all; in fact, her creative enacting of the anointing ritual is unique in scripture. Unfortunately, in all of the Gospel accounts, it is described with the bare minimum of words, leaving much up to our imagination. But we can wonder, for example, what motivated her to disregard social convention, and with extraordinary courage, to enter into this tight enclave of male disciples, and approach Jesus directly. We must

13. Hart, *The Beauty of the Infinite*, 25.

14. Ibid., 24.

15. Ibid., 25.

admire her boldness in taking on the formal role of a prophet, and marvel at the truly prophetic imagination that inspires her to, of all things, anoint Jesus. Though he is, of course, the Anointed One, Jesus' identity as Messiah is not elsewhere comprehended in Mark's Gospel until the centurion's confession at the cross (Mark 15:39).[16] We can reflect on the materials she has chosen for this task: nard we know to be among the finest perfumes of the time, and this is emphasized by the alabaster flask that contains it. But with what words would we describe this fragrant scent, or the form of its alabaster container? And the breaking open of this fine vessel: surely this is part of her dramatic intent too, revealing that she is pouring out its contents, not in part, but in entirety. Having done so, the fragrance that has anointed the head of her Lord fills the house. Her beautiful work is complete, and so, Susan Miller observes, "the woman is silent . . . leaving her action to speak for itself."[18]

As we have already observed, the disciples have little interest in these elements of the woman's beautiful act, and seek to dismiss her, but Jesus curates her work differently, focusing our attention on it, making it the centerpiece in the scene. Why does Jesus respond this way, and what might we learn from his endorsement of this extravagant offering of beauty? There are all sorts of things we might say here. We are reminded, of course, of the centrality of beauty in the Christian narrative; of the beauty of God's character; of the way in which God inscribes this beauty upon creation; and of the importance of beauty in our worshipful response to God. We have also reflected already on the way in which beauty is integrally woven into the biblical narrative that precedes Jesus.

But here, late in Mark's Gospel, as shadows loom, Jesus approves of the fittingness of the woman's action, and our focus is drawn particularly toward the extravagant beauty displayed in the cross, where "the splendid form of God's self-giving love" is expressed.[19] This, I believe, is where the crux of the matter lies, for the disciples' objection is not simply to the woman's act of beauty *per se*, but to its unmerited extravagance. And yet, we find in relation to the cross of Christ, that this act of aesthetic extravagance is not only merited, but essential.

16. Miller, *Women in Mark's Gospel*, 128.

17. See Evans, *Mark 8:27—16:20*, 360.

18. Miller, *Women in Mark's Gospel*, 132.

19. Vanhoozer, "Praising in Song," 116.

To describe something as "extravagant" often suggests an excessiveness, an inappropriateness in proportion. By contrast, beauty has often been characterized by an appropriate sense of proportion in classical thought. Elaine Scarry expresses this association well: "beautiful things give rise to the notion of distribution, to a lifesaving reciprocity, to fairness not just in the sense of loveliness of aspect but in the sense of 'a symmetry of everyone's relation to one another.'"[20]

Interestingly, when Jesus speaks of the "beautiful thing" done by this woman (v. 6), he uses the word *kalon*, which carries with it a sense of something being "fitting" and "good," as well as "beautiful." How can this be, when the act being described seems far from fitting in its excessive costliness?

But the cross, Richard Viladesau comments, "challenges us to rethink and to expand our notion of the beauty of God, and indeed of 'beauty' itself."[21] It is in relation to the cross of Christ, that we can understand how the woman's offering can be extravagant, and also good, fitting and beautiful. For the strange beauty displayed in the cross breaks open our containers of reciprocity, fairness, and symmetry. Rather, in the life and death of Jesus Christ, God pours God's self out for the sake of the world, and in so doing, is God.

Revealed to us in the cross is a beauty that is selfless, extravagant, excessive, "a stumbling block to Jews and foolishness to Gentiles" (1 Cor 1:23); the life of the Son is unjustifiably "poured out for many, for the forgiveness of sins" (Matt 26:28). What moment in the Gospels expresses and anticipates this beauty more evocatively and movingly, than the extravagant act of beauty performed by this woman? And how could this work express such an asymmetrical beauty, unless it was extravagant?

At this point, we must make an obvious, yet important, observation. Neither the beauty displayed on the cross, nor the beauty of the anointing action, are self-interested outpourings. In contrast with other unnamed women in Mark's Gospel who approach Jesus with requests, Miller notes that this woman instead brings a gift, "an offering of love to Jesus."[22] So also the extravagant gift of the Son, given because "God so loved the world" (John 3:16).

20. Scarry, *On Beauty and Being Just*, 95.

21. Viladesau, *The Beauty of the Cross*, 9.

22. Miller, *Women in Mark's Gospel*, 131.

Hart helps unpack further the significance of this selfless character of the beauty of the cross. Because of its association with transcendence, it has sometimes been thought that beauty "can point in only one direction, away from the world," and upward toward the transcendent realm.[23] Understandably, divine beauty and worldly poverty would then seem to be divergent. However, such an account of transcending beauty is contradicted by the character of God revealed to us in Jesus Christ. "Christian thought, with its trinitarian premise," Hart argues, "must follow the path of beauty outward into the world, even into states of privation."[24]

Perhaps it is because, in Western culture, the arts have tended to be the special preserve of the materially affluent and intellectually enlightened, that we associate the extravagance of beauty with self-gratifying luxury. However, the beauty of the cross reveals a different sort of extravagance: a beauty that is full and lavish, yet generous in its orientation toward the other. In this sense, our own extravagant artistic expressions need not be seen at odds with the poverty with the world, but rather referring back to this divine beauty. Christians will also discern this beauty in creation, Hart suggests, which with "an unsettling prodigality . . . lavishes itself upon even the most atrocious of settings,"[25] thus reflecting the "dynamic involvement" of the infinite God within the finitude of the created order.[26]

We also note that this beauty displayed in the cross, while selfless, is not self-negating; it is a redemptive beauty that finishes not in death or nothingness, but in the resurrection life. Miller suggests that the generosity of the woman's gift of perfume also foreshadows "the abundant life all will receive in the new creation."[27] Though this scene is bracketed by narratives of violence and betrayal, the woman's action "breaks into a hostile environment in the same way that the kingdom of God suddenly becomes manifest in a world ruled by evil."[28] The extravagance of her action against a backdrop of scarcity prompts us to look forward, reminding us of the surplus of beauty and the beautiful surplus anticipated in biblical accounts of God's coming kingdom.

23. Hart, *The Beauty of the Infinite*, 323.

24. Ibid.

25. Ibid., 15.

26. Ibid., 20–21.

27. Miller, *Women in Mark's Gospel*, 140.

28. Ibid., 130.

We have covered a lot of ground here, and in case the implications of this discussion are not immediately apparent, I'd like to conclude with some reflections on artistic vocation, in light of the questions we have considered.

Firstly, while we would tend to quickly dismiss the objection of the disciples, I have suggested that the question they pose is an important one, not least for Christian artists. Just as, from a Christian perspective, we would not want to see art and aesthetics as isolated from the rest of human existence, nor can we allow the artistic vocation to be divorced from the rest of our vocation as disciples of Jesus. Nicholas Wolterstorff describes our vocation as Christians as one of responsibility toward God, including for our neighbor and for creation. He makes the point plainly: "The artist is not to pick up his responsibilities when he lays aside his art—he is to exercise his responsibilities in the very production of his art."[29]

For many of us, including artists, this may not be a welcome point, and Wolterstorff goes on to suggest why this might be the case: "Undoubtedly it is on this point of art and responsibility that the Christian image of the artist diverges most sharply from the heaven-storming image of post-Enlightenment Western man. For where the Christian sees the artist as a responsible agent before God, sharing in our human vocation, Western man in the Gauguin-image sees him as freed from all responsibility, struggling simply to express himself in untrammelled freedom . . . Indeed, it is often suggested that if the artist so much as thinks in terms of responsibility his flow of creativity will be stanched."[30]

Of course, the belief that we can disconnect art from the wider world in which we find ourselves is, as de Gruchy puts it, a "dangerous illusion." "Art is always embedded in culture," he argues, "even when it is counter-cultural in its aim. It does not exist in an autonomous sphere separate from the rest of life without any public accountability."[31]

From a Christian perspective, then, art and artists do not operate in a realm beyond questioning, and artistic vocation does not exempt us from the call to discipleship, and its responsibilities. Limited as the disciples may have been in their vision, their questioning of the extravagance of the woman's action reminds us that a concern for the poor, and a thirst for God's justice, is integral to following Jesus, and this commitment must be allowed to inform and question our artistic commitments. While we do not

29. Wolterstorff, *Art in Action*, 78.

30. Ibid.

31. De Gruchy, *Christianity, Art and Transformation*, 198–99.

want art to become an ideological enterprise, nor can we allow the pursuit of beauty to become self-centered or idolatrous, ignorant of our hurting world. As de Gruchy argues, a certain "sanctification of our aesthetic sensibility" is needed, bringing us a sense of "good taste" that "helps us to know the difference between an extravagance that is unjust and the creation of splendor that humanizes, restores dignity, evokes hope, and thus contributes to renewal and transformation."[32]

But while I have sought to preserve the legitimacy of the disciples' questioning, I have also argued that their perspective is somewhat lacking. An appreciation of beauty and aesthetics has often been absented from Christian discipleship. Too often, the church has marginalized the artist, whether through puritanical purging of visual art, or through a more subtle neglect and disempowerment. I'd dare to suggest that this has often particularly been the case among those most fervently devoted to the poor, and the cause of social justice. We can only conclude with regret that this has been an unfortunate diminishment of our Christian witness.

By contrast, we have celebrated the beautiful action of this woman, not simply for its aesthetic appeal, but for the way it appears to somehow participate in the extravagant beauty revealed in the cross. While cautioning us against confusing the "redemptive possibilities of art" with the unique "redemption wrought in Christ," Begbie observes that "God's redemption in Christ clearly has an aesthetic dimension to it, and there would seem no good reason to deny that we can share in this dimension of divine activity through artistic endeavour."[33]

In a world made ugly by the hand of injustice, expressing the beauty of God's redemptive work in Christ through the creative arts is an essential part of the church's witness. This need not be seen as taking place in tension with Christ's call to serve the poor, but rather as an important response to this call. Indeed, responding to the needs of another can be redemptive for both parties; it need not be a fetter for the artist, but an opportunity. This could come through direct artistic engagement with issues of poverty and injustice; the scope for artistic contribution in these areas, though often unappreciated, is boundless. However, as I have tried to make clear here, even aside from such focused efforts, works of art and creativity in themselves have a valuable place in the transformative work of God's new creation. For

32. De Gruchy, "Holy Beauty," 24.

33. Begbie, *Voicing Creation's Praise*, 212–13.

after all, the vision toward which we live is not only one characterized by wellbeing, but also by extraordinary beauty (e.g., Rev 21).

Finally, we have considered the extravagance of this woman's action. There is a certain sort of extravagance that I have not endorsed here, the self-centered indulgence that Wolterstorff perceives to be systemically embedded into the fine art world. He describes the institution's "insatiable appetite for additional works [that] drives its agents into acts of plunder and rapacity," and its "system of distribution [that] provides rich opportunity for those who are interested not at all in art but only in financial self-aggrandizement."[34]

In contrast to such extravagance, I have sought to affirm the "excessiveness" of this woman's action in light of the example of Christ. We have already reflected on way in which this woman's selfless outpouring expresses something of the extravagance of the cross, and all followers of Jesus are invited to do the same. "Be imitators of God," Paul writes, ". . . and live a life of love, just as Christ loved us and gave himself up for us as a fragrant offering and sacrifice to God" (Eph 5:1–2). Vanhoozer suggests that "the Christian life acquires a beautiful shape when it takes on the shape of the cross. Inner beauty expresses itself outwardly through works of love, through works of self-emptying humility and self-giving action."[35]

For the artist, selfless and extravagant acts of beauty make a bold statement in a global society increasingly defined by the desires of consumerism, the lure of wealth, and the fear of scarcity. In such a culture, art always runs the risk of becoming simply another commodity to be traded. However, the divine beauty upon which we have reflected resists such capitalization, and so also should our expressions of beauty.[36] The extravagance that I have advocated for art is not a matter of decadent gallery openings and lofty sale prices, but rather the extravagance of a gift to the other, pouring ourselves into works of beauty that will bring blessing to others, rather than to ourselves.

Such an attitude may do little for our artistic aspirations to make a name for ourselves, but in this respect, I find the conclusion of the anointing scene quite remarkable. For on the one hand, Jesus honors this woman, saying "Wherever the gospel is preached throughout the world, what she has done will also be told, in memory of her" (v. 9). Such praise from Jesus

34. Wolterstorff, *Art in Action*, 192.

35. Vanhoozer, "Praising in Song," 120.

36. See Hart, *The Beauty of the Infinite*, 431–39.

is without parallel in the Gospels. Could there be a higher affirmation for her extravagant act of beauty? And yet, in the Synoptic Gospels, she re mains anonymous. "She has made it," we might say . . . but who is she? Her anonymity is likely due, at least in part, to the cultural biases of the time, but in a poetic sort of way, it also seems strangely apt. Because, for all the lavish expense of her gift, she has not purchased a name for herself in his tory, but rather, has extravagantly given of herself to Jesus, in whose story she will forever be remembered.

The question I have wrestled with in this essay is challenging and complex; I have not sought to resolve it, but rather, to be drawn into it. To be a follower of Jesus means, among other things, to live attentive to the cry of the poor. However, it also means to live attentive to the beauty of God, which does not distance itself from poverty and injustice, but seeks to transform it.

Accordingly, in expressing our love for Jesus and for the poor, we are invited to bring to Jesus beautiful things, creative things, artistic things, as generous and extravagant offerings. To do so may involve great risk or great cost, but we do so, not for our own sake, but trusting that through us—to borrow Paul's words—the "fragrance of the knowledge" of Christ may fill the world (2 Cor 2:14).

Bibliography

Begbie, Jeremy S. *Voicing Creation's Praise: Towards a Theology of the Arts*. Edinburgh: T. & T. Clark, 1999.

Brueggemann, Walter. *The Prophetic Imagination*. Minneapolis: Fortress, 2001.

———. *Theology of the Old Testament: Testimony, Dispute, Advocacy*. Minneapolis: Fortress, 1997.

De Gruchy, John W. *Christianity, Art and Transformation: Theological Aesthetics in the Struggle for Justice*. Cambridge: Cambridge University Press, 2003.

———. "Holy Beauty: A Reformed Perspective on Aesthetics within a World of Ugly Injustice." In *Reformed Theology for the Third Christian Millennium*, edited by Brian A. Gerrish, 13–26. Louisville: Westminster John Knox, 2003.

Dyrness, William A. *Visual Faith: Art, Theology and Worship in Dialogue*. Grand Rapids: Baker Academic, 2001.

Evans, Craig A. *Mark 8:27—16:20*. Word Biblical Commentary 34B. Nashville: Nelson, 2001.

Hart, David Bentley. *The Beauty of the Infinite: the Aesthetics of Christian Truth*. Grand Rapids: Eerdmans, 2003.

Miller, Susan. *Women in Mark's Gospel*. London: T. & T. Clark, 2004.

Scarry, Elaine. *On Beauty and Being Just*. Princeton: Princeton University Press, 2001.

Vanhoozer, Kevin J. "Praising in Song: Beauty and the Arts." In *The Blackwell Companion to Christian Ethics*, edited by Stanley Hauerwas and Samuel Wells, 110–22. Malden, MA: Blackwell, 2004.

Viladesau, Richard. *The Beauty of the Cross: The Passion of Christ in Theology and the Arts, from the Catacombs to the Eve of the Renaissance*. New York: Oxford University Press, 2008.

Wolterstorff, Nicholas. *Art in Action: Toward a Christian Aesthetic*. Carlisle: Solway, 1997.

5

Living Close to the Wound

Libby Byrne

To "mend the world" is no small task especially when brokenness stretches so deeply into our human story. When we consider the scope of the damage that exists within our world and in our own lives it can seem that is beyond our capacity to re-imagine the world as whole, unbroken—as it was in the beginning. In the face of the very practical work that is so urgently required to repair the damage that we have inflicted upon the planet and upon each other, the hope that art could "mend the world" seems no more than a lofty ideal doomed to failure.

But despite the limitations inherent in our human capacity, there lies within us a deep desire for wholeness and it is out of this desire that the idea to "mend the world" arrives. The first step on the journey is to acknowledge that there is a wound and it is woven into the very fabric of our human experience. To be constantly drawing attention to the wound in our humanity is not a popular calling. In an age where we value the self-actualizing potential of the individual over and above the strength of our community, continuing to draw attention to our cultural and spiritual wounds seems to be less than popular if not countercultural.

Within this essay I will explore the premise that in contributing to the work of mending the world, it is the calling of the artist to live close to the wound. I will locate this contention within the nexus that seems to exist between art, theology and philosophy, in order to describe the prevailing conditions required for the artist to work toward the task of mending a broken world. I will then give examples of how these theories work in practice with particular reference to the work of Anselm Kiefer and finally my own studio practice.

MELANCHOLY

To "mend the world" firstly requires that we turn our attention toward the experience of *being* in the world. Resisting the temptation to live for the future in constant pursuit of our own personal happiness enables us to embrace the experience of being in the world and we are able to become more deeply aware of the value of our own unique place in the universe. As we turn our attention away from ourselves and consider the wider human story we begin to understand that to really live within the gift of our being, is to live in a place of exile and melancholy.[1]

Matthew Del Nevo draws this assertion regarding the nature of our human experience from Augustine's basic premise: "You (Father God) made us for yourself and our hearts are restless until they rest in you."[2] Del Nevo suggests that the nature of our estrangement from God places us in the position of living in exile within the world; hence our existence is essentially one of continual restlessness and melancholy. He then draws on John Keats' idea that the world is a "vale of soul-making" and connects this with the experience of melancholy thus concluding that a climate of melancholy is necessary in the work of deepening the imagination and creating the conditions in which it is possible for our soul to be blessed.[3]

Del Nevo draws a clear distinction between the soul and the self, saying that the "Self has to do with the first person singular . . . [and] sees its individuality as singular, that is, worthy and deserving of admiration and preference."[4] Soul is not a given nor is it reliant on our own worth, yet our experience of soul is made possible by the way we choose to live within the world. Whilst the ego driven self is able to exist in isolation, it is the experience of soul that enables us to live in connection with one another and with God. For Del Nevo soul is about living a life that is blessed, not by anything that can be earned but by creating "the conditions for it to be

1. Del Nevo, *The Valley Way of Soul*, 26.
2. Augustine, *Confessions* 1.1.1, cited in Del Nevo, *The Valley Way of Soul*, 26.
3. Del Nevo, *The Valley Way of Soul*, 45.
4. Ibid.

bestowed."[5] When we pay attention to the serious work of "soul-making" we are awakened to the importance of melancholy as it thickens our own experience of blessing and strengthens the connections that we have with others on a soul-to-soul level.

It is in the light of melancholy, that darkness is able to be illuminated sufficiently so as to reveal the true nature of our existence in exile. Mel ancholy creates a softening in the landscape. Free from the harsh light of happiness, the artist is able to be vulnerable enough to receive the gift of an image born out of loss. According to Del Nevo, melancholy is different to sadness or depression as it opens us up to other people. In the same way, images born in the light of melancholy have the capacity to open us up to ourselves, connecting us in the breadth and depth of our human experience of loss and wounding. In doing so they give us an opportunity to acknowl edge the losses that might otherwise have remained secret.

Vulnerability

It is possible to consider the wound as something more than loss; more than unwelcome damage in the midst of an otherwise perfect creation. John O'Donohue suggests that the wound can be also considered a point of vulnerability.[6] He goes on to say that it is the work of the artist to regu larly return again and again to this point of vulnerability in an attempt to excavate something new. In order to be healed, this wound needs to find a new form and it is within the darkness of the wound that new life swells. It is from the wound, the point of most awkward vulnerability, that the artist works to excavate life in a new form.

In this sense, the wound can be considered an unexpected opening in the surface that makes it possible for us to see the beauty that resides within darkness. If we are tempted to prematurely seal the opening of a wound, the new form is unable to emerge and take shape in the world. The artist is called to spend time living close to an open wound, attending to the layers and waiting for signs of life from within the darkness.

In this process it is important to risk looking past what may be evident on first sight. The first veil of a wound may be very difficult to see and require a careful response. We might be tempted to want to change the

5. Ibid.

6. O'Donohue, *Divine Beauty*, 196.

awkward shape of the wound into something simpler and easier. Speaking of the development of a Crucifixion series, Brett Whitley says of his process, "One of the hardest things is to discipline oneself . . . concentrate on one vision until it discloses its third and fourth veil—to keep seeing past what you have just seen."[7] As the first veil of the work presents itself, we rely heavily on tacit knowing to determine how to stay with this emergent form.[8] It is our trust in the process that infuses us with the courage to be disciplined and attentive at this point of vulnerability; to reach beyond the limitations of what we have previously known in pursuit of something new that has integrity, which is a real and uncomplicated statement of truth.[9]

At this stage of the process we are open to the possibility of really seeing the shape of our own vulnerability and so our attention to the work becomes a prudent consideration of what may still be needed in the work as it takes form. We must consider how best to work with our vulnerability in light of "the good of the thing being made."[10] It is possible to be seduced into the need to use the canvas to inscribe our personal experience and thus undergo a cathartic release from our own suffering but to do this, is to make the work from the position of *self* rather than from the *soul*.[11] Genuine acceptance of the shape of our vulnerability opens us to the experience of melancholy, the natural climate in the "vale of soul making," and our desire to be whole, to rest in God, is replenished.

The Empty Tomb

It is confronting to bear witness to an open wound and in the moment when I first see the surface of this disturbance it is easy to fall into the desire to do whatever I can to be rid of the damage. Burying the debris or concealing it in darkness would seem to be a way to avoid the experience of grief.

The tomb is the place where the wounded Christ was concealed, no longer visible for three days and nights. Matthew Fox challenges the notion that the tomb was a place of desolation and claims the image of the empty tomb as a powerful symbol of God's creative energy in the world, describing

7. Crumlin, *Beyond Belief*, 118.

8. See Polanyi, *The Tacit Dimension*.

9. Whitley, cited in Crumlin, *Beyond Belief*, 118.

10. Williams, *Grace and Necessity*, 47.

11. Del Nevo, *Valley Way of Soul*, 45.

it as "the primary womb from which Christ is reborn."[12] The tomb, in which humanity concealed its deepest wound in the death of Christ, actually held the creative potential to become the womb from which "all things are made new" (Rev 21:5).

In the same way, the artist who seeks to "mend the world" will need to work within a metaphorical tomb anticipating that within this place, chaos can be transformed by creativity and new life will be issued forth. "The luminous beauty of great art so often issues from the deepest, darkest wounding."[13] Art offers a vehicle in which we are able to enter the tomb with the wound of our humanity and then engages us while we wait for a new image to be formed and ultimately resurrected. Or to put it more simply, "Art heals by accepting the pain and doing something with it."

Sacrament

The artist who is obedient to the discipline of the work is likely to experience a profound attunement to reality. Within the stillness of the tomb we are free to relinquish any imagined sense of control. We are invited to embrace the reality "that I do not know really who I am; therefore I have to let go of who I am not."[15] "Letting go of who I am not" offers us the freedom that is inherent in a blank canvas. No longer constrained by who we perceive we *should* be we are able to consider who we *could* be when we are unrestricted by the limitations of our own imagination. We are becoming attuned to possibilities that exist for us within the artwork itself.

Good art happens when the artist is able to resist inscribing herself in a work and becomes a witness to the arrival of an image, merging with it in a relationship that is sacramental in nature.[16] Such a relationship requires us to be willing to let go of the need to be in control of the product and simply be obedient "to the unfolding logic in the process of making, as the work discloses itself."[17] Art functions to take the attention away from

12. Fox, *A Spirituality Named Compassion*, 133.

13. O'Donohue, *Divine Beauty*, 190.

14. McNiff, *Art Heals*, i.

15. Freeman, *Return to the Centre*.

16. Del Nevo, *The Valley Way of Soul*, 128–36. Del Nevo discusses the poetic spirit of the author merging with the work in a relationship that is sacramental with particular reference to the poem "Devotion" by Yves Bonnefoy.

17. Williams, *Grace and Necessity*, 52.

ourselves, enabling us to relinquish our own thoughts and our claim on any imagined version of ourselves as being in control of that which is created. When we let go of the need to *know* what is happening in the work all that is required of us is to be present to the expanding possibilities. Unknowing expands in the soul as a deep breath expands in the lungs. If we are able to recognize the gravitas inherent in the moments of unknowing before the canvas, then we are able to risk stepping out of the way long enough for Art to actually happen.

ANSELM KIEFER AND THE "SCHOCK"

In an interview with Tim Marlow at the Louisiana Museum of Modern Art Anselm Kiefer said of the creative process, "It always starts with a Schock."[18] Born in Germany in 1945 Kiefer grew up amongst the *schock* of post war rubble and was deeply aware of the cultural heritage left by the Nazi regime and the Holocaust. In a time when it was taboo to speak of the atrocities of this recent war, Kiefer chose to attend to the wound of his cultural heritage producing monumental artworks honouring the memory of the Jewish people and their place within our human family. In particular his regular referencing of train tracks leading into landscapes that have been formed from molten lead, make it impossible for us to ignore the plight of those who have lived and died in concentration camps throughout human history. Though they refer to a particular experience, place and time these works are not representations of the landscape. They have been formed of lead, dirt, drainpipes and straw and then executed on a monumental scale and so they are capable of actually become the landscape to which they refer, here and now. Rather than viewing from a distance, we are witness to the real presence of this work. We find ourselves living in the midst of a cultural and spiritual wound, a holy wound; and we are called into silence.

Kiefer believes that as an artist, his responsibility is always to the work itself. It is not his intention to make political statements that will change the way in which we think about the wounds of humanity, but simply to present the work to us as accurately as he can. He is always obedient to the process as it unfolds before him. It could be argued that as material objects, his canvases do not have the capacity to change the world. And yet as they exist and they reverberate within the world calling us into an experience of

18. Kiefer and Marlow, "Louisiana Museum of Modern Art."

"seeing" this work with all of our senses, we are changed. The work alone cannot change the world, but when we meet the work in a sacramental re lationship we are changed and so therefore is the countenance of the world.

Kiefer's work always demands a sensuous encountering as he awk wardly layers the materials on a monumental scale. He is effectively sculpt ing the landscape out of paint and raw materials and in doing so he presents us not with a final product, but with the process as a place where we can be in exile. Claiming that art is never finished, Kiefer allows the process of making to continue to unfold within the museum or the gallery. He allows the work to decompose on the walls before us and as we see the detritus that falls within the framework of the canvas, we are reminded that exile is a transient state. His work speaks to the "essential reality" that the veil of our human existence will also fall away as we find our home in God. Rowan Williams describes this possibility and says, "Art seeks to reshape the data of the world so as to make their fundamental structure and relation visible."[20]

When we take the time to see Kiefer's work as a "sensuous encounter ing engaging all of our senses in the work of curiosity, appreciation and inquiry" it becomes part of our knowing about the world and it stimulates within us a climate in which we are free to hope that the world can be changed and that which is broken can be mended.[21] As a German Catholic Kiefer risks engaging his process with sacred Jewish text, often referencing Isaiah and the Kabbalah. He takes the risk of scrawling inscriptions of text upon some of these images, but in doing he takes a clear position of need ing to know something, of being open to learning from the painting about the place of these texts within the landscape of life after the holocaust.

Kiefer's use of materials suggests the possibility that he has a sacra mental relationship with his work. Having been brought up in the Roman Catholic Church, Kiefer describes his first communion as a crucial mo ment in his life. Reflecting on this experience with Tim Marlow, Kiefer remembers being a ten year old boy who was earnestly preparing for the experience of the sacrament and serious in his hope that the ritual would lead to spiritual illumination. Despite his attentive engagement with the ritual and the celebrations Kiefer was left uninspired and disappointed by the event. He now considers that the experience of missing something in

19. Williams, *Grace and Necessity*, 18.

20. Ibid.

21. Seely and Reason, "Expressions of Energy," 34.

the sacrament of the Eucharist could have contributed to his desire to work as an artist. For Kiefer, art making is a spiritual occupation because it is about making a connection between things that are separated.[22]

Kiefer regularly risks letting go of convention in order to make connections with the life that he believes is inherent in the materials. In pouring molten lead onto canvas and paint Kiefer lives into the belief that "Risk is an essential need of the soul . . . a form of danger which provokes a deliberate reaction . . . and represents the finest possible stimulant."[23] His deliberate use of dangerous materials over many years has provoked some excessively difficult landscapes that demand our attention and the recollection of cultural wounds that we might rather dismiss.

However, our collective hope is that time spent in the presence of the wound will help "mend the world." Having spent many years following Kiefer's work as he bore witness to the experience of the Holocaust, my own hope that something would be *mended* was finally brought to fruition in his 2007 exhibition "Aperiatur Terra."[24] It was in this exhibition that Kiefer risked exploring a promise from Isaiah within a landscape that had previously served him as iconographic of the Holocaust. In the shadow of the railway tracks, Kiefer discovered a pathway into a field of poppies as he wondered aloud and scrawled into the sky, "The earth breaks open and brings forth a Saviour" (Isa 45:8). Simon Schama, of *The Guardian*, said of this work, "From deep beneath the loam of memory heaped over the canvas, Kiefer's vast, rutted wastelands have germinated brilliant resurrections."[25] In doing so, Kiefer's work was able to *mend* something that had been broken in the world and having seen the work with all my senses, I was changed.

Courage

Having been changed in the moments of viewing this work, I spiral quickly back into the tomb of my studio with the desire and the courage to attend to my own wounds. The climate in the studio needs to be attuned to this work in the same way that the soul is attuned. The studio needs to be

22. Kiefer and Marlow, "Louisiana Museum of Modern Art."

23. Weil, *The Need for Roots*, 33.

24. "Aperiatur Terra" was exhibited at the NSW Gallery between 19 May and 29 July 2007.

25. Schama, "Trouble in paradise," 12.

a *safe enough* place for melancholy to dwell, whilst offering the physical containment necessary for unexpressed beauty and desire to be released from within the darkness of a wound and ultimately united with the source of our desire—that is God: "Our hearts are restless until they rest in you." The studio is a place of restless desire seeking to be birthed and so the studio is never really a *safe* place because there is always risk in birthing something new. However, the studio can be a secluded place, a sacred place in which longing and desire are able to find a home and lead us to a new understanding of our human experience. The creation of a series of work in the studio allows the artist to "think in a medium."[27]

The *Life Map* Series

Bearing witness to the fruits of Kiefer's capacity to attend to the wound in humanity gave me courage to consider the possibility of healing the wounds in my own story by attending to them with canvas and oils. In 2001 whilst working as a full time painting student, I was impelled toward the challenge of visually mapping my own life in the hope of finding a home for the patterns of longing and desire, grief and joy that seemed to have marked my experience. However when I suggested this to my teacher I was strongly discouraged and he warned me that I was likely to become lost in the midst of a project that may never be finished. But Kiefer had taught me that to be *finished* was not something to desire or expect in the process of painting and so I was able to begin.

Initially designed as a series of four panels it was soon evident that to be honest about the depth and breadth of my life experiences I would need to create a long panel that was capable of undergirding all of these images. This longer panel worked to gather all that I thought I had known and held it within the thickness and darkness of my own vulnerability. As I was physically stretched to paint this long and dark work I realised that I was being taken "deep into the call of all the unfinished and unsolved."
emerged from this place by creating a sixth panel, offering a three dimen sional perspective in an attempt to bring the work to a close. But rather

26. Augustine, as cited in Sullivan, *Art Practice as Research*, 26.

27. Sullivan, *Art Practice as Research*, 26.

28. O'Donohue, *Benedictus*, 35.

than finish that which was unfinished and unsolved, this was the canvas in which I was able to draw breath.

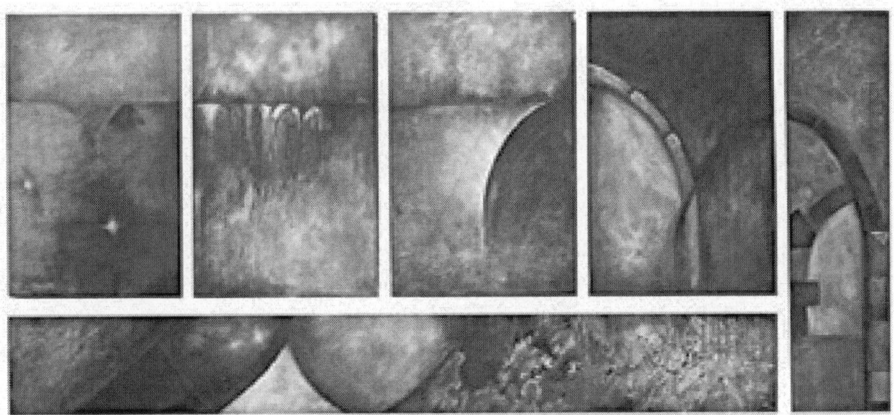

Image 3: Libby Byrne, *Life Map: Six Panels* (2001). Oil on canvas, 210 x 135 cm.

The mystery in the lower canvas seemed to compel my attention with an invitation to consider what healing may be possible in the darkest corner of the series if I were to explore and expand the darkness in a larger canvas. Having spent three solid weeks immersed in the creation of this series, I was exhausted. I was unsure if I had the emotional reserves to return to the darkness and in many ways I wanted to flee into the simplicity of cleaning my bathroom, a task that had been ignored since the work on the *Life Map* had begun. I stood in the middle of the shared studio at school ready to let go of the idea altogether, when a young woman walked through the room carrying a very large, very blank canvas. It was in that moment that desire was reborn and I knew I would not clean the bathroom until this next piece was done.

Having gathered stretcher bars and canvas I returned to the studio that was still strewn with the debris from the *Life Map* series. Looking for a place to settle amongst the restless energy, I aligned myself with the energy that was held within the materials and in doing so I discovered compassion; firstly for the image and then for myself. I discovered the power of opacity in the darkness of this painting. It was impenetrable to light, though not ever black. As it had been made through the layering of melancholy and materials, it held within it a pulsating energy and surprising beauty. I had risked allowing the darkness in the *Life Map* space to expand and in doing so I learnt that it was also contained. The leading edge of the darkness is clean and clear and is able to anchor the whole painting in the wound of this dark despair. With this line firmly in place, a second line is able to steadily descend and intersect with the darkness creating a safe enough space for the light of hope. Hope and despair intersect and in doing so, create the concave edge of a vessel in which the essence of life happens.

In this one piece I had been able to simplify and the complex messages in the Life *Map* series and then amplify the essence of the relationship be tween light and dark, hope and despair. As the materials were felt, worked, ordered and reordered all of my senses were activated in the process of making meaning and in that I was able to discover compassion in the de sire to be gentle with myself and the image. It has been a big commitment and a huge risk to birth this work and finally I stood back from the image, from the expression of the wound and was able to breathe deeply. Finally I had discovered one thing that I knew to be true—hope and despair work together in my life embracing all that is, was and is to come.

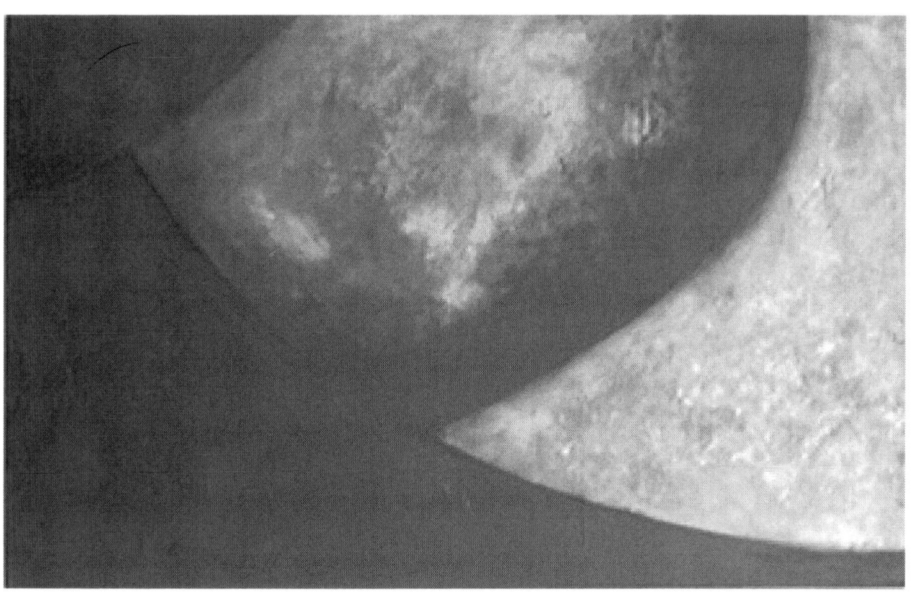

Image 4: Libby Byrne, *Vessel* (2001). Oil on canvas, 195 x 120 cm.

The Hem of the Garment

To create a climate in which I am able to attend to the unfolding logic within the pattern of a wound, the studio needs to be regularly cleansed of distraction. Cleaning the studio after the completion of a series of work can be a ritual akin to the dressing of the wound. It creates a moment in which I am able to leave the past behind and create an open space in which "all things are made new" (Rev 21:5). But even as this cleansing takes place in the studio, I am making room for the essence of the work in my soul. Letting go of the material image paradoxically allows the essence of this new form to become part of my soul and my knowing and this travels with me over time.

Almost ten years after completing the *Life Map* series and the *Vessel*, this image re-emerged as a source of hope in a time of crisis. In February 2010, I was diagnosed with Multiple Sclerosis. In those early days of illness my sight was limited by the onset of Optic Neuritis. The story of the hemorrhaging woman who was healed was in the forefront of my mind as I longed to be cured of this illness. In essence, the story is characterized by the sensuality of touch. As both of my eyes were affected with neuritis, touch had become the essence of my engagement with materials. Limited in my capacity to see colors and details I once again took my lead from Kiefer, this time deciding that the only way to come into contact with the hem of this garment here and now, was to sculpt it out of paint.

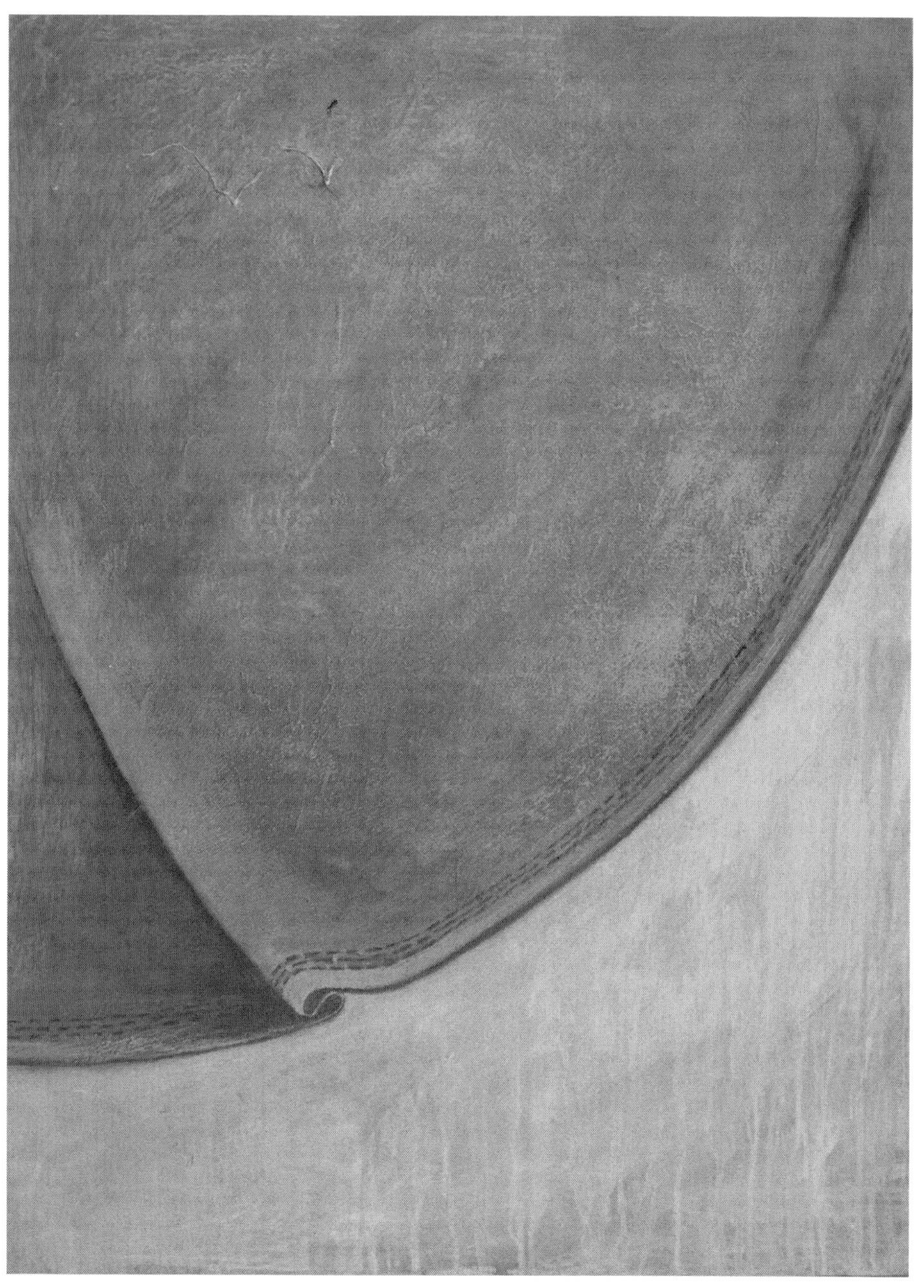

Image 5: Libby Byrne, *Hem of the Garment* (2010). Oil on canvas, 56 x 103

Layers of jasper and bone white acrylic paint hemorrhaged and mingled on the canvas as I created a surface into which I could work with my hands. As I felt my way across this slimy mess, I was relieved to discover a familiar concave line and I knew that in that moment I had connected with the hem. I had reached out to this hem in my hope and my despair and as I ran my fingers along the line I was connected to both. It was in this stage of the process that the painting illuminated the presence of Christ before me, above me, beside me and behind me. As I was touching the work, I was touching his hem and in doing so I was being healed. That is not to say that I was cured of the illness but the open wound of my longing for the presence of Christ was healed as I met him in this simple concave line amongst the paint. "The maker's obedience is to the thing made, to the unfolding logic in the process of making, as the work discloses itself."[29] Within my obedience to this line, the power of the work was able to disclose itself. This obedience to the image was something that I could never have imagined in the initial hemorrhaging. It was however an experience of deep attunement to the presence of Christ within the materials and the emergent image.

Conclusion

It takes courage to live this close to the wound. It takes courage to risk working with materials in such a way that they have the potential to obliterate any beauty that begins to emerge from darkness. It takes courage to step back from the canvas, the crucible of unformed material and breathe deeply whilst awaiting alchemy. To say that I am glad that Anselm Kiefer has had the courage to do this in his work is an understatement. The reverberation of Kiefer's work in my world has stimulated me to risk exploring my own sacramental relationship with materials and images. As I choose to live close to the wound in my own crucible of unformed materials I am open to the possibility of being transformed, made more whole than I have been before. The images that have emerged from this place have taught me to tolerate the experience of damage whilst taking into account the shape and presence of a holy wound, as I live the life that is available to me in this "*vale of soul-making*."[30]

29. Williams, *Grace and Necessity*, 52.

30. John Keats, cited in Del Nevo, *The Valley Way of Soul*, 45.

Bibliography

Crumlin, Rosemary. *Beyond Belief: Modern Art and the Religious Imagination*. Melbourne: National Gallery of Victoria, 1998.

Del Nevo, Matthew. *The Valley Way of Soul: Melancholy, Poetry and Soul-Making* Strathfield: St Paul's, 2008.

Fox, Matthew. *A Spirituality Named Compassion*. Rochester: Inner Traditions, 1999

Freeman, Laurence. *Return to the Centre: Silent Retreat at Monte Olivetto, Italy* Contemplative Life, 2010. 4 compact discs. Recorded June 2010.

Kiefer, Anselm, and Tim Marlow. "Louisiana Museum of Modern Art: Anselm Kiefer on Art and Religion." Online: http://www.youtube.com/watch?v=_jyEGWIYsps&feature=results_video&playnext=1&list=PL35B22D8F09B8A

McNiff, Shaun. *Art Heals: How Creativity Cures the Soul*. Boston: Shambala, 2004

O'Donohue, John. *Benedictus*. London: Bantam, 2007.

———. *Divine Beauty: The Invisible Embrace*. London: Bantam, 2003.

Polanyi, Michael. *The Tacit Dimension*. New York: Doubleday, 1966.

Schama, Simon. "Trouble in paradise." *The Guardian*, 20 January 2007, 12. Online: http://www.guardian.co.uk/artanddesign/2007/jan/20/art.

Seely, Chris, and Peter Reason. "Expressions of Energy: An Epistemology of Presentational Knowing." In *Knowing Differently: Art Based and Collaborative Research Methods* edited by Pranee Liamputtong and Jean Rumbold, 25–46. New York: Nova Science, 2008.

Sullivan, Graeme. *Art Practice as Research: Inquiry into Visual Arts as Research*. California: Sage Publications, 2010.

Weil, Simone. *The Need for Roots: Prelude to a Declaration of Duties Towards Mankind* New York: Routledge, 2001.

Williams, Rowan. *Grace and Necessity: Reflections on Art and Love*. London: Continuum, 2005.

6

The *Sudden Imperative* and *Not the Male Gaze*

Reconciliatory Relocations in the Art Practice of Allie Eagle

Joanna Osborne *and* Allie Eagle

Allie Eagle was one of a group of women who instigated the women's art movement in New Zealand in the mid-late 1970s. Contributing to a movement that was international in scope, Eagle curated one of New Zealand's first all-women shows at the Robert McDougall Art Gallery in Christchurch in 1974, and introduced some of the first feminist analyses of art history for a New Zealand context in *An Exhibition of Six Women Artists,* in 1975. Her influential art practice during the seventies voiced concerns that were integral to the wider feminist movement as well as reflecting her views as a lesbian separatist. One of Eagle's seminal works from 1978, *This woman died: I care,*[1] made a poignant comment on the need for safe legal abortion.

In 1980, Eagle had a life changing spiritual experience that brought about an ideological process of reconsideration and relocation from lesbian separatism to Christianity. Eagle's recent *Sudden Imperative* project addresses this political, theological and personal change.

1. *This woman died: I care (died trying to abort herself),* 1978. Watercolor, pastel and graphite on paper, 72 x 54 cm. Auckland Art Gallery Toi O Tamaki. Purchased 1993.

Joanna Osborne: The first stage of Allie Eagle's *Sudden Imperative* project was completed in 2003, resulting in five large scale watercolor and pigment impregnated encaustic wax portraits of women and Briar March's film *Eagle and Me.*[2] Having completed a number of small exhibitions and a major commission for the Waitakere City Council Chambers in 2007 took time away from her art practice to care for her elderly mother in her final years. She returned to the *Sudden Imperative* in late 2009.

Image 6: Allie Eagle, *Child Jesus in the Temple: a community parable for the City of Waitakere* (2007). Watercolour, charcoal and encaustic wax on board, 700 cm. Waitakere Council Chamber foyer.

The *Sudden Imperative* project is governed by a process of re-contextualization and re-evaluation that Eagle undertakes of her earlier lesbian separatist feminist political activism in the 1970s. In these works, gendered, political, biblical and interpersonal narratives inform a contextual theological and iconographical framework in which to re-frame her early feminist position. Each portrait reflects a colored page from the "wordless book," allegorically representing different facets of Christian soteriology. Eagle then positions a selection of works from the 1970s as conversation partners for each painting within the series, consciously re-contextualizing some of her early political and theological views. The two paintings we will focus on here—the black and the white panels entitled *Scarlet Cord Tumatahuki o Ehetere*—can both be read to include reconciliatory concerns in the way they reflect aspects of Eagle's own story of faith, and at the same time comment on wider socio-political issues.

2. See www.allieeagleandme.com.

Image 7: Allie Eagle, *Scarlet Cord* (The Black Panel: Rahab) (2003). Watercolor, acrylic and reductive sanding on gesso panel with pigment impregnated encaustic wax, 190 x 122 cm. Artist's collection.

Image 8: Allie Eagle, *Te Tumatahuki o Ehetere* (The White Panel: Esther) (Watercolor, oil paint, gold leaf and acrylic using reductive sanding on gesso panel with pigment impregnated encaustic wax, 190 x 122 cm. Artist's collection.

Eagle's paintings also contain the reflection or stories of her sitters. In recent years, her methodology has involved an extensive amount of preliminary input in the form of recorded or filmed and photographed interviews that she conducts in her drawing sessions. Her return to the second stage of the *Sudden Imperative* project has seen this methodology become intrinsic to the project, building upon Eagle's already inclusive and communally-driven practice. Eagle will talk briefly about the preliminary work she has conducted drawing and interviewing men with the view to paint another set of five large-scale allegorical portraits to complement the women. Here we begin chronologically as Eagle unpacks her pivotal feminist position of the 1970s.

~

Allie Eagle: This is a journey about mending. I needed to make some works for now that revisited and reframed my 70s works. I felt strongly that the study or examination of those earlier political works needed to be seen alongside work that reappraised those years. I believe the reappraisal I sought to bring has a sense of reconciliation and healing in it—wholeness for brokenness.

As a young artist establishing myself in Christchurch in the 70s, I shared many concerns for the broken world of women with many other women who had come out of rough domestic situations. I "came out" as a lesbian with my partner, and we had our alliances clearly positioned within a global movement of lesbian feminists ("lesbian feminist separatists" to be exact).

In my view, men were the big problem in the world. They got all the perks and they left us out of them. I believed at one point that "all men were rapists except those who had not raped yet!" That was how I saw men then. (We were disenfranchised women amassing an inventory of crimes by men against women. It was a time when a watershed of bitterness had dammed up and strong strategies for change were developing in feminist ideologies everywhere).

This was a time too of identifying the problem and separating from the male world in order to define our own sense of worth and identity. One of our strategies meant the separation from our heterosexual feminist sisters. Within this strategy of separatism we developed our own lesbian culture and ethos by living and sharing our lives together. We joined the larger feminist movement on most of the wider issues of the women's movement.

We lobbied for gay rights, and needed the larger women's support for that. We also worked hard on issues like the women's right to choose safe and free abortions; even though pregnancy was not an overriding issue with us in our lesbian world, as we were not in relationships with men, we still identified with the struggle as an alliance force. We were part of the first wave of setting up women's rape crisis centers as well as a women's refuge in Christchurch.

Women's equity issues were being clearly defined. The place for wom en artists to have a "piece of the pie," as it were, in an art world that was dominated and controlled by men—that is where I put a lot of my energy.

Image 9: Allie Eagle, *Self-portrait* (1974). Graphite on paper, 64 x 43 cm. Collection of Christchurch Art Gallery Te Puna o Waiwhetu.

J.O.: Your contribution as a curator was to initiate the first feminist critiques of art history in New Zealand, which was also instrumental in the development of a politics of art practice in the mid-to-late 70s.[3]

A.E.: Yes, after my art school years in Canterbury in the 60s, and a brief stint at teaching art at secondary schools, I went to work at the Robert McDougall Art Gallery in Christchurch. It was here that I was able to make a dent in the patriarchal New Zealand art world regarding the world of women artists. I was given some curatorial freeway by a sympathetic boss who allowed me to curate women's art shows and locate contemporary women's work for the collection. This in itself was seen by many as disturbing: the idea of making a case for women-only exhibitions annoyed a few critics. They seemed to think that there was no difference between men's and women's art, whereas we could see that there were many levels of context for the production of art that differed greatly between the sexes. Many art gallery contemporary collections and exhibitions held the work of solely men, and it felt for many of us that a woman's worldview was entirely missing from these collections. Many feminists wrote articles and conference papers to ask questions and posit new understandings of what a woman's worldview was. (This was prior to any women's or gender studies being available at a tertiary level). We had women-only exhibitions and trawled the whole country to find women who would dare to give expression to their feminist concerns. I was critically involved in staging a large exhibition open only to women during the 1977 Women's Convention in Christchurch. This was an empowering time for us as women. Lesbians were proclaiming their identity and right to determine their own sexual preference. It was a time when women artists were able to identify many aspects of our lives that had not found visual or written or oral expression, and this particular art event had foot traffic, over three days, of well over 5000 women. The entire event was a powerful experience. After the convention the exhibition was open to men as well as women. The response was mixed, and though some men *got* what we were doing, others were very antagonistic.

J.O.: How did you see your spirituality at the time? Tell us about your engagement in goddess spirituality as one of the strategies you employed as a feminist.

3. See *Exhibition of Six Women Artists*; Dann, *Up from Under*, 112–28; Eagle, "Allie Eagle in the NZ Women's Art Movement."

A.E.: The arrival of "the Goddess" seemed to occur pretty naturally or super naturally, if you like, and came as a result of our combined musings.

J.O.: The movement to "reclaim the Goddess" was international in scope and can be clearly traced through the women's art movement in New Zealand. The Women Artists' group in Christchurch were the first in this country to embrace goddess imagery and ritualistic practices in their art making. How did this strategy function? It seems that individual artistic pursuits within this strategy varied widely, ranging from the research into ancient practices and civilizations in search of a motif or metaphor for solidarity and female power, to genuine spiritual quests and practices.[5] How did that outwork in your art-making and personal spiritual practice?

A.E.: Well we figured that as women we were spiritual as well as political, and that we had spiritual needs that could not, and must not, be met through entrenched patriarchal religious systems. It was not hard to "get" that the Church had 2,000 years of subjugation of women. We began by making up our own rituals. It was a matter of feeling our way through, to make images and rituals and performance that reclaimed the Goddess. Heather McPherson introduced me to the book *The White Goddess: A Historical Grammar of Poetic Myth* by Robert Graves. And then later we discovered Mary Daly and Shulamith Firestone. Bit by bit we unpicked non Judeo-Christian sources of ancient art history and anthropology and started to weave our own stories using goddess mythology as our base. Pretty soon there was serious academic research and even anthropological digs and visits going on everywhere. We were a network of mostly white middle-class women intent on finding our primitive roots. But there was also serious research being undertaken by our Māori "sisters." It was a time of "cultural, feminist strategies." In no time it was a really powerfully-shared concept. Artists like Judy Chicago in the States were making work full of vitality that embraced a newly-emerged goddess-centered theology and embraced community involvement.

J.O.: A significant aspect of this feminist strategy within art practices was a sense of connectedness to the earth. Artists used their own bodies and interacted in site-specific or ritualistic ways in the land. There was an interest in challenging the nature/culture duality that is often associated with patriarchal structures. Your work *Stone belly woman* would fit into this category,

4. McPherson, "Have you heard of Artemisia?," 37.

5. See Orenstein, "Recovering her Story," 174–89; Christ, "Why Women Need the Goddess," 211–19.

wouldn't it? At the same time you regard *Stone belly woman* as a positive inclination within your Christian spiritual journey don't you?

Image 10: Allie Eagle, *Stone belly woman: (SPIRIT BODY LAND connections)* (1979). Photographic documentation. Artist's collection.

A.E.: Yes, it was a "first," even though in hindsight I see an emerging new motivation too, or at least my pre-Christian self gathering strength by doing this kind of work. It was an enactment that anticipated the need to be cleaned up in a spiritual sense. The work itself was a one-off ritualistic action and had a purpose. It was a work to mark an ending and to denote a new beginning. Under the umbrella of art, as was the nature of much performance art, this "piece" was perhaps one of the first in New Zealand of performance-based art.

J.O.: Allie, you embraced goddess spirituality, as a personal and political practice, and an artistic pursuit but by the end of 1977 your adherence to the formation of this cultural feminist strategy you had built was shifting wasn't it? Among a broad range of concerns, including the provocative piece *Empathy for a Rape Trail Victim* in your 1978 exhibition *Three Women Artists*, you line up a series of goblets, falling and spilling liquid, to represent an increasing disillusionment with goddess spirituality, or Wicca, and in the same space on the opposite wall, you line up drawings of broken plates and two women in the water parting ways.

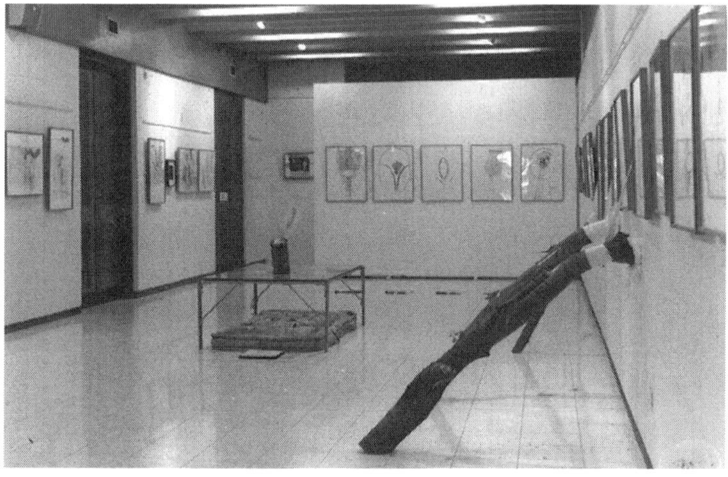

Image 11: Allie Eagle, Installation in *Three Women Artists: Allie Eagle/ Jane Zusters/Anna Keir* (1978). CSA Gallery, Christchurch. Photographic documentation. Artist's Collection.

Image 12: Allie Eagle, *Empathy for a Rape Trial Victim* (1978). CSA Gallery, Christchurch.

A.E.: Yes, there was great tension there for me. We were anarchic in our relationships. I don't think that I was conscious in '77 that I might one day throw in the towel on this commitment because in some ways that momentum of work and attention I was getting for the work kept me digging deeper. But our relationships or my relationships were not fuelled with old-fashioned ethics of fidelity or faithfulness or any of those good old virtues. I found myself increasingly getting into hot water in my personal relationships because there were no parameters. Sometimes the glimmering coals of my childhood Christianity seemed more attractive than what I was living. I was coming to an end in myself.

J.O.: Can we discuss one of your self-portraits from 1979?[6] The state of mind you have depicted in this work could be said to mark this disillusionment, or discontent, you came to have with your lesbian separatist position. Your face is frightened and flushed, your eyes are pierced with anxiety, and the background is an ominous thick and muddied dark space. You have mentioned that this was a pivotal work with regard to the spiritual changes to follow.

6. Allie Eagle, "Self-portrait," 1979, Unknown Collection.

Image 13: Allie Eagle, *Self-portrait* (1979). 74 x 55 cm. Unknown collection.

Image 14: Allie Eagle, *Memory of the wind that swept us, changed us* (1977). Watercolor, 64 x 43 cm. Collection of Rosemary Ronald.

A.E.: Yes, a deep unrest had set in by 1979. New Zealand feminists had held four huge women's conventions over the last decade and I started to feel uncomfortable with my stance. The successes I felt I gained for the gay and lesbian movement, and for the women's art movement, were tracked and marked by my own relationships and life by little bouts of doubts and pangs of conscience, and then by review and reappraisal. Two of the critical people involved in this reevaluation were my partner's two sons who were growing up and needed sound male role-modeling, which in our opinion didn't exist. Or did it? I was found wanting. We were too iconoclastic, too much into the breaking down of heterosexual images of male and female, and of "God-given" mandates of marriage, to be able to really speak holistically into the lives of these two boys. Two overseas departures from my partner, their mother, caused me to rethink the safety of our brave new world. I felt unsafe in my own rhetoric, in my worldview, and I began to seek safety for the boys and myself in the old forms of comfort that I had known as a child—in Holy Scripture and, dare I say, in a relationship with a man, the man called "Jesus."

J.O.: Mary Daly critiqued Christianity as an inherently patriarchal system that was oppressive to women. While she may have been on the right track in addressing significant theological oversights, her critique framed ortho dox Christianity as irredeemable. She called for a "post-Christian" radical lesbian separatism that held patriarchal Christianity as inherently evil. you, Daly was a key text. Your shift away from Daly's theology to a form of evangelical Christianity was a significant leap. I have heard you say more than once "I went from the bosom of matriarchy to the bowls of patriarchy," referring to these years of change and your teaching placement at a Catholic boys school. How did you reconcile such a jump?

A.E. I had enjoyed the writing of Mary Daly to begin with, and then I wrestled with it. It was reaffirming to find bold scholarly theological work that could reinforce our own theories. But Daly's stuff became untenable for me, poisonous almost. It dried out the root of all understanding about forgiveness and other forms of grace. The fruit of the Spirit was missing. I discovered the *Magna Charta of Woman* by Jessie Penn-Lewis and she at least posited the position of women within Christianity with a light that gave me a stepping board back into faith. My mother was praying for me! And the experience of actual repentance and forgiveness through Christ was very palpable for me. Reading the Bible again as I sought understanding was very fluid and it was as if "scales were being removed from my eyes." Despite all my misgivings about patriarchy, Christ was real for me. Patriarchy was patriarchy. It existed. But Jesus was different. He talked to the woman at the well. He broke the patriarchal order of things. I got it by a leap of faith. I am healed somehow of the complaint. Although in society the chauvinistic malaise still persists, I am more engaged now in asking questions from an even temper. Talking *with* men, not *at* them or *about* them, is the way I would want to forward change or healing in the world. And I think here of the business of sitting with men and painting and drawing them.

7. See Ruether, "The Emergence of Christian Feminist Theology," 9; Martin, *Feminist Question*, 161.

8. See *Allie Eagle and Me.*

Image 15: Allie Eagle, *Tough Call* (The Red Panel: Mary) (2003). Watercolor, oil paint, gold leaf and acrylic using reductive sanding on gesso panel with pigment impregnated encaustic wax, 190 x 122 cm. Artist's collection.

Image 16: Allie Eagle, *Cover* (The Gold Panel: Anna) (2003). Watercolor, oil paint, gold leaf and acrylic using reductive sanding on gesso panel with pigment impregnated encaustic wax, 190 x 122 cm. Artist's collection.

Image 17: Allie Eagle, *Heaps* (The Green Panel: Sarah) (2003). Acrylic glazes and pencil on gesso panel with pigment impregnated encaustic wax, 190 x 122 cm. Artist's collection.

J.O.: Let's talk about the *Sudden Imperative*, a project that addresses this transition you talk about. The first painting of the series, your self-portrait *Scarlet Cord* (depicted earlier), seems to me to convey a moment of decision or a transition inherent in the phrase "sudden imperative." A nude figure with her face shrouded stands with one hand raised in a gesture of surrender, the other hand clutching a suitcase. Although you have preserved anonymity with the shrouded face, it is your self-portrait. And the figure also carries the identity of Rahab—one of the five different biblical characters you have attached to each portrait in turn.

A.E.: The hand risen, the other hand clutching "baggage," and the shrouded head, are all emblems: I have got baggage, I am blinded, I lift my hand up to surrender. "God help me miserable sinner that I am!" (Oops, I just used the "sin" word!) Yes, I wanted to find a pose or a gesture that most defined that moment. The female form in this painting is middle-aged, but my first encounter with God at that point of delivery—well I was a lot younger—like the drawing of one of the young women in the water and the eagle hurtling into the picture, that was me then.

J.O.: Your autobiography and 70s position conceptually informs the depiction of repentance in the *Scarlet Cord* as a personal conviction. Rather than read a personal political predicament into this work, I have taken seriously your concealed face and have read your figure as "standing in for the other" in the general sense. Your covered face also reads as a statement of faith. Particular personal convictions do not hinder a wider reading of the structural or the more universal understandings or implications within a soteriological process.

Scarlet Cord readdresses a series of works from the 1978 exhibition *Three Women Artists*. The work you especially have in mind is entitled *Memory of the wind that swept us, changed us* (depicted earlier), a lyrical watercolor depicting two young women wading in water. Within the exhibition, it was situated among a string of ten works that expressed a lament for disintegrating personal circumstances—parting figures struggling in the tide, scattered clouds, hard black lines, soaring hawks, sinking ships, translucent washes of blue. *Memory of the wind that swept us, changed us*, along with the other pieces, seem to mark the beginning of an acknowledgment of inner ambivalence. In revisiting this particular work, ambivalence is transposed into a statement of faith as *Scarlet Cord* depicts a moment of soteriological transition. The biblical character Rahab plays an intermediary role as you refer to segments of her narrative that carry meaning for you and relate to your own. You also open up new readings of the biblical text by placing Rahab within your own narrative and within a post-colonial New Zealand context.

The work we mentioned earlier, *Stone Belly Woman*, is intended to be read in conjunction with *Te Tumatahuki o Ehetere*, the white panel and third painting of the *Sudden Imperative* series (depicted earlier). The title of this work and the text within the painting is in Māori. "Ehetere" is loan word for Esther in the Māori and "Tumatahuki" is part of a building structure, the "upright rods between the posts of a native house, for supporting the laths to which the reeds are fastened."[9] *Te Tumatahuki o Ehetere* contains the symbolism of cleansing and textual references to preparedness within which could be set the determination to act for the good of others. It is a work that represents righteousness, according to the "white" of the wordless book. In this work your friend and colleague Cushla Parekowhai stands in a pool of flood-churned water holding the pose of Rembrandt's *Hendrickje Bathing*, and is identified as the biblical character Esther by an inscription of gold leaf at the base of the painting. The pool of water, Te Puna Rere (the waterfall that springs or the flowing spring) is a pond nestled in the bush on your wetland at Te Henga, and was the site of your earlier work *Stone Belly woman*.

A.E.: The *stone belly* suite of photos were made in late 1979 and they were in the same wellspring as *Memory of the wind that swept us, changed us*. Both works consider the spiritual quest that was always there, the desire to be made whole—to be cleansed. I had always brought images of the figure in water into my painting. Whereas in the first 70's instance it is a ritual enacted out, in the second, in *Te Tumatahuki o Ehetere,* there is somehow a fulfillment of this call. I think when we were at *play ritualistically* in the 70s there was an integrity in the searching that was really very valid—pilgrim's steps if you like. The wordless book is the framework I use to recontextualize my seventies work.

J.O.: To me, the two works, *Scarlet Cord* and *Te Tumatahuki o Ehetere* carry a reading that could represent a soteriological event. Reading them together in this way they catch something of the meaning of salvation as "rescue" and "restoration."[10] In Charles Spurgeon's programme for the wordless

9. Williams, *A Dictionary of the Mā*[set macron over a]*ori Language*, 453.

10. Middleton and Gorman, "Salvation," 55.

book, he identified black with "error" or "sin" and white with "wholeness" or "righteousness." An understanding of the stages of the Christian salva tion process is structured through the use of color. While the conventional "wordless book" now includes five colored pages, they can be pared back to an original three—black, red and white—to represent the doctrine of salva tion. Gold and green, and sometimes blue, were added later to more fully represent the gospel narrative. Traditionally this evangelical resource was used to explain the Christian message to those who could not read, or to children. It was often used as a missionary's device. Spurgeon first spoke of his use of "wordless book" in a sermon on Psalm 51.[11] I see you using the wordless book to compositionally and theologically structure the *Sudden Imperative*. But the series is by no means a set of illustrative examples of the stages implied by Spurgeon's programme for the book. I see you using them as a structural device for your own contextual purposes. With their respec tive references to 70's works and spaces, the paintings contain distinctive autobiographical stances on the salvation event.

A.E.: Correct. That "event" was about having a deep experience of the nature of Jesus. It takes time for us as humans to distil our ideas and to refine our beliefs. And it takes a bit of courage to say "I was wrong," or, "I didn't get it quite right there." I think I got a bit tired of seeing my earlier works always read in the way that they were intended as socio-political works challenging patriarchy and so on. They were being studied at university and high school just in their own 70s context and no one was really seeing the connectedness with the later work I have done. It seemed the best thing to do was produce some heavyweight work that readdressed some of these earlier issues and worldview alongside my regenerated work.

Sudden Imperative: Men

J.O.: To complete this project, you have the same visual soteriological and biblical framework in place for an accompanying series of large-scale wa tercolor and encaustic wax portraits of men. Yet you have been building up to these paintings with substantial research and preliminary drawing. Here again you state that your 1974 self-portrait (depicted earlier) as the radical feminist is the starting point for understanding your current suite of male portraits. But rather than focusing on an exploration of the pivotal

11. Spurgeon, "The Wordless Book."

moments of change and relocation within your own journey, this project has a conversational focus and a relational centre. There is a reconciliatory element that underpins your "repentant men" series. You are interested in the exploration of self-reflection, a quality you express that is not the "fixed and focused gaze of men leaping into jeeps, or running on to football fields," but a quality you wish to explore that you describe as "not the male gaze—but the spiritual gaze."[12]

Image 18: Allie Eagle, *Insight: (Not the Male Gaze) Can we talk now Daddy?* (2010–2011). Installation of oil pastels at the Temple Gallery, 2011. 56 x 38 cm each. Artist's collection.

A.E.: Putting that time in with my male subjects (so far two years at least) was a way of demonstrating an engagement with men and their lives, and in a sense an act of demonstrating the healing of the anger I had against men. In a sense, there was an affirmation of those changes that took place in me every time a male entered my studio space for a portrait sitting. I guess the ten years service of teaching at a boys school did some of that, but I needed to somehow enact or position myself as having both my art and teaching practices involved in a healing catharsis that would unlock some

12. Eagle, "Searching for a Repentant Man," 12.

of the old dross, and dissolve it somewhat. That sexism still exists, that men are still fairly reserved about expressing their feelings, that chauvinism is still about—all of these things, including the way that men objectify women and dominate the workplace, are really no longer my *truck*. Yes, they are concerns, but it is by being present with my male sitters/subjects that I uncover a more incisive and compassionate reality for myself. I'm more interested in grace these days. "It is not the male gaze, it is mine of them; a woman artist who wants to regard a man not as an object or thing, but as a person, where there is an inquiry that simply asks: How is it with you, brother?"[13]

Both sets of paintings and all the pastel drawings of men and my interviews are a way to discern the inner workings of people. Feminism for me was initially a series of serious complaints. The personal was political. And yes, with analysis, it produced some constructive strategies including a way of looking at how men viewed women. Putting the boot on the other foot and having me take a good hard look at men should not be as much disturbing as it is moving and telling. That's what I hope.

The men series could be summarized like this: I dedicated nearly two years to listening (using a recording device) to a disparate group of (about 50) male sitters who regularly visited my studio as subjects. I peered at, listened to, drew, and painted these men. Intimate and ongoing friendships were forged. My goal was to create a body of portraits of men that re-addressed my changed attitudes and understandings of them. (I aim to have one hundred oil pastel male portraits, plus five big paintings, for the final exhibition.)

It is important to note that, for me, the radical lesbian separatist feminist artist life ended in 1980, and increasingly over the next 30 years there was a big upheaval of ideas and feelings going on in me. I worked with and taught men and boys. I reappraised my old position. But I had never addressed or dedicated any body of work to that transition. So the *Insight: (Not the Male Gaze) Can we talk now daddy?* series is, in a sense, a 30 culmination of that change in mindset regarding men.

The contrast is meant to be apparent; the big pictures of women are all people in a state of flux and transformation, and so too it is for the men.

13. Ibid., 13.

Bibliography

Allie Eagle and Me. Film, directed by Briar March. New Zealand: Screen Innovation Production Fund, 2004.

Christ, Carol P. "Why Women Need the Goddess: Phenomenological, Psychological, and Political Reflections." In *Theorizing Feminisms: A Reader*, edited by Elizabeth Hackett and Sally Haslanger, 211–19. Oxford: Oxford University Press, 2006.

Dann, Christine. *Up from Under: Women and Liberation in New Zealand 1970–1985*. Wellington: Allen & Unwin, 1985.

Eagle, Allie. "Allie Eagle in the NZ Women's Art Movement." Allie Eagle and Me. 2008. Online: http://www.allieeagleandme.com/eduResource/AEwomensMove.html.

———. "Searching for a Repentant Man." In *Allie Eagle Insight: (Not the Male Gaze) Can We Talk Now Daddy?*, by Allie Eagle, 12–15. Reikorangi: River Pa Studios, 2011.

Exhibition of Six Women Artists: Organised by Robert McDougall Art Gallery, Christchurch, in Conjunction with International Women's Year [Essay and research, collation of work: Alison Mitchell]. Christchurch: Gallery, 1975.

Martin, Francis. *The Feminist Question: Feminist Theology in the light of Christian Tradition*. Grand Rapids: Eerdmans, 1994.

McPherson, Heather. "Have you heard of Artemisia?" In *A Women's Picture Book: 25 Women Artists of Aotearoa (New Zealand)*, edited by Marian Evans et al., 37. Wellington: Government Printing Office, 1988.

Middleton, J. Richard, and Michael J. Gorman. "Salvation." In *The New Interpreter's Dictionary of the Bible*, edited by Katherine Doob Sakenfeld, 5:45–61. Nashville: Abingdon, 2009.

Orenstein, Gloria Feman. "Recovering Her Story: Feminist Artists Reclaim the Great Goddess." In *The Power of Feminist Art: The American Movement of the 1970s, History and Impact*, edited by Norma Broude and Mary D. Garrard, 174–89. New York: Abrams, 1994.

Ruether, Rosemary Radford. "The Emergence of Christian Feminist Theology." In *The Cambridge Companion to Feminist Theology*, edited by Susan F. Parsons, 3–22. Cambridge: Cambridge University Press, 2002.

Spurgeon, Charles H. "The Wordless Book." Sermon, delivered at the Metropolitan Tabernacle, Newington, UK, January 11, 1866. The Spurgeon Archive. Online: http://www.spurgeon.org/sermons/3278.htm.

Williams, Herbert W. *A Dictionary of the Māori Language*. Wellington: Government, 1957.

7

Building from the Rubble

Architecture, Memory, and Hope

Murray Rae

In the aftermath of the second world war as Europe and the world slowly learned of the horrors that had taken place at Auschwitz, Dachau, Belsen, and elsewhere, and in which the German people had been at least partially complicit, there were those who argued that on account of such atrocity there could be no more philosophy and no more art. Prominent among them was Theodor Adorno who famously declared that "To write poetry after Auschwitz is barbaric."[1] Adorno's declaration became a slogan around which expressions of the horror and incomprehensibility of the Holocaust were gathered, a chastening, salutary reminder that the depravity perpetrated under the Nazi regime was perpetrated by our own kind, by fellow human beings. The degree to which ordinary citizens were persuaded by Hitler's rhetoric and went along with his violence, albeit they were only partially aware of its terrible extent, implicated the human race as a whole. *We human beings* are capable of this.[2] To write poetry or to

1. Adorno, "Art, Culture and Society," 17–34. Reprinted in O'Connor, ed., *The Adorno Reader*, 210. The declaration that there could be no more philosophy and no more poetry was in fact a very particular response to the Holocaust and does not represent Adorno's view of the prospects for philosophy or art in general, as his own further contributions to philosophy and aesthetic theory reveal.

2. One of the central problems confronted in Adorno's philosophy was the question of how it is possible that humankind "instead of entering into a truly human condition, is sinking into a new kind of barbarism." Horkheimer and Adorno, *Dialectic of Enlightenment*, xi.

create art in the aftermath of this horror would be to conceal the full extent of our inhumanity and to suppose, absurdly, that we could make amends. Adorno's slogan suggests, rather, that a humanity capable of such evil had squandered irrevocably any claim upon the true, the good and the beautiful, while the pretention to make any sense of what had happened would be an intolerable affront to the victims. As Terry Smith has put it, "All artists can do is contemplate, in immobile silence, the enormity of the devastation that had been wrought."[3] For a time Adorno rejected even an art that tried to show the horror. Smith again explains that such efforts "risked . . . the danger that their very artistry might provide pleasures, however indirect and inadvertent, to those receiving the political messages, thus blunting the artists' obligation to the victims of the Holocaust: to show that it was, above all, unthinkable, inconceivable."[4]

Adorno qualified his position in later reflection, acknowledging that the suffering of the victims "has as much right to expression as one who is tortured has to scream; hence it may have been wrong," he says, "that after Auschwitz no more poems may be written."[5] Among efforts to represent the screams of the tortured, Adorno approved especially Samuel Beckett's play *Endgame* which, he says, "trains the viewer for a condition where everyone involved expects—upon lifting the lid from the nearest trashcan—to find his own parents . . . Beckett's trashcans are the emblems of culture restored after Auschwitz."[6] It would seem, following Adorno's line of thought, that in respect of the atrocities of Auschwitz, there can be no redemption. We can neither make amends, nor be allowed to forget. That conviction, however, does bestow an ethical responsibility upon us. Adorno comes to the view that philosophy, and art too, presumably, must accept a "new categorical imperative," so to arrange its thought and action that "Auschwitz would not repeat itself, [that] nothing similar would happen."[7]

Unfortunately, however, it does not belong to the power of philosophy or art, or theology for that matter, to see to it that nothing similar happens again. The common recurrence of murder, of genocide, of war, and of terror, testifies to a brutality within our human race that we have not been able

3. Smith, *The Architecture of Aftermath*, 69.

4. Ibid. Smith takes the point from Adorno's "Commitment" in Adorno, *Notes to Literature*, 85–86.

5. Adorno, *Negative Dialectics*, 362.

6. Adorno, "Trying to Understand Endgame," 119–50. Also in O'Connor, ed., *The Adorno Reader*, 343. I owe these references Smith's discussion of Adorno in *The Architecture of Aftermath*, 68–70.

7. Adorno, *Negative Dialectics*, 365, cited in Zuidervaart, "Theodor W. Adorno."

to heal. We may say with some justification that human brutality of this nature is abnormal, but we have also to acknowledge that it does occur again and again. The terrorist attacks of the ninth of September, 2001, for recent instance, as also the murderous rampage on Utoeya Island in Norway in 2011, do not match the horrors of Nazism in their murderous extent, but the hatred leading to their conception and the chilling efficiency of their execution reveal a depth of evil in some human hearts just as shocking and incomprehensible as that which conceived the Holocaust.

Almost immediately upon their comprehension of the scale of the destruction wrought on 9/11, the people of the United States and more broadly in the Western world began to ask how we could make amends. What was to be done in the face of terror? How should we respond? The question was posed first to politicians and it was the mayor of New York, Rudi Giuliani, who managed to find some words of reassurance—reassurance that there was a way forward, a way to cope. People went also to the churches, searching for words with which to express their grief and hoping that there might be some solace in God. Beyond that they looked to the military to make amends. Above all, in the Western world—in the so-called "Christian" West—we looked to the military to make amends.

While the military has been entrusted with the task of dealing with terrorism and putting things right, we have looked to artists for guidance about what should be done in the abyss of ground zero left in the middle of Manhattan. We have looked to architects to tell us what should happen next. After the rubble was cleared and meticulous efforts made to salvage the remains of the three thousand victims at the World Trade Centre site, something had to be done to memorialize, to rebuild, and to express America's response to the terror that had come into its midst. Architects found themselves as key players in America's search for a way forward in response to and beyond the evil that had been done. Rafael Viñoly, one of the architects eventually involved in submitting proposals for the redevelopment of Ground Zero, recognized very early the responsibility that artists would be called upon to assume. Viñoly wrote in the *New York Times* just two weeks after 9/11: "There is a sense of void among us. A void that is charged with the weight of emotion, the fears of risk and the expectation that we can overcome. In a curious parallel, that void is the common territory of art. It is the place where the unexpected power of invention can reach beyond the limits of logic and set a new direction."[8]

8. Viñoly, "Fill the Void with Beauty" cited in Smith, *The Architecture of Aftermath*

Of course the artists called upon to build something new from the rubble of ground zero were dealing only in part with a void. They were dealing, to be sure, with the void left where the twin towers had once stood, with sixteen acres of empty real estate, and they were dealing with the emptiness left among the friends and families of the three thousand people who had died. That had somehow to be acknowledged and respected. But alongside these voids the architects had also to deal with a mass of competing, perhaps irreconcilable, demands; the demands of Larry Silverstein, the property developer who holds the lease on the World Trade Centre site and who wanted his ten million square feet of office space back; the demands and expectations of the Lower Manhattan Development Corporation appointed by the governor of New York to oversee the rebuilding process and to see to it that the interests of the city as a whole were taken into account; the demands of those like Mayor Giuliani who wanted the sixteen acres set aside as a memorial to the victims and for no building, other than a memorial, to be set upon it; the demands of the Port Authority who still owned the land and who were responsible for the transport infrastructure of New York and for rebuilding the transport hub destroyed when the twin towers collapsed; the architects had also to deal with the demands of those who escaped the crumbling towers, and of those thousands of people who lived and worked nearby all of whom "felt that they were entitled to some say in what was to be built where the twin towers had stood."[9] The competing demands and expectations might have seemed overwhelming and impossible to meet. Suzanne Stephens, however, who writes for the *Architectural Record*, spoke on behalf of her architectural colleagues. "After this cataclysmic event," Stephens reports, "many architects felt that they must do *something*, and that is to do what they know best—design. Theirs was an optimistic resolve; that innovative architecture may offer a way to heal ourselves as well as Manhattan's mangled downtown."[10] Whether architecture can offer a way to heal ourselves will be a matter for further consideration as we proceed, but let us begin by investigating in more detail the initial progress made at ground zero.

9. I take the point from Goldberger, *Up From Zero*, xiv. One measure of the public demand to have a say in the rebuilding process is the thousands of people who turned up to the numerous forums held around New York to debate the prospects for Ground Zero, including 4000 attendees at a Town Hall Meeting in July 2002 called "Listening to the City."

10. Stephens, "Fantasy Intersects with Reality at Ground Zero," 12.

Two early responses offered markedly contrasting proposals. Mayor Giuliani’s plea that the site be left empty except for a memorial to the victims won support from some, particularly from the families of those who had died. In contrast, a good many people, according to poll results, supported former mayor Ed Koch’s call, made within hours of the attack, to rebuild the towers just as they had been before—in defiance of the terrorists! Team Twin Towers, an advocacy group led by film and television executive Randy Warner, produced plans for replica buildings with increased structural and security features. But this was the response of those unchastened by what had happened, of those who believed that the most important thing to be done was to reassert American power and the superiority of American values, or at least the values of those powerful political and business interests that had overridden widespread public protest to build the towers in the first place. The proposal to rebuild replica towers was a response of those forgetful of the communities and small businesses that had been erased from the map in order to make way for the twin towers when first constructed, and forgetful of the inhospitable, dehumanizing and widely derided features of the original World Trade Centre buildings.[11]

The unchastened hubris of Team Twin Towers’ proposal was exceeded, however, by the sculptor James Turrell who claimed, “I am interested in seeing the working culture of New York continue. People want a memorial now because they’re feeling emotional, but emotions pass, all emotion passes, and then the memorial has no meaning. The new buildings should be higher than the old ones, and there should be three of them.”[12]

What does it take to mend the world? First of all, I suggest, it requires that we see and understand clearly the nature of our brokenness. Understanding “the fragility of capitalism both as a system and as the occasion and design spirit of this particular building”[13] would be one lesson to begin with. Another lesson would be that reconciliation, Christianly conceived, is the work of one who did not strive for glory but emptied himself and took the form of a servant (Phil 2:7). Learning such lessons is something that Team Twin Towers and James Turrell signally failed to do. While they did have supporters, most involved in the debate have recognized that art and

11. For an account of the controversy surrounding the building of the World Trade Centre, see Glanz and Lipton, *City in the Sky*, 62–87.

12. Cited in Smith, *The Architecture of Aftermath*, 162. Smith’s source is the citation in Solomon, “From the Rubble, Ideas for Rebirth,” B37.

13. Smith, *The Architecture of Aftermath*, 150.

architecture cannot proceed at Ground Zero as if there were nothing to be learned about our own participation in and contribution to the brokenness of our world.

In the years following 9/11 there were literally hundreds of architectural visions put forward, some solicited under the terms of several design competitions and others volunteered by architects and planners apparently sharing Suzanne Stephens's confidence that innovative architecture, if not able to offer a means to heal ourselves, could at least provide an appropriate memorial to the dead and give voice to America's, or New York's, indomitable spirit.

The official design competition staged jointly by the Lower Manhattan Development Corporation and the Port Authority eventually narrowed down seven design teams who presented nine schemes. On December 18, 2002 these schemes were unveiled at the Winter Garden adjacent to Ground Zero. It is important to understand that these schemes were not well-developed proposals for actual buildings. The competition brief called for innovative design studies expressive of a vision for the site that could then be developed at a later date through actual building designs.

After a couple of weeks of deliberation the panel assembled to assess the various schemes announced that the winning scheme was that presented by the renowned Polish born, Jewish, American architect Daniel Libeskind. Libeskind had been invited to be a member of the advisory panel charged with assessing the entries but had been unable to attend the preliminary meetings. As an afterthought, apparently, he decided to enter the competition himself.[14] At the Winter Garden on December 18, Libeskind was the first to present his scheme.

Libeskind went up to the lectern. His first words were not about architecture at all. "I believe this is about a day that altered all of our lives," he said. And then he went on to describe his own arrival in the United States forty-three years earlier. "I arrived by ship to New York as a teenager, an immigrant, and like millions of others before me, my first sight was the Statue of Liberty and the amazing skyline of Manhattan," Libeskind said. "I have never forgotten that sight or what it stands for."[15]

Libeskind continued:

> When I first began this project, New Yorkers were divided as to whether to keep the site of the World Trade Center empty or to fill

14. So reports Goldberger, *Up from Zero*, 7.

15. As cited in ibid., 8.

> the site completely and build upon it. I meditated many days on this seemingly impossible dichotomy. To acknowledge the terrible deaths which occurred on this site, while looking to the future with hope, seemed like two moments which could not be joined. I sought to find a solution which would bring these seemingly contradictory viewpoints into unexpected unity. So, I went to look at the site, to stand within it, to see people walking around it, to feel its power and to listen to its voices. And this is what I heard, felt and saw.
>
> The great slurry walls are the most dramatic elements which survived the attack, an engineering wonder constructed on bedrock foundations and designed to hold back the Hudson River. The foundations withstood the unimaginable trauma of the destruction and stand as eloquent as the Constitution itself asserting the durability of Democracy and the value of individual life.[16]

I have quoted Libeskind at length because it is this speech, as much as his architectural scheme that won Libeskind the competition. He managed to convince the judges and indeed the gathered audience that he, better than any of the other entrants, understood the problem and the challenges that lay before all who had an interest in what happened at Ground Zero. "Libeskind did not talk about square footage or economics, and he barely used an architectural term in his presentation. He talked about commemo ration, memory, mourning, and renewal, and he did it with the zeal of a preacher. 'Life victorious,' were his final words," and he sat down to "sus tained applause."[17]

One of the first tasks of an artist, I suggest, is to help us to see and to understand better the reality that lies before us and around us. Whether one agrees with Daniel Libeskind in every particular of his analysis, he provided more convincing evidence than any other architect that day that he understood the memories, the anguish, and the hope that required ex pression in whatever was to be done at Ground Zero. He understood that if there is to be healing we have first to understand the nature and extent of our brokenness.

There are reasons why this Polish born, Jewish immigrant to America could present a better understanding of the situation that any of his rivals in the competition. Libeskind's most notable work to that point had been the Jewish Museum in Berlin. In that building Libeskind had shown himself

16. Cited in Smith, *The Architecture of Aftermath*, 180.

17. Goldberger, *Up from Zero*, 9.

capable of breaking Adorno's silence. This Jewish architect had given Germany a building, a work of art, that upheld the memory of Holocaust, gave voice to the victim's screams and yet could say as well that light and hope are not extinguished.

Libeskind describes "three basic ideas that formed the foundation for the Jewish Museum design. First, the impossibility of understanding the history of Berlin without understanding the enormous intellectual, economic, and cultural contribution made by its Jewish citizens. Second, the necessity to integrate physically and spiritually the meaning of the Holocaust into the consciousness and memory of the city of Berlin. Third, that only through the acknowledgement and incorporation of this erasure and void of Jewish life in Berlin, can the history of Berlin and Europe have a human future."[18]

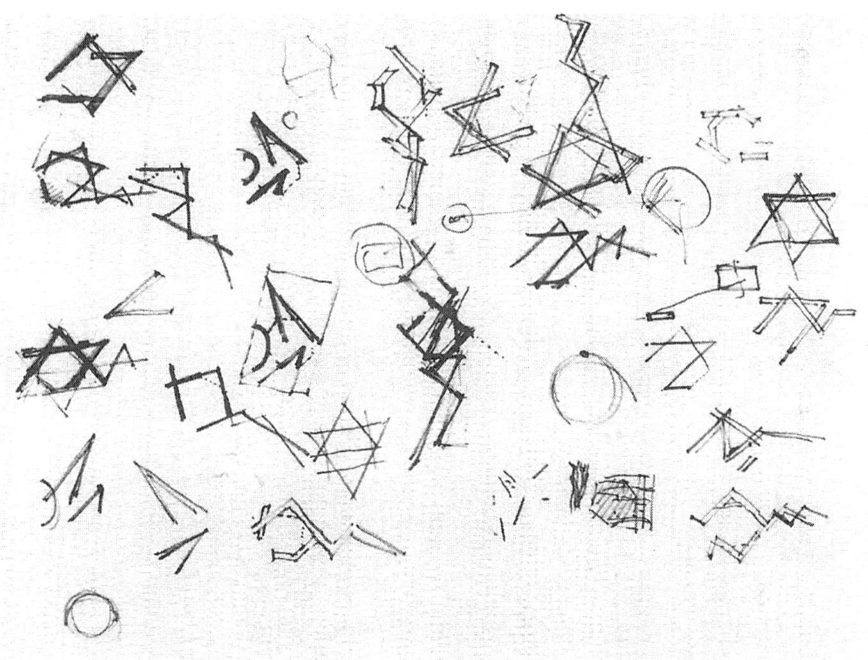

Image 19: Daniel Libeskind, *Star of David.*

Libeskind's initial concept drawings for the museum take up the motif of the Star of David, but the star is broken, contorted, deformed. Eventually,

18. Libeskind, *The Space of Encounter*, 23.

in the architecture itself, the star is unfolded; the form is disrupted but not lost.[19]

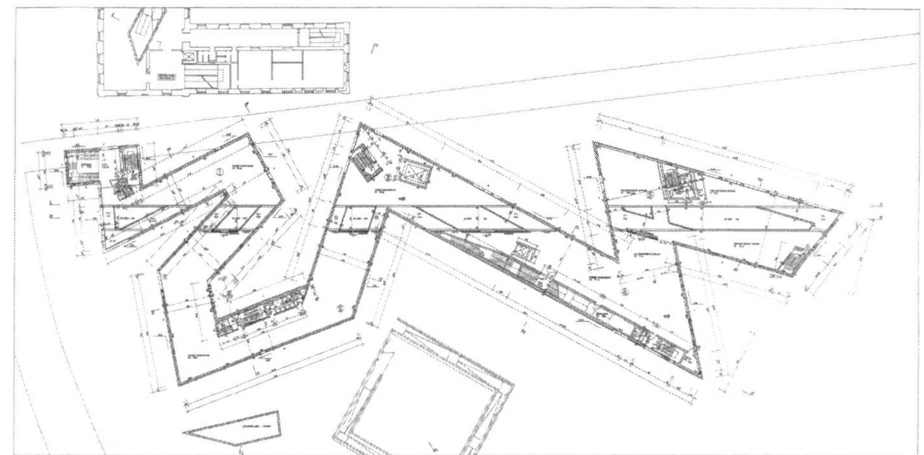

Image 20: Museum Plan © SDL, Courtesy Studio Daniel Libeskind.

Libeskind further explains that the Museum "is a project about two lines of thinking, organization and relationship. One is a straight line, but broken into many fragments; the other is a tortuous line, but continuing indefinitely."[20] The straight line, representing perhaps the unwavering de termination of genocidal logic, intersects the broken but infinite line of the Star of David, and where it does so it forms a series of voids running the full height of the museum's layered galleries. The voids speak of the fate of those six million Jews who became victims of a logic that was itself nihilistic, empty, and utterly bereft.

19. The zigzag countours of the building derive also from Libeskind's sketch of imagi nary lines on a Berlin city map connecting the site with the street addresses of prominent members of Berlin's Jewish history—Henrich von Kleist, Heinrich Heine, Mies van der Rohe, Rahel Varnhagen, Walter Benjamin, and Arnold Schönberg. See the explanation in, for example, Schneider, *Daniel Lineskind Jewish Museum Berlin*, 36.

20. Libeskind, *The Space of Encounter*, 23.

Image 21: Jewish Museum Berlin Void © Torsten Seidel, Courtesy Studio Daniel Libeskind.

Image 22: Holocaust Tower © Bitter Bredt, Courtesy Studio Daniel Libeskind.

Terry Smith explains that on entering the building the visitor is confronted with a steep stair leading down into an abyss. On reaching the bottom, one is faced with the entrances to three underground streets. No directions are offered, no clues make any sense of what lies before, although each street does have a single destination. "Turning right up a short passage, the Holocaust void is entered only through a heavy concrete door, which is then closed. The unheated, uncooled space inside is shaped into a large wedge by twenty-seven-foot-high unadorned concrete walls. You can just make out the sounds of the city outside as it goes about its business. Above, a thin strip of white light, reflected from some unseeable source, rims the top of one wall."[21]

Libeskind cites the words of a survivor:

> "What do you suppose that white light in the sky that you saw from the crack in the cattle car on your way to Stutthof really was?" the interviewer asked Elaine some thirty years later in her Brooklyn home. "You see, in order to survive you must believe in something, you need a source of inspiration, of courage, something bigger than yourself, something to overcome reality. The line was my source of inspiration, my sign from heaven. Many years later, after liberation, when my children were growing up, I realized that the white light might have been fumes from a passing airplane's exhaust pipe, but does it really matter?"[22]

From the basement entry point the visitor ascends through the labyrinthine exhibition spaces, themselves windowless except for the top floor where one looks out upon the city of Berlin. The lower galleries are punctuated, however, by shards of glass and light, reminiscent of Kristallnacht, in which flames engulfed Berlin's synagogues and left the streets littered with shattered glass. But, as is evident from the façade of the building, the shards of light appear through lines that, if pieced together, would form the Star of David. Light, hope, and a reminder of divine election are given, even in the midst of brokenness.

21. Smith, *The Architecture of Aftermath*, 81–82.

22. Eliach, *Hasidic Tales of the Holocaust*. Cited in Libeskind, *The Space of Encounter*, 49.

Image 23: Jewish Museum Berlin next to original baroque building © Bitter Bredt, Courtesy Studio Daniel Libeskind.

Recall the narrow downward stair by which one enters the Jewish museum. Descent as the motif of memorial, particularly the memorial of terror, was utilized again in Libeskind's scheme for Ground Zero and has subsequently been developed by designers Michael Arad and Peter Walker. In his presentation at the Winter Garden, Libeskind explained, "We have to be able to enter this hallowed, sacred ground while creating a quiet, meditative and spiritual space. We need to journey down, some 70 feet into Ground Zero, onto the bedrock foundation, a procession with deliberation into the deep indelible footprints of Tower One and Tower Two."[23]

Descent is the movement of grief; it is also the movement of chastening, of humility, and perhaps of repentance. Recall here Adorno's conviction that all of us are implicated in the Holocaust. It is our race that has done this, the human race. The memorial of 9/11, whatever else it might convey, should remind us that we are all caught up in the fallenness of our

23. Libeskind, "Studio Daniel Libeskind."

world and we are all responsible. Triumphalism has no place. Rebuilding the towers as they were before, only higher, and this time three of them[24] would show only that we have learned nothing. It is salutary that the modifications to the replica towers proposed by Team Twin Towers were an increase in structural strength and increased security. The recommendation in the face of terror was to brace ourselves for more attacks but to make ourselves more impregnable, more unassailable. Writing just two days after 9/11 Nicolai Ouroussoff, a columnist for the *Los Angeles Times*, offered a contrasting view:

> America is now faced with two fundamentally divergent choices. The first, a natural impulse, would be to lash out at our enemies while barricading ourselves in an impregnable fortress. After the devastation caused by the Oklahoma City bombing in 1995, for example, the U.S. Government Services Administration issued strict new security guidelines for the design of new government buildings. Dozens of new courthouses have been built since then. Often, the results were imposing concrete structures, grim symbols of a society under siege. The other option requires more courage. It would call for creating an urban landscape shaped by qualities of openness and empathy, not paranoia.[25]

As the re-development of Ground Zero and the surrounding neighborhood progressed, Ourousoff's plea for an "urban landscape shaped by qualities of openness and empathy, not paranoia" came in the form of the question whether there would be space for a mosque in the vicinity of Ground Zero. While the proposal to build an Islamic Community Centre two blocks from the World Trade Centre site prompted vociferous opposition from some, the Islamic Centre has now been built. It includes a range of publicly accessible community facilities and a memorial to the victims of 9/11. It remains to be seen whether the gestures of openness and empathy represented architecturally in the building are embraced by the surrounding community.

When John Whitehead, chairman of the Lower Manhattan Development Corporation, opened proceedings at the Winter Garden presentation of the design schemes for Ground Zero he began with the following remarks: "The original World Trade Centre was more than a set of buildings.

24. We noted above that this was proposed by James Turrell as was something similar by "Team Twin Towers."

25. Ouroussof, "Towers' Symbolic Image," A32. I owe the reference to Smith, *The Architecture of Aftermath.*

It stood for global commerce over global conflict. These teams have produced world-class work that embraces and extends the ethos of the World Trade Centre. Underlying these diverse plans is the common theme of rebirth. Beyond the powerful aesthetic statement that these designs make, they also convey powerful messages—they must speak to our children and our children's children about who we are and what we stand for."[26]

Architecture has had this role for as long as we can remember, ever since Abraham pitched his tent near Bethel and built an altar there to the Lord (Gen 12:8). "As for me and my household," that altar made clear to Abraham's offspring, "we will serve the Lord" (Josh 24:15). I suggested earlier in this chapter that mending the world depends on our coming to see and understand the nature of the world's brokenness. It depends on our coming to see and understand our need of healing, to understand who we really are. I have tried to illustrate the ways in which the work of architects, if it is to contribute to the mending of our world, has also to begin with a proper understanding of our selves and of our brokenness.

Architecture itself cannot heal our brokenness. But what we build, and how we build it can reveal the extent to which the Spirit is at work within us, nudging us toward forgiveness and reconciliation and a true mending of the world.

26. Cited in Goldberger, *Up from Zero*, 6.

BIBLIOGRAPHY

Adorno, Theodor W. "Art, Culture and Society." In *Prisms*, translated by Samuel and Shierry Weber, 17–34. Studies in Contemporary German Social Thought. Cambridge: MIT Press, 1981.

———. *Negative Dialectics*. London: Routledge, 1973.

———. *Notes to Literature*, Volume 2. New York: Columbia University Press, 1992.

———. "Trying to Understand Endgame." *New German Critique* 26 (1982) 119–50.

Eliach, Yaffa. *Hasidic Tales of the Holocaust*. New York: Oxford University Press, 1982.

Glanz, James, and Eric Lipton. *City in the Sky: The Rise and Fall of the World Trade Centre*. New York: Holt, 2003.

Goldberger, Paul. *Up From Zero: Politics, Architecture and the Rebuilding of New York*. New York: Random House, 2004.

Horkheimer, Max, and Theodor Adorno. *Dialectic of Enlightenment*. New York: Herder & Herder, 1972.

Libeskind, Daniel. *The Space of Encounter*. New York: Universe, 2000.

———. "Studio Daniel Libeskind." No pages. Online: http://www.renewnyc.com/plan%5Fdes%5Fdev/wtc%5Fsite/new%5Fdesign%5Fplans/firm_d/default.asp.

O'Connor, Brian, editor. *The Adorno Reader*. Oxford: Blackwell, 2000.

Ouroussof, Nicolai. "Towers' Symbolic Image." *LAT*, September 13, 2001, A32. Online: http://articles.latimes.com/2001/sep/13/news/mn-45326.

Schneider, Bernhard. *Daniel Libeskind Jewish Museum Berlin*. 3rd ed. Munich: Prestel, 2004.

Smith, Terry. *The Architecture of Aftermath*. Chicago: University of Chicago Press, 2006.

Solomon, Deborah. "From the Rubble, Ideas for Rebirth." *NYT*, September 30, 2001, B37.

Stephens, Suzanne. "Fantasy Intersects with Reality at Ground Zero." In *Imagining Ground Zero: Official and Unofficial Proposals for the World Trade Centre Competition*, edited by Suzanne Stephens et al., 12–25. London: Thames & Hudson, 2004.

Viñoly, Rafael. "Fill the Void with Beauty." *NYT*, September 23, 2001. Online: http://www.nytimes.com/2001/09/23/arts/art-architecture-the-aftermath-fill-the-void-with-beauty.html.

Zuidervaart, Lambert. "Theodor W. Adorno." In *Stanford Encyclopedia of Philosophy*, edited by Edward N. Zalta, n.p. Online: http://plato.stanford.edu/archives/win2011/entries/adorno/.

8

The Interesting Case of Heaney, the Critic, and the Incarnation

John Dennison

I

Irish poet Seamus Heaney has secured his position as one of the foremost practitioners in the English language of the last fifty years. His relative pre-eminence in the Trans-Atlantic commerce in poetics, however, is due in no small part to a considerable body of prose writings, collected in four volumes, but also distributed throughout numerous periodical articles and interviews. It is here that Heaney's career-long preoccupation with the poet's public responsibilities is expounded, forming—over the course of more than four decades—a remarkably consistent conceptual structure centered on the problems and possibilities of poetry in the face of history's certain violence. Particularly since the award to Heaney in 1995 of the Nobel Prize for Literature, this strong apology for what he affirms—with a characteristic blend of earnest affirmation and calculated reticence—as the "adequacy" of poetry, has expanded into a transcendental cultural poetics, his account of the good of the arts in the post-Christian, consumerist and technocratic age.[1]

1. The ideal of "adequacy" recurs throughout Heaney's prose poetics, but is particularly prominent in his mature thought. See, for example, Heaney, *The Redress of Poetry* (1995), 8; Heaney, *Crediting Poetry*, 27–28.

What is notable about this account is not only the degree to which it attracts considerable public interest and, in some measure, assent, but also the fact that it is characterized by a pronounced commitment which in its affirmation of certain fundamentals approximates religious faith. We might further note that he has frequently expressed his trust in poetry in terms drawn from Christian scripture, doctrine and devotion, a habit that goes back at least to the mid-1960s, and that reflects the influence of Leavis and Arnold's sacerdotal criticism as much as it does Heaney's Catholic background and education.[2] He is drawn repeatedly to statements of poetic theory that are both memorably phrased and that are also normative, or at least definitive, formulations; there is, we might say, a catechistic quality to his marked capacity to interiorize a text, what Neil Corcoran describes as his "high powers of absorption."[3] As his poetics reach their most emphatic, most systematic expression in the early 1990s, the religious tenor of his commitment becomes pronounced, a characteristic that has also marked his later pronouncements. "The humanities, then, are as much a faith as a discipline," says Heaney upon receiving the 2008 Cunningham Medal; "When I talk about them I am more like somebody affirming a belief than somebody demonstrating a proof."[4] Such comments should prompt us to explore further what Heaney criticism generally has failed to do: to take seriously the pronounced *religious* register of Heaney's affirmations, and to probe the conceptual shape and import of his trust in poetry, not least because his is a voice that, as far as contemporary apologies for the good of poetry and poetics are concerned, has commanded considerable attention.

To this end, some critics have been encouraged toward the conclusion that what we find in Heaney's poetics is an active, if heterodox and often apophatic, extension of Christian theology through the arts. Certainly, some of these are hampered in their approach by an all-too evident desire to bring the Catholic catechumen and Head Boy of St Columb's back within the fold, even if that means temporarily shifting the theological fence-posts.[5] Others have offered more nuanced interpretations of Heaney and Christian thought in which the emphasis on the importance of Christian theology is

2. For a full textual analysis of Seamus Heaney's formation and his debts to Arnold and Leavis, see my "Seamus Heaney and the Adequacy of Poetry."

3. Corcoran, *The Poetry of Seamus Heaney*, 225–26.

4. Heaney, "Holding Patterns," 18.

5. See Evans, *"Strong Enough to Help"*; Noble, "Seamus Heaney," 266–68; Pike, "'Read Poems as Prayers.'"

salutary. Thus, while his reading implies a strong alignment between the critic's method and Heaney's poetics, Malcolm Guite in *Faith, Hope and Poetry* is careful to emphasize his approach is constructive rather than his torical and critical in its description of the truth-bearing potential of the human imagination, an emphasis that in turn frees up his theological ex egesis.[6] Pointing out the neglect of the specifically theological in Northern Irish poetry, Gail McConnell is sensitive to the degree to which Heaney's "theologically charged endeavour is secular in practice," a predicament that, she implies, highlights the potentially idolatrous and vacuous nature of such trust in poetry (her extrapolation of Heaney's poetry as the site of convergence between a New Critical hermeneutic and a Catholic "iconic" hermeneutic is finally not grounded sufficiently in Heaney's developing poetic practice and thought).[7]

Most importantly here, reacting to what he perceives as a general critical failure or unwillingness to take seriously the metaphysical trajec tory of Heaney's mature thought, John Desmond in his book *Gravity and Grace* argues that we must ask "what is the fundamental *ground* for such notions [as language, identity, transcendence, and poetry's relationship to culture] in Heaney's work? [. . . W]hat are the real ontological and reli gious bases for Heaney's epistemology of poetry and his hope for the future [. . .]?"[8] Those "ontological and religious bases," Desmond insists, undergird what he rightly identifies is Heaney's essentialized, metaphysical notion of humanity, and his description of poetry as a "grace."[9] Similarly, the poet's notion of transcendence is not, á la Jung, finally delimited by the historical and psychological; it reflects, Desmond argues with reference to Catholic humanist poet Czesław Miłosz, a certain realistic insistence that "the 'di vine in man' is grounded in a supernatural source that makes possible some liberation from necessity in history."[10] In other words, he maintains that for Heaney the possibility of transcending history is not a mere construct or projection. When it comes to language and reference, Desmond likewise

6. Guite, *Faith, Hope and Poetry*. Given the biographical and historical aspects of Heaney's poetry, his abiding concern with the poet's public responsibility, and the degree to which his later poetry (from, say, *Seeing Things* onward) is entwined with the prose po etics, it is arguable whether one can offer such a strongly theological exegesis of Heaney's work without reckoning with the nature of the poet's own commitments.

7. McConnell, "Towards a Theology of Poetry," 70–85.

8. Desmond, *Gravity and Grace*, 2.

9. Ibid., 3–4.

10. Ibid., 8–9

insists Heaney espouses not the nominalism and constructivism of post-structuralist semiotics but a linguistic realism "in the tradition of Christian realism," a covenantal commitment to an *a priori* transcendent order of significance and value.[11]

While Desmond is careful to note Heaney does not frame these in explicitly theological terms, he concludes that such fundamentals are focused in, and ultimately logically presuppose, the doctrine of the incarnation.[12] He implies, moreover, that Heaney's work rests in no small measure on fiduciary assent to the reality that doctrine describes, although Desmond more immediately emphasizes the poet's commitment, particularly from the late 1980s onwards, to "the light," the Miłoszian affirmation of humanity's divinity in the search for meaning.[13] Certainly, Heaney's prose poetics and certain exemplary poems return repeatedly to motifs of mediation between the historical and super-historical; Desmond is rightly sensitive to what he terms the "ontological axis of [Heaney's] poetry, the intersection or crossroads between what he has called the "glimpsed ideal" and the specific mundane realities recorded in his major poems."[14] As will be considered in detail, this is a pattern Heaney has himself theorized at length: the imaginative "activity of poetry" inclines toward the transcendental, an effort of counterweighting reality, a counterweighting that is efficacious because it holds together a formal manifestation of "free, uncensored impulse" with an unflinching acknowledgement of "the actual."[15]

It is such strong equilibrious patterns, almost systematic in their shape, that encourage Desmond in making an extensive parallel between the thought of Heaney and the French philosopher, activist, and mystic, Simone Weil, whose posthumous collection of heterodox theological aphorisms supplies part of Desmond's title.[16] This parallel, which effectively pushes his exegesis of Heaney's poetics (the second number in Baylor University's *Studies in Christianity and Literature*) toward a constructive theologizing through the arts, is allowed to gloss Heaney's expansive affirmations, his habitual use of Christian theological and devotional language, and appropriation of Christian doctrines to his apology for poetry. Indeed, the

11. Ibid., 10–14.
12. Ibid., 3–4, 9.
13. Ibid., 7, 9.
14. Ibid., 3.
15. Heaney, *The Redress of Poetry* (1990), 3, 8.
16. Weil, *Gravity and Grace.*

fact that Heaney moves beyond any simple analogy with Weil's theological descriptions, not only suggesting that poetry displays a "similar impulse" to counterweigh the "gravity" of the fallen world, but more, arguing that poems' equilibrious responses to political conflict "are particular instances of a general law which Simone Weil announced [. . .] in [. . .] *Gravity and Grace*"—such would seem to secure Desmond's assumption that Heaney's poetic vision is "compatible with [. . .] the essential doctrines of the faith," and more, that "the Christian doctrine of the Incarnation forms the theological basis of Heaney's aesthetic," albeit one troubled by stoicism.[17]

Desmond is, certainly, onto something important, something basic to any full apprehension of Heaney's poetics; indeed, as will become clear, Christian doctrine, and in particular what Heaney has called "the stark, astonishing proposition" of the incarnation, is more fundamental to his belief in the good of poetry and arts than even Desmond perceives.[18] But for such an account to work, too much—both from Heaney's own writing, and from Christian doctrine—must be omitted. While the correspondence with Weil that he intuits is important, in assuming that Heaney's theological references, religious language and metaphysical affirmations reflect an abiding Christian belief Desmond is finally insufficiently attuned to the degree to which Heaney's belief in the good of poetry is shaped by the conventional wisdom that Christian theology can only be demythologized projection. As such, for Heaney, Christianity—indeed, religion generally—constitutes a cultural resource we late Moderns must knowingly appropriate.

This, then, is what might be called—with half-earnest homage to Heaney's prose—the Interesting Case of Heaney, the Critic and the Incarnation, a triangulation by which, via Desmond's exegesis, we are drawn into fuller consideration of the relationship of Heaney's expansive cultural poetics to Christian theology (and perhaps, in turn, into further reflection on the limits and pitfalls of doing theology through the arts).[19] Desmond appreciates what is at stake in examining the religious character and conceptual structures of Heaney's prose poetics: that it will allow us to discern in what sense he regards the arts as ameliorative, or even redemptive. Doing so properly will also present us with a salutary case-study in post-Christian transcendentalist poetics. That is, attending to the development and structures of

17. Desmond, *Gravity and Grace*, 3, 44; Heaney, *The Redress of Poetry* (1990),

18. Heaney, *Finders Keepers*, 414.

19. My chapter title riffs on that of Heaney's "The Interesting Case of Nero, Chekhov, and a Knocker," the essay opening his prose collection *The Government of the Tongue*

Heaney's thought will allow us to apprehend how this influential account of the arts' world-mending powers is not so much extensive with Christian soteriology as finally delimited by the biblical and theological descriptions it knowingly appropriates; it will allow us to see the degree to which Heaney's trust in the adequacy of poetry turns on a refracted after-image of Christian doctrine, particularly that of the incarnation.

II

In 1972 Heaney offers his first account of a personal poetics, his brief essay "The Trade of an Irish Poet." "On the one hand," Heaney insists, "poetry is secret and natural, on the other hand it must make its way in a world that is public and brutal."[20] While reflecting the brutality of this, the bloodiest year of the Northern Irish Troubles, the conceptual separation of secret, natural poem and public, brutal world also provides Heaney with a conceptual means of securing the autonomy of poetry against ideological and political instrumentalism. Although largely rhetorical, Heaney's duality anticipates what becomes a fundamental of his poetics: that, however fully it may internalize the quarrels of that reality, poetry's response to the world cannot be complicit in—cannot be subject to—the denigrations of what he increasingly comes to invoke as "history."[21]

The crisis of the Troubles thus stimulates Heaney's own theorization of poetry's distinctiveness from, and adequacy to the world, where that world is conceived of in terms of finitude, contingency, violence and suffering. While the neo-Romantic and modernist poetic paradigms that Heaney inherits in his undergraduate formation initially prove problematic in application, it is this dualism of poetry and history that emerges from the crucible of the early Troubles as a notably consistent and substantial feature of the prose poetics, one that by the 1980s conforms to a certain redemptive logic.[22] Generally speaking, the higher and more expansive Heaney's account of poetry is, the more resolutely negative his account of human existence becomes, and the more he is at pains to articulate exactly how poetry is nonetheless an adequate, ameliorative response.

20. Heaney, *Preoccupations*, 34.

21. Heaney first invokes the oppositional relation of poetry and history in "Violence and Repose," 13.

22. Again, for a detailed examination of this transition in Heaney's early poetics, see my "Seamus Heaney and the Adequacy of Poetry," chapters 2 and 3.

Importantly, this clarification of Heaney's thought, resolving on this moral duality of poem and world, and culminating in a general, transcendental humanist statement in poetics, coincides with the poet's immersion in a personal process of secularization.[23] "Through the popularising of the insights of anthropologists and mythologists," Heaney explains in Catholic doctrines can now be understood as value-bestowing "fictions" or "structures."[24] Such constructs have been (to adapt a line from his contemporaneous poem "The Skunk") "Mythologized, demythologized," terms that, where Heaney is concerned, have their historical roots in Matthew Arnold's advocacy of Higher Criticism as much as in Bultmann's subsequent kerygmatic Christology.[25] It is this conventional wisdom that underlies—indeed, sanctions—Heaney's transcendentalist poetics, marked as these increasingly are by religiosity and sacerdotalism.

By the mid-1980s, that early rhetorical emphasis on the world "public and brutal," has expanded and ossified into a profoundly pessimistic association of history, finitude, and the human condition, so that Heaney's affirmations of poetry's autonomy are logically predicated on this account of life in the public domain. In the first of his 1986 T. S. Eliot lectures, he insists: "The fact is that poetry is its own reality and no matter how much a poet may concede to the corrective pressures of social, moral, political and historical reality, the ultimate fidelity must be to the demands and promise of the artistic event."[26]

No doubt this expresses the necessary, felt separation between the vitality and liberty of the imagination, and the exigent, given demands of the poet's context. Yet it is more fundamentally the assertion of poetry's real autonomy, the securing of "the artistic event" out of which some restorative good might come. Neil Corcoran rightly identifies that Heaney's "theory of the function of poetry as excess demands that it exceed historical contingency rather than be merely collusive with, or subject to it."[27] Which is why the poet does not hesitate to insist, "as Lazarus in bliss insisted to Dives in torment, that a gulf does exist. A poem floats adjacent to, parallel to, the historical moment. What happens to us as readers when

23. See here Heaney's 1979 address to the Modern Languages Association, "Current Unstated Assumptions About Poetry," 645–51.

24. Druce, "A Raindrop on a Thorn," 30.

25. Heaney, *Field Work*, 48.

26. Heaney, *The Government of the Tongue*, 101.

27. Corcoran, *Poetry of Seamus Heaney*, 214.

we board the poem depends upon the kind of relation it displays towards our historical life."[28]

Here, the conceptual distinctions of the prose poetics begin to conform to a kind of redemptive logic. Not only does Heaney frame his "gulf" between the poem and history in metaphysical terms, where his allusion to Jesus' parable in Luke 16:19–31 implies an opposition of heavenly poetry and hellish history; his comments also display a certain theological sensibility reminiscent of Charles Hart's *The Student's Catholic Doctrine*, Heaney's high school catechistic text, in which great care is taken to delineate the logic of the relationship realized between God and the creation in the incarnation.[29] The logic emerging is this: once you have committed to a restorative, even redemptive account of poetry's function, it is necessary to emphasize both the poem's otherness from life, and its redeeming relation—its restorative assumption of the stuff of history.

Accordingly, Heaney's dualistic structure assumes a doubled aspect. Once separated from history, what ensures poetry's positive efficacy is an internal economy of beauty and truth, transcendent utterance and unflinching realism: "The poet's double responsibility to tell a truth as well as to make a thing would henceforth be singly discharged in the formal achievement of the individual poems."[30] Heaney's comment on Robert Lowell again suggests a certain theological exactness about what we might call the poem's two natures, the distinct yet indivisible aspects of a poem set apart from—and for the sake of—the world. And here again, Heaney is re-appropriating the distinctions and structures of Hart's *Student's Catholic Doctrine*, which so carefully explains the logic of the one Savior's two natures, human and divine, historical and eternal.[31]

It is on the basis of this adapted structure that Heaney can concede: "In one sense the efficacy of poetry is nil—no lyric ever stopped a tank." It is on that same basis that he can go on to declare: "In another sense, it is unlimited. It is like the writing in the sand in the face of which accusers and accused are left speechless and renewed."[32] Heaney expounds the basis of that analogy, the story in chapter eight of John's Gospel in which the Pharisees bring to Jesus a woman caught in adultery. Ingeniously, he focuses on

28. Heaney, *The Government of the Tongue*, 121.

29. Hart, *The Student's Catholic Doctrine*, 38–47.

30. Heaney, *The Government of the Tongue*, 135.

31. Cf. again Hart, *The Student's Catholic Doctrine*, 38–39.

32. Heaney, *The Government of the Tongue*, 107.

the detail of Jesus writing on the ground to advance another version of a recurrent motif in his prose, the poem as a space outside of time: poetry, like the writing of Christ, "does not propose to be instrumental or effective. Instead, in the rift between what is going to happen and whatever we would wish to happen, poetry holds attention for a space, functions not as distraction but as pure concentration."[33] The responsive, responsible poem is both truthful and transcendental, apprehending the brutal stuff of history, yet doing so by holding everything in check in a lyric "break with the usual life."[34] It thus makes inwardly present a salutary, self-reflexive space of renewal.

Heaney constructs his analogy in such a way that the nuances of Jesus' just authority and redemptive intervention adhere to his account of poetry: "like the writing in the sand in the face of which accusers and accused are left speechless and renewed." And those nuances bring to light the religious impulse of Heaney's formulations: in placing poetry between "what is going to happen and whatever we would wish to happen," his poetics gesture toward eschatology—toward a lasting renewal of "the usual life"—even as he limits any realizations to an inner sphere, a space of "pure concentration." The re-appropriation of Christian scripture and theology at this point is masterful, a sacerdotal theorization of what Desmond concludes is the way "many of Heaney's later poems are profoundly incarnational in the Christian sense."[35] Presumably, by "profoundly incarnational," Desmond does not mean that Heaney's poems participate in the saving work of the Triune God (otherwise we would surely have to qualify that "Christian sense"); but if he then—after Heaney's parable in poetics—intends "incarnational" to be understood metaphorically (poems transcend, but do not break with "the usual life"), then it is no longer quite so profound, and is certainly not immune—as Desmond wishes Heaney's poetics to be—from the labels "skeptical, stoical, or post-Christian."[36]

33. Ibid., 108.

34. Ibid.

35. Desmond, "Seamus Heaney as a 'Christian' Poet," 61.

36. Ibid., 61.

III

Heaney's poetics find a culmination in *The Redress of Poetry*, his inaugural address, in 1989, as Oxford Professor of Poetry. Reformulating his dualistic conception of poetry around the richly suggestive term "redress," Heaney's account derives its notable energy and precision in large part from *Gravity and Grace*, a collection of aphoristic theological sentences by Simone Weil. Within her dualistic heterodoxy, the metaphor of "gravity" refers to the tragic, innate descents of humanity, in some ways identical with the orthodox idea of sin.[37] Importantly, for Weil, humanity's subjection is most acutely expressed in its temporal finitude: "Time does us violence; it is the only violence."[38] Weil's dualistic soteriology sets the judicial image of the scales in motion with principles of physics, divine Grace levering up and restoring to equilibrium a creation beset by evil.

The prior receptivity of Heaney's thought to Weil's is unquestionable; he seizes upon the suggestiveness of Weil's soteriological metaphor—the cross as the fulcrum of God's counterweighing redemption—extrapolating freely from constructive theology to his own poetics: "in the activity of poetry a similar impulse persists, to place a counter-reality in the scales, a reality which is admittedly only imagined but which nevertheless has weight because it is imagined within the gravitational pull of the actual."[39]

The doubled metaphor thoroughly explicates the redemptive logic of his poetics: "The redress of poetry is effected primarily by work that sets itself upright by virtue of free, uncensored impulse"; how then, if so necessarily autonomous, can poetry counterweigh the world? "Because it is imagined within the gravitational pull of the actual"; because it "must contain within it the co-ordinates of the reality which surrounds it."[40] Again, the ascription to poetry of a kind of two-natures doctrine finds its soteriological completion in poetry's efficacious transcendence over "the actual."

Of course, the extent of such religious connotation, so precisely wielded, suggests it is not only convenient, or appropriate to the occasion, but also indicative of an earnest commitment. And such unconcerned

37. Weil, *Gravity and Grace*, 1–4; note also Gustav Thibon's introductory explication of her theology: "There is no doubt that here below matter and evil exercise 'all the causality which belongs to them'; the spectacle of the innumerable horrors of history is enough to prove that the kingdom of God is not of this world" (ibid., xxxii).

38. Ibid., 74.

39. Heaney, *The Redress of Poetry* (1990), 4.

40. Ibid., 8, 4, 11.

appropriation of Weil's theology is partly what leads Desmond to affirm Heaney as theorizing and exemplifying an idealist metaphysical poetics centering on an idea of incarnation.[41] But the relation of Heaney's poetics to Christian doctrine is notional and structural, not confessional and theological. Indeed, Heaney's appropriation of Weil's language incorporates into the poetics theological affirmations that expose—rather than ratify—the limits of his constructive effort. For Weil, the true balancing act can only be the cross of Christ, God's levering up of his fallen creation: "When the whole universe weighs upon us there is no other counterweight possible but God himself . . . Evil is infinite in the sense of being indefinite; matter, space, time . . . There can be no other. It has to be at the intersection of the world and that which is not the world."[42]

This is profoundly illuminating of the logic of Heaney's poetics: if poetry is in any way to be a metaphysical "counterweight" to the world, it must be substantially (indeed, *ontologically*) other than that reality, while also effecting an "intersection" of timelessness and history. As Heaney's schoolboy catechism puts it, "No creature, however, least of all fallen man, was capable of making," "satisfaction adequate to the sin."[43] And yet, that same redemptive logic rebukes Heaney's trust in what Weil calls "imagination which fills the void" and that she, at least, deems part of the problem: "The thought of death calls for a counterweight, and this counterweight—apart from grace—cannot be anything but a lie."[44]

What troubles Desmond's interpretation most, then, is not the tendency to accommodate too easily Heaney's thought to Christian orthodoxy (assuming substantial continuity between theological and poetic structures), nor the insistence that Heaney is not Gnostic (for in the negative rendering of history and contingency his prose poetics surely are).[45] Rather, he fails to reckon properly with the degree to which Heaney's sacerdotal poetics pre

41. Desmond notes his is not "a study of the influence of Weil on Heaney per se"; nevertheless, his theological analysis of Heaney's idealist metaphysics proceeds by interpreting first Weil and then Heaney on particular points, effectively "glossing" the latter with the former's oeuvre. At the very least, this approach is troubled by the fact that there is no evidence Heaney is deeply schooled in Weil's thought; his recourse to her work is confined to his use, in this one lecture, of *Gravity and Grace*.

42. Weil, *Gravity and Grace*, 84–85.

43. Hart, *Catholic Doctrine*, 37.

44. Weil, *Gravity and Grace*, 16.

45. Desmond, *Gravity and Grace*, 9. Regarding Desmond's accommodation of Heaney to Christian orthodoxy, see also his "Seamus Heaney as a 'Christian' Poet."

suppose an extensive acquiescence to the assumption that Christian theology describes—constructs—transcendental "fictions" and "structures" that in their basic aspect are immanent and therapeutic, *and knowingly so*. Such, indeed, is the work of the poet who, as Heaney approvingly quotes from Wallace Stevens, "'creates the world to which we turn incessantly [. . . and] gives life to the supreme fictions.'"[46] Desmond is right to insist that Heaney espouses not the nominalism and constructivism of post-structuralist semiotics but a linguistic realism and commitment to a prior order of value, as far as this idealist metaphysics goes.[47] But Heaney's accession to this notion of supreme fictions (and his brief, subsequently revised, entanglement with "the deconstructionist critics, with their unmaskings and destabilizings"), ultimately highlights the ongoing, unresolved and at points tenuous epistemological effort of such post-Christian constructions.[48]

Noting such allows us to see the ways in which Heaney's experience of secularization is more extensive and substantial than Desmond allows (and as such, is less simply resolved).[49] Interviewed in 1991, Heaney explains his appropriations of religious language in terms of his own secularization and deliberate spiritual reconstruction: "The religious language was entirely radiant and mysterious—but it was unquestioned. Then you come to the detached, self-secularised period, and you say: eternal life? It's all language, you know. There's no afterlife . . . And then, suddenly, you say: well, wait! Eternal life can mean utter reverence for life itself. And that's what there is . . . The sacred value is actually eternal life. So that language is perfectly proper. It can be used again."[50]

This is not the recovery of metaphysical knowledge, nor the liberating humiliation of late modern rationality by prevenient, self-offering grace; it is the knowing, calculated demythologization of this vocabulary and its being put to use in an effort of meaning-making. This is not an individualized, transformed Christianity, but rather a post-secular humanist reappropriation of convenient truths. And it is not just that this language has been deregulated and reclaimed in a humanist effort to substantiate "sacred

46. Heaney, *The Redress of Poetry* (1995), 2.

47. Desmond, *Gravity and Grace*, 13–14.

48. Heaney, *The Redress of Poetry* (1990), 10; the attempt to side-step post-structuralism is subsequently deleted from the collected version of this lecture. For a full treatment of Heaney's revisions to previously published prose, see my "'To construct something upon which to rejoice,'" 116–37.

49. Cf. Desmond, *Gravity and Grace*, 3–5, 8–11.

50. "A Soul on the Washing Line," 126.

value"; it is, more, that a metaphysical immanence that it now seems was *always* there has been exposed: "It's all language, you know," "that's what there is." The consolation of Christian belief, Heaney elsewhere caricatures, is facile and evasive, "some bland rhapsody about God in his heaven and all is right with the world . . . We are to rejoice, yes; but as T. S. Eliot clearly and unconsolingly stated, we have to construct something upon which to rejoice."[51] What nearly rescues this statement from orotundity is its dead seriousness: this is "what there is," a construction in artful language of de liberate joy, in the face of proof that everything is, in Weil's terms, "apart from grace."

Although the collection from which it comes, *Seeing Things* widely been celebrated for its shift toward transcendentalism, the poem "Squarings, i" lays bare precisely this post-Christian vision.[52] Heaney has described the poem as "about the capacity for illumination, splendour and elation," "a sense that a weight had been lifted off and that some light has entered in"; having written it while working on a selection of Yeats's poems, he connects it with "The Cold Heaven."[53] Yet the poem turns on ponderous deliberations that are strikingly Eliotesque; indeed, opening with a frag mented scene of a dwelling wrecked and open to the elements—"Bare wall stead and a cold hearth rained into"—the poem frames an over-exposed, negative image of the Nativity, suggestive of Eliot's "Journey of the Magi":

> And after the commanded journey, what?
> Nothing magnificent, nothing unknown.
> A gazing out from far away, alone.[54]

If this is Heaney's own "Journey of the Magi" it is not the recollections of a witness who, having struggled toward the magnificent, has had his self-assumed faith and knowledge undone in the encounter.[55] Rather, the judg ment on Christ's birth is unequivocal: "it is not particular at all, | Just old truth dawning: there is no next-time-round." Most interesting here is what happens to the religious and transcendent vocabulary: "Bright puddle where the soul-free cloud-life roams"; "Unroofed scope. Knowledge-freshening

51. Heaney, "Keeping Time," 259–60; cf. Eliot, *Collected Poems*, 95.
52. Heaney, *Seeing Things*, 55.
53. Murphy, *Reading the Future*, 89–90.
54. Heaney, *Seeing Things*, 55.
55. Cf. Eliot, *Collected Poems*, 110.

wind."[56] Each phrase intimates absence, but, more devastatingly, derives force from the Hopkinsesque conjunction of terms connoting fullness and transcendence (and in this sense the poem does indeed recall the merciless hyper-luminescence of Yeats's "The Cold Heaven").[57] In the same way, Heaney's wider rehabilitation of religious constructs and soteriological analogies, made in order to articulate his high—yet finally immanent and limited—account of the spiritual adequacy of poetry, draws down the shadow of humanity's aloneness in the face of history, even as it lends his affirmations the cultural uplift and afterglow of Christian creedal affirmation.

IV

Crediting Poetry represents the acme of Heaney's account of poetry's adequate response, offering the most precise delineation of the conceptual shape of his poetics. True to form, it is two-fold: the poem is true to the world, with "that documentary adequacy which answers all that we know about the intolerable." "But," he continues, "there is another kind of adequacy which is specific to lyric poetry," a confirmation of human being in "linguistic fission and fusion, . . . the buoyancy generated by cadence and tone and rhyme and stanza."[58] And again, this doubled adequacy of poetry rests on a belief in the poem as an order substantially other than, or above and beyond, the world: "Poetic form is both the ship and the anchor. It is at once a buoyancy and a holding . . . [This is] what the necessary poetry does, . . . touch the base of our sympathetic natures while taking in at the same time the unsympathetic reality of the world to which that nature is constantly exposed."[59]

A certain logical circularity emerges, for this central tenet of Heaney's crediting of poetry—"the sufficiency of that which is absolutely imagined"—is also the logical and metaphysical predicate of his efforts to substantiate poetry's redemptive function.[60] Heaney's own experience of

56. Heaney, *Seeing Things*, 55.

57. Cf. Yeats, *The Collected Poems*, 140. Cf. also the opening poem of Heaney's most recent collection: "'Had I not been awake'" recounts a more positive, less complex experience of the numinous, in this instance, not light, but the wind; the poem nevertheless turns on a similarly emphatic refusal of the "ever | After." Heaney, *Human Chain*, 3.

58. Heaney, *Crediting Poetry*, 27–28.

59. Ibid., 29.

60. Ibid., 20.

secularization and the wider cultural decline of metaphysical certainties apparently admit no other option: the sufficiency of poetry must be upheld. In this sense, Desmond is right to describe Heaney's mature thought as idealist, committed to "a hope for greater human fulfilment"; but therein lies the limit of his thought and the difference from Christian belief: prevenient grace is not—is not even co-extensive with—an ideal.[61]

Burdened with such received wisdom, there is something entirely appropriate to the poetics about the equivocal, restrained ideal of adequacy: poetry is "a clarification, a fleeting glimpse of a potential order of things "beyond confusion," a glimpse that has to be its own reward."[62] The remarks, improvising on Robert Frost's poem "Directive," signal Heaney's strong assent to that poet's formulation of the poem as "a momentary stay against confusion," which in turn echoes an older, far less modest account of poetry's imaginatively redemptive power: Matthew Arnold's pronouncement that, now that the Christian creeds have been exposed as "divine illusion," we must turn to the consolation and revelation of Scripture-as-poetry, and—by extension—of transcendent, joyful literature; it is in poetry that we "will find *an ever surer and surer stay*."[63]

As Paul Muldoon suggests, Heaney's idiomatic attraction to such terms as "stay" and "adequate" reflect his own late twentieth century, post-Christian return to his undergraduate formation in an Arnoldian trust in the ameliorative resource of literature.[64] "Poetry keeps, saves, and stays," Heaney enthuses in a recent interview, offering a "ritualized symbolic rendering of reality" in moments of crisis.[65] It "constitutes for a group, for a culture, the fundamental values of the spirit in that group. If you take it into yourself it founds your values for you."[66] That last oddly sacramental phrase is complemented by Heaney's more recent improvisation of analogies between poet and priest.[67] The "salvific function" of the poet is seen in his or her suffering commitment "to speak to the inner hearing, in the

61. Desmond, *Gravity and Grace*, 47.

62. Heaney, *The Redress of Poetry* (1995), xv.

63. Frost, "The Figure a Poem Makes," in *Collected Poems*, n.p.; Arnold, *Essays in Criticism*, 1.

64. Muldoon, *The End of the Poem* (2006), 394; Muldoon, *The End of the Poem* (2000), 5.

65. Kearney, "The Staying Power of Poetry," 14.

66. Murphy, *Reading the Future*, 93.

67. As exemplified by Heaney's address opening the inaugural T. S. Eliot Summer School, London, 27 June 2009.

language, in themselves and in the reader."[68] Correspondingly, Heaney describes poetry's inner "salvation" in which the poem is "the eye of a verbal needle through which the growing person can pass again and again," "a path by which the individual can enter, repeatedly, into the kingdom of rightness."[69] His improvisation here on Jesus' discussion of the Kingdom of God in Luke 18 recalls Arnold's improvisation on Jesus' discourse in Luke 17: "Religion says: *The kingdom of God is within you*; and culture, in like manner, places human perfection in an *internal* condition . . . It places it in the ever-increasing efficacy and in the general harmonious expansion of those gifts of thought and feeling, which make the peculiar dignity, wealth, and happiness of human nature."[70]

The parallel suggests how appropriate it is to extend to Heaney's cultural poetics also his remark from 1999 that "my poetry is somehow my religious substitute, as Matthew Arnold says."[71] If Heaney's prose reflects a "displaced Catholicism," such description needs careful qualification: it is not simply that Heaney's childhood Catholicism was displaced into the poetics; rather, that catechetic formation was displaced by one historically predicated on the abandonment of Christian doctrine.[72]

V

Heaney's short essay on Miłosz from 1999 turns on a passage, the type of which has already been established as a hermeneutical touchstone for Heaney's trust in the adequacy of poetry. Miłosz's imagination, Heaney explains, "is supplied and made ample by a fundamentally religious vision, the one based on the idea of Incarnation. What this entails is an assent to the stark, astonishing proposition that through the incarnation of the Son of God in the figure of Christ, the eternal has intersected with time, and through that intersection human beings, though creatures of time, have access to a reality out of time."[73]

68. Murphy, *Reading the Future*, 93.
69. Heaney, "Bags of Enlightenment," B6.
70. Arnold, *Culture and Anarchy*, 11–12.
71. Wylie and Kerrigan, "An Interview with Seamus Heaney," 132.
72. Cf. Corcoran, *The Poetry of Seamus Heaney*, 210.
73. Heaney, *Finders Keepers*, 414.

Heaney’s exposition is striking for its orthodoxy. In its catechistic unfolding of the logic of Christian salvation, and its implied acknowledgement of the scandalous offence of Christian doctrine to the hegemony of modern reason, it cannot only derive from Heaney’s deep respect for his Polish exemplar. The mere inclusion of this doctrinal explanation, and the fact that Heaney chooses to elaborate it theologically in terms of the eternal and the temporal, suggest his remarks are self-reflexive. He appears to recognize the extent to which this “astonishing proposition” constitutes an informing antecedent to his own account of poetry’s two-fold adequacy; the extent to which, too, this answer of his school-boy catechism describes and addresses the immortal longings of his prose poetics: the desire that through the countervailing, momentary stay of the poem, “though creatures of time” we might “have access to a reality out of time.”

It is not so much, then, that Heaney—as Eliot says of Arnold—that “there is only one stay,” the divine Word-made-flesh and representative, Jesus Christ, but rather that he has largely acceded to the prevailing wisdom that all such metaphysical and religious notions are necessarily mythopoetic projections.[74] Recalling how in his experience secularization “screened out the first visionary world,” Heaney reflects: “you learned that, from the human beginnings, poetic imagination had proffered a world of light and a world of dark, a shadow region—not so much an afterlife as an afterimage of life.”[75] On this account, whether the “unconscious poetry” of religion or the momentary stay of a poem—both are the self-confirming constructions of “the impulse towards transcendence.”[76] At the same time, Heaney’s own response to this “impulse to transcendence,” namely his decision to credit the two-fold adequacy of the history-encompassing, world-balancing poem, is profoundly informed by—indeed, logically predicated on—an emptying of belief, an absence lodged in Heaney’s personal experience and pervasive to the underlying character of his thought: “You can lose your belief in the afterlife, in the particular judgement at the moment of death . . . but it’s harder to lose the sense of an ordained structure, beyond all this fuddle. Poetry represents the need for an ultimate court of appeal. The infinite spaces may be silent, but the human response is to say that this is not good enough, that there has to be more to it than neuter absence.”

74. Eliot, *The Use of Poetry and the Use of Criticism*, 119.

75. O’Driscoll, *Stepping Stones*, 472.

76. Ibid., 470.

77. Ibid., 470.

Again, however resolute the constructions of the poetic imagination, for Heaney such efforts are always knowing, too-aware of their transcendental aspiration and procedure, and as such, finally predicated on absence, on the acknowledged impossibility of *all* such constructions of transcendence in any sense other than an inner, imagined sense: that what answers the human longing for something "beyond all this fuddle" can only be an "afterimage of life."

Heaney's faith in poetry is thus shaped by the absence of that "ordained structure" that entered him as a catechumen. Indeed, his account of poetry's adequacy is finally delimited and exposed by that informing absence. For he cannot reconstruct in his prose the relation of eternity and history that is declared in the doctrine of the Incarnation: there, not only does eternity enter history, but God in the Incarnate Word *assumes the condition of history*, and *all* that entails, in an exhaustion and transformation of that deleterious reality. Approximating that *communicatio idiomatum* would require a more complete union of the poem and history than Heaney is prepared to make, enduringly committed as he is to the moral purity and existential liberty of the poetic act. Despite the longing to exceed circumstance, his thought tends to the ongoing strain of a gnostic poetics, repeatedly shoring up the untenable autonomy and transcendence of poetry.

In this way, Heaney's prose poetics constitute (to extend his analogy) a fractured "afterimage" of Christian doctrine. The more completely the poetics appropriate and approximate that doctrine, the more the immanence, the logical strain, and the metaphysical and ethical limits of Heaney's conclusions are exposed, so that the answers of his school-boy catechism chastise his "idea of poetry's answer."[78] And here, Heaney's own comments on Elizabeth Bishop's early poem "The Monument" offer an apt, worked-up, fit-for-purpose gloss on the history, scope, and post-Christian burden of his prose poetics: "This monument [. . .] promises nothing beyond what it exhibits, and yet it seems to be standing over something which it also stands for. Once again, a withdrawn pressure, an inscrutable purpose or missing element is what the resulting structure exists to express or shelter"[79]

78. Heaney, *The Redress of Poetry* (1995), 191.

79. Ibid., 171.

Bibliography

Arnold, Matthew. *Culture and Anarchy: An Essay in Political and Social Criticism* London: Smith, Elder, 1882.

———. *Essays in Criticism: Second Series*. London: Macmillan, 1888.

Corcoran, Neil. *The Poetry of Seamus Heaney: A Critical Study*. London: Faber & Faber, 1998.

Dennison, John. "Seamus Heaney and the Adequacy of Poetry: A Study of His Prose Poetics." PhD diss., University of St. Andrews, 2011.

———. "'To construct something upon which to rejoice': Seamus Heaney's Prose Revisions." *South Carolina Review* 43, no. 1 (2010) 116–37.

Desmond, John. *Gravity and Grace: Seamus Heaney and the Force of Light*. Waco: Baylor University, 2009.

———. "Seamus Heaney as a 'Christian' Poet." *Christian Scholar's Review* 31 (2001 66.

Druce, Robert. "A Raindrop on a Thorn: An Interview with Seamus Heaney." *Quarterly* 9 (1979) 24–37.

Eliot, T. S. *Collected Poems 1909–1962*. London: Faber & Faber, 1974.

———. *The Use of Poetry and the Use of Criticism: Studies in the Relation of Criticism to Poetry in England*. London: Faber & Faber, 1933.

Evans, John. *"Strong Enough to Help": Spirituality in the Poetry of Seamus Heaney*. Oxford: Farmington Institute for Christian Studies, 1997.

Frost, Robert. *Collected Poems of Robert Frost*. London: Cape, 1943.

Guite, Malcolm. *Faith, Hope and Poetry: Theology and the Poetic Imagination*. Farnham: Ashgate, 2010.

Hart, Charles. *The Student's Catholic Doctrine*. Dublin: Burns, Oates & Washbourne,

Heaney, Seamus. "Bags of Enlightenment." *Guardian*, 25 October 2003, B4–6.

———. *Crediting Poetry: The Nobel Lecture*. Oldcastle: Gallery, 1995.

———. "Current Unstated Assumptions About Poetry." *Critical Inquiry* 7 (1981)

———. *Field Work*. London: Faber & Faber, 1979.

———. *Finders Keepers: Selected Prose 1971–2001*. London: Faber & Faber, 2002.

———. *The Government of the Tongue: The 1986 T. S. Eliot Lectures and Other Critical Writings*. London: Faber & Faber, 1988.

———. "Holding Patterns: Arts, Letters and the Academy." In *Articulations: Poetry, Philosophy and the Shaping of Culture*, 11–23. Dublin: Royal Irish Academy,

———. *Human Chain*. London: Faber & Faber, 2010.

———. "Keeping Time: Irish Poetry and Contemporary Society." In *International Aspects of Irish Literature*, edited by Toshi Furomoto et al., 247–62. Gerrards Cross: Smythe, 1996.

———. *Preoccupations: Selected Prose 1968–1978*. London: Faber & Faber, 1980.

———. *The Redress of Poetry: An Inaugural Lecture delivered before the University of Oxford on 24 October 1989*. Oxford: Clarendon, 1990.

———. *The Redress of Poetry: Oxford Lectures*. London: Faber & Faber, 1995.

———. *Seeing Things*. London: Faber & Faber, 1991.

———. "Violence and Repose." *Hibernia*, 19 January 1973, 13.

Kearney, Simone. "The Staying Power of Poetry." *Irish Literary Supplement* (2007)

McConnell, Gail. "Towards a Theology of Poetry: Seamus Heaney's Icons and Sacraments." *Irish Review* 43 (2011) 70–85.

Muldoon, Paul. *The End of the Poem: "All Soul's Night" by W. B. Yeats, an inaugural lecture delivered before the University of Oxford on 2 November 1999*. Oxford: Oxford University Press, 2000.

———. *The End of the Poem: Oxford Lectures*. London: Faber & Faber, 2006.

Murphy, Mike. *Reading the Future: Irish Writers in Conversation with Mike Murphy*, edited by Clíodhna Ní Anluain. Dublin: Lilliput, 2000.

Noble, Tim. "Seamus Heaney: The Deep Grammar of the Human Condition." *Month* 24 (1991) 266–68

O'Driscoll, Dennis. *Stepping Stones: Interviews with Seamus Heaney*. London: Faber & Faber, 2008.

Pike, P. "'Read Poems as Prayers': Seamus Heaney and the Christian Tradition." PhD diss., Lancaster University, 1999.

"A Soul on the Washing Line." *The Economist*, 22 June 1991, 122–26.

Weil, Simone. *Gravity and Grace*. Translated by Emma Craufurd. London: Routledge, 1987.

Wylie, J. J., and John C. Kerrigan. "An Interview with Seamus Heaney." *Nua: Studies in Contemporary Irish Writing* 2 (1998–1999) 125–37.

Yeats, W. B. *The Collected Poems of W. B. Yeats*. 2nd ed. London: Macmillan, 1950.

9

New Media Art Practice

A Challenge and Resource for Multimedia Worship

Julanne Clarke-Morris

Art cannot mend the world, but through art, and through us, God can. With the power of the Spirit, new media art can lead hearts and minds into the knowledge and love of God, and into a deeper understanding of our proper human response to that love. In this essay I will discuss how multimedia worship installations can draw us into relationship with God and God's truths more effectively, by using the critical practice of new media art disciplines.

Using two video installation works from the early 2000s as a primary illustration, I will investigate how the assumptions and expectations of vir tual reality immersion art, installation art, and site-specific art can resource contemporary worship to more effectively engage the person who walks in off the street.

An illustration: *Lumen ad Revelationem*, 2002

Lumen ad Revelationem was a contemplative liturgical art installation presented in the 12th-century crypt of Christ Church Cathedral, Dublin, in 2002. It appeared as a demarcated space illuminated by video projections within the Cathedral's large cruciform crypt, a shadowy underground space, which extends under the length and breadth of the building.

The visitor enters the crypt's dimly-lit, yet crisp and tidy stone-edged space, down a stone staircase from the cathedral interior. A forest of Romanesque arches stretches through the cavern, making it a series of intimate spaces rather than one grand hall.

The installation of video projections is sited in an alcove of arches near the centre of the crypt. The first noticeable feature is a constant low dull sound, something like a distant wave, which gradually becomes recognizable as a low, rumbling street sound.

Moving into the installation, the visitor encounters two of the crypt's Romanesque arches filled with blue-toned video projections where ordinary Dubliners went go about their everyday activities, at a very slowed pace, on the city's streets.[1] With the low rumbling soundtrack and the single color range, there is a feeling of monotony, a depiction of ordinary life as dull and mundane. Before the arches sits a simple black plinth topped by a punctured metal plate designed to hold votive candles, a few of which already burn there. A pile of thin beeswax candles sit nearby with an invitation to stop and light one.

In order to experience the installation fully, the visitor had to first physically slow down. To grasp the slowed-motion street scene, the viewer was compelled to pause and reflect. Before the work could really be revealed, they had to stop long enough to light a candle, to be right where they were, and pay attention, even if only for a moment. As soon as the candle was lit and placed into the holder, a new projection emerged within the mundane blue scene. A giant orange carp swam languidly across the blue arches. An enormous bee tottered inside the brilliant yellow chalice of a rhododendron bloom. A gigantic magnolia bulb turned and unfurled in the breeze. For each candle lit, a single image appeared, and remained visible for less than sixty seconds. As each new image emerged, a surge of sumptuous sacred choral music overflowed into the street's dull roar.[2]

1. The street footage, its sound and the appearance images were all slowed to twenty percent of life speed. My decision to use slowed footage in this piece came from my discovery that slowed footage captures the delicate movements of animals and the action of wind on plants more expressively. I later appreciated the sophisticated use of slowed footage in capturing the nuance of human expression in video artist Bill Viola's works such as "The Greeting" (1995) and "Emergence."

2. Commonly known in English as "Rachmaninoff's Vespers," this piece was written

Here was the crux of the installation—that the one who takes the time to stop and wonder may be given a fleeting glimpse of the extraordinary. In that moment of stillness, they are offered a glimpse of heaven, of the beauty of creation magnified, of an allusion to the ever-present, yet unseen, reality of God.

This installation was in some ways very simple. Numerous editing and construction choices, informed by both contemporary new media art theory and liturgical antecedents, went into forming the succinct nature of the work.

"New Media" Art Disciplines vs. Mass Media

Before I continue with a discussion of the value of critical new media art practice, it is important to acknowledge that many forms of digital and multimedia practice are currently being used in worship.

Problematically, when digital media is used in church contexts, it often draws on the aesthetics and production values of commercial graphic design. This mode of communication places these Christian media productions into a cultural context that needs to be seriously considered in the conception of the work. When worship artists use the slick "MTV" aesthetics utilized by television networks or other commercial interests, that decision will have an impact on reception of the work. If multimedia in worship simply replicates a populist mainstream commercial style, it places the Gospel message into a discourse that is commonly used for manipulation and is highly subject to an emphasis on the trivial.

In comparison, installation art, site-specific art, interactive digital art and virtual reality art are useful for worship artists, because of the intentions and communication conventions they bring to the task of creating an experience. Each of these forms is constructed with a critical intention, yet an openness to dialogue and genuine co-creative interaction with the viewer. Installation art carries with it the assumption that multiple perspectives and interpretations are not only possible, but highly desirable.

The success of artists such as the US band OK Go (who have rejected the commercial music production machine and continued to make their

by Sergei Rachmaninoff in 1915 using texts from the Russian Orthodox *All Night Vigil* liturgy. I recorded the music used in this installation in Christ Church Cathedral, Dublin, sung by the Cathedral choir.

own installation artworks as videos for their music) shows that these value distinctions are recognized by viewers.

What follows here is an investigation of specific qualities in new media art disciplines that may prove useful in the conception and development of worship installation art.

Virtual Reality and Immersion Art

Virtual reality art focuses on building an entirely new three-dimensional environment as a form of art. In his book *The Metaphysics of Virtual Reality*, Michael Heim describes "immersion" and "full body immersion" as two of the seven essential forms of virtual reality.[3] These concepts have been broadly taken up by new media artists.

Immersion as an art concept goes back to nineteenth-century German composer Richard Wagner who was among the first to talk of an artistic work as a total or whole experience, what he called a "gesamtkunstwerk." The *Larousse Encyclopedia of Music* describes Wagner's mature theatrical works as not only "creating an atmosphere," but also as "plunging the listener into a new world."[4]

In some cases, immersive virtual reality art means that an existing three-dimensional environment is transformed to become a different world, as a fully walk-in work of art. As in *Lumen ad Revelationem*, this is often achieved by imposing video projections into a space. In other immersion works, a discrete virtual environment can be entered into via a digital device such as a screen or headset.

One example is the 1995 ground-breaking work *Osmose* by Canadian artist Char Davies, which used a headset and breath control to take the participant into a distinct 3-D virtual world and allow them to navigate through it. The work drew on Davies' experience as a diver in her construction of its three-dimensional layers of pond, forest and cloud.[5] Some who

3. Heim, *The Metaphysics of Virtual Reality*, 110–12.

4. Anonymous, "The Symphony and Opera in Germany," 325.

5. "There are a dozen world-spaces in *Osmose*, most based on metaphorical aspects of nature. These include Clearing, Forest, Tree, Leaf, Cloud, Pond, Subterranean Earth, and Abyss. There is also a substratum, Code, which contains much of the actual software used to create the work, and a superstratum, Text, a space consisting of quotes from the artist and excerpts of relevant texts on technology, the body and nature" (Davies, "Osmose").

have entered into the work experienced a "metaphysical" freedom from bodily limitations.

In his book *Grace and Necessity: Reflections on Art and Love*, Rowan Williams names the ability to create new worlds as one way that artists can aid our understanding of the creative power of God. Art can contribute to theology in that it helps us to see the quality of creation that is imagining a world into being.[6]

While for Protestant and Pentecostal Christians full-immersion liturgical art is something quite new, it is a common experience for Eastern Orthodox Christians. Liturgies enacted in contemporary Greek and Russian Orthodox cathedrals and monastery churches immerse worshippers in an interior space completely plastered in imagery on every surface but the floor.[7] In these buildings, painted frescoes, icons and mosaics form a seamless reality that visually recalls the story of the faith and the constant presence of the heavenly cloud of witnesses. The Eastern Orthodox understanding of liturgy is that human worship temporarily joins in with the never-ending praise and worship of heaven.[8]

Installation Art—Transforming Space

Installation usually refers to an arrangement of sensory elements in a three-dimensional space, designed to transform both the space and the meaning of its constituent parts. It often includes everyday objects, natural materials, digital media, video, projected images, sound, interactive features and performance. Installations aim to engage the participant in a response to the changed space and to the way the new arrangement of objects change their meaning in relationship to one another.

So, like liturgy, installation art often assumes that the final truth will lie in the human response, not in any of the particular elements used. In other words, the artwork is made, at least in part, by the work of the people

6. Williams, *Grace and Necessity*, 166–67.

7. While the whitewashed interiors of Protestant churches do not engage worshippers in this kind of visual feast, they make an ideal site for the temporary video projections used in multimedia liturgy. White-walled churches provide worship installation artists with a visually blank slate, so that temporary projections can fill the space with powerful images, which remain too fleeting to become stale.

8. Jensen, *The Substance of Things Seen*, 85. *Lumen ad Revelationem* used Rachmaninoff's music in a way that remained true to this aspect of its original intention.

who come to experience it. The people's response to the artist's intentions embedded in the work becomes the artwork itself.

In 2001, I presented a worship installation work entitled *Illuminations* in the twelfth-century crypt of Christchurch cathedral Dublin, which relied on the perspective, timing and movement of each viewer to create that person's unique experience of the work.

The installation set out to transform and enliven the dry and dark stone crypt and draw out the tree-like qualities of its Romanesque stone pillars. It contained visual cues from the crypt, including from its funerary history; the space still houses numerous tomb monuments and at one time included graves.

Multiple video projections filled a large circular enclosure of eight pillars, bringing the bright green leafy under-canopy of a summer woodland into the crypt in the middle of a dreary winter. Sounds from the projected forest (including gusts of wind, rustling leaves and snatches of birdsong) reflected up into the arches from speakers positioned beneath iron gratings on the crypt floor.

The leafy video projections wrapped softly around the architecture without forming hard edges, molding onto the building's arches and transforming them from solid blocks of stone into luminous moving fields of color. Biblical and contemporary poetic texts using the tree of life or the forest as metaphor appeared within the foliage, while faces from the crypt's monuments appeared in the green, blended with a live human face.

In drawing on historic and visual elements from the crypt, the installation reflected echoes of the space back to itself, and co-opted them for a new meaning.[9] Light in the darkness, life in death, summer in winter, a forest sprung up in the valley of dry bones.

For most, it was simply a cause to stop and wonder. For many, it was an invitation to wonder in a different way to what viewers might be expecting when they entered the cathedral. The images and texts appeared on separate cycles, which meant that no single experience of the installation would be the same or more complete than another. The relationship between sounds, images and texts was always changing, and depended on the position the visitor chose to observe the installation unfold.

9. In another part of the crypt, a projection blended images of a man floating in cross-shaped pose in a river, with images of rushing water, a baby's face, a descending white bird, and the faces of angels from the crypt's monuments re-filmed beneath the water projection. These baptismal images played on the crypt floor near the archeological site of an extinct river.

Notes in the visitors' book offered a range of responses—from indignation at the green lighting on the crypt's nineteenth-century sculptures, to comments offering profound gratitude for the experience. One spiritual director was mesmerized. Children loved the installation and played with it by running in front of the projections and enjoying the play of their shadows on the ceilings and walls. A group of "emo" style young people on tour from London lingered for some time in the space and pronounced it "trippy." It was received with excitement by many in the art community who were otherwise closed to faith.

Installation Content: Intentionality versus Open-ended Enquiry

Worship installation art aims to transform the visitor's expectations of what might appear, thus throwing open a new space wherein the Spirit might work. Installations are always intentional, yet often designed to elicit an open-ended enquiry or undetermined response. Like most contemporary art (perhaps excepting overtly political art) installations tend to avoid any quality that can be perceived of as didactic, or limited to a single, correct or pre-determined response. The intentional openness to a range of meanings goes even further than that. Early U.S. digital installation artist Bruce Nauman explains that installation art often exists to "provide the framework in which a work of art can unfold."[10]

With worship art there's no question that the intention is evangelical—it sets out, at the very least, to engage participants in what Robin Jensen calls "an awareness of a deeper and more profound reality."[11] This intention means there will be need to be limits that are placed on the work; ways we don't want it to go. That task needs to be done at the editing stage, to eliminate intuitive interpretations that will lead the work astray. However, only the most inappropriate directions an interpretation might take should be edited out. Like in liturgy, there needs to be a healthy degree of freedom for the Spirit to speak through the art into the hearts of others.

These insights on the role of the receiver are not new to communications theory. The recipient of any communication will interpret and respond in ways that may change the meaning of the work. However, that

10. In Mèredieu, *Digital and Video Art*, 58–59.

11. Jensen, *The Substance of Things Seen*, 85.

dynamic needs to be especially well-considered and provided for in this art form. A benefit of well-considered openness is the fact that people know when they are being given a tied-down message and when there is more freedom. In particular, the generations under forty will immediately sense the influence of wrapped-up doctrine, or a push to sign on the dotted line. More often than not they will quickly disengage when faced with a hard-edged representation of "truth"—unless they are already on board. Installation art challenges Christian worship artists to find ways of speaking our truth into a world of thinkers from a respectful distance, in dialogue and with patience.

SITE SPECIFICITY

Since the 1970s, art practice has been increasingly shaped by a two-way relationship between artworks and their location, which is described as "site specific." Initially appearing as a consideration for sculpture (and then dance) designed for a particular space, site specific art draws on the physical, psychological, historical and cultural features of an artwork's location, and allows the location to become a dynamic factor in the work. In worship art too, not only the physical features of a site should be considered, but the current and historic uses of the space, its position as a cultural site, its history of ritual and its social functions. In effect, the approach of site-specificity assumes a dialogue between the site and the content of the work.

Churches and church buildings carry rich histories of intentionality in the use of the space, which means worship artists begin with a complicated palette. Whether you choose to counteract the site and its echoes, or to use them, they must be sensitively considered if the resulting artwork is to communicate in a coherent way. When multimedia worship art fails to take its site critically into account, its communicative power can be reduced.

One liturgical installation I visited in a Swiss Protestant Church in 2006 provides a good example. A labyrinth and an accompanying set of reflective stations were arranged in the open space provided by the cavernous whitewashed church interior. Here the assumption of the worship curators (to use Mark Pierson's term[12]) seemed to be that their church building was a neutral space. However, the unrelentingly bright environment and physically exposed nature of each station made it impossible to engage in

12. Pierson, *The Art of Curating Worship*.

reflection at leisure without feeling under surveillance. The space commu nicated something more powerful than the stations it was housing, taking attention from the work and interfering with the kind of attention neces sary to provoke revelation or epiphany in the participant.

More sophisticated attention to the site specifics of that installation would have greatly improved its effectiveness. The labyrinth might have been defined by fabric walls, or some other method employed (such as presenting it at night with controlled lighting, placing visual baffles into the space such as potted trees or swathes of fabric) to create more intimate nooks and crannies and break down the panoptican quality of the space.

My liturgical approach to site specificity has been strongly influenced by French philosopher Gaston Bachelard's 1964 philosophical text *Poetics of Space*, which investigates the human experience of intimate spaces. He characterizes the different spaces in a house as having specific poetics. As a space, an attic provokes different thoughts and perceptions to a cellar, or a brightly lit sunroom.

Lumen ad Revelationem was influenced by Bachelard's chapter on miniature, where he quotes Victor Hugo's description of the tiny world inhabited by insects in a summer field. Bachelard insists that the poetic human imagination can lead into an understanding of the great truths of existence. Lying in a field on a summer's day, a child may discover that her own small body is enormous when she compares herself to the tiny insects she can see scurrying beneath the blades of grass. Then, as she looks up from this reflection, she begins to imagine what her true scale may be in comparison to the sky. In that poetic moment, the small child can find herself grasping the nature of eternity.

New Media Worship and Aesthetics

New media worship installations will communicate more effectively with aesthetic coherence. Similarly, the communicative power of this form can be let down on aesthetic technicalities.

Beauty is an important feature of worship installation art, as it is in other visual arts or musical compositions used in worship. There is a danger for multimedia liturgical installations to use objects and make arrangements with a conceptual framework that pays insufficient attention to aesthetics. Vulgar objects not fully understood can jar against the inten tions of the work, or a lack of intentionality about the arrangement of space may leave gaps in the experience that requires the participant to suspend their disbelief too far. That said, beauty in itself is not necessarily always a virtue. However if ugliness or vulgarity is present it needs to be properly understood for what it communicates.

The lure of beauty is another danger that can cause the worship installation artist to stray from the work's intended purpose. Beauty itself does not operate within a moral compass, but can be found serving merely decorative, vulgar, or evil ends and so worship artists need to be on guard against seduction by beauty. One example is in the work of Irish painter Francis Bacon whose paintings are artistically sophisticated and offer a kind of macabre beauty. Yet his insistence on a morbidly flesh-bound understanding of human existence readily leads to a godless conclusion.

Multimedia Worship Installation and Ethics: Use of Resources

When installation and temporal art appeared in the 1960s-70s, it challenged the commodification of art objects by standing outside the realm of monetary exchange. You couldn't easily buy or sell a temporary arrangement built into someone else's gallery, so by being non-object based, these art works were freed from being consumed as investment opportunities. Instead they were encountered as experiences.[13] Like liturgy, there should be no charge or monetary value placed on worship installation art. It is a gift.

Theological criticism of artistic opulence and the inappropriate assignment of resources to the arts will always be with us. Despite the beautiful biblical example of the woman who anointed Jesus with expensive perfume (Matt 26; Mark 14), it remains valid to question how many resources should be poured into worship installation art, both human and financial. As with any art form, the ecological impact of the materials used must be another serious consideration.

Worship installation art that is valuable to the Christian community and that forms part of the bigger picture of the ministry of the church will avoid some of the pitfalls of excess. If multimedia installation art forms

13. As installation art has matured, inevitably dealers, collectors and art institutions have found ways to commodify it, but the original value is still held to in much of this practice.

an integral part of a church's outreach and communication strategy, or provides the opportunity for a fresh expression for artists and media technicians, it will be of greater value than if it is the work of an isolated individual. If the materials used are assessed for their environmental impact as well as for aesthetics and cultural content, the work will have greater spiritual integrity.

Christian installation artists whose work operates within the tensions of glorifying God and serving God in the poor will be better able to find the right balance on these questions. The nineteenth-century Oxford Movement of liturgical renewal in the Church of England provides one example. While its Anglo-Catholic tradition of worship had a luscious and expensive aesthetic, it offered a glimpse of heaven to the inner-city poor whose lives were otherwise bereft of beauty. While they favored "high" forms of worship, Anglo-Catholic communities were also visiting people in the slums and advocating for just wages, fair rents and humane working conditions.

Conclusion

This essay has only touched the surface of a field which is rich with possibilities for inter-disciplinary research and development. Virtual reality art practice has the potential to both inform and be informed by traditional Christian installation art forms. These include areas not covered here, such as immersive worship traditions, historic and contemporary approaches to pilgrimage, ways of the cross, guided visits to sites of spiritual significance and other interactive forms of Christian spiritual practice.

In summary, what I have tried to indicate here is that as a relatively new art form, worship installation art needs to draw more intentionally on the critical practice of new media arts. Virtual reality, immersion, installation and site-specific art disciplines all have critical perspectives to add to the resources of Christian liturgical traditions in the planning and execution of worship installation art. In addition, worship installation art would be better served by more conscious attention to aesthetics, communications context and resource use.

BIBLIOGRAPHY

Anonymous. "The Symphony and Opera in Germany." In *The Laroussse Encyclopedia of Music*, edited by Geoffrey Hindley, 322–29. London: Hamlyn, 1976.

Davies, Char. "Osmose." Immersence. Online: http://www.immersence.com/osmose.

Heim, Michael R. *The Metaphysics of Virtual Reality*. New York: Oxford University Press, 1993.

Jensen, Robin M. *The Substance of Things Seen: Art, Faith and the Christian Community*. Grand Rapids: Eerdmans, 2004.

Mèredieu, Florence, de. *Digital and Video Art*. London: Chambers Harrap, 2005.

Pierson, Mark. *The Art of Curating Worship: Reshaping the Role of Worship Leader*. Minneapolis: Sparkhouse, 2010.

Williams, Rowan, *Grace and Necessity: Reflections on Art and Love*. London: Continuum, 2005.

10

Silence, Song, and the Sounding-Together of Creation

Steven Guthrie

This is my Father's world, and to my listening ears

All nature sings, and round me rings the music of the spheres.

—"This Is My Father's World," Maltbie D. Babcock

We live in a world that has grown both silent and deafeningly loud. This is the paradox of our contemporary aural environment. On the one hand, the modern West has nurtured the conceit that in all the material world, humanity alone possesses a voice—and so our ears are deadened to much of the creation.[1] On the other hand, we have simultaneously filled every crevice of the heard environment with sound and noise. In the great composer Arnold Schoenberg called the radio (along with the

1. The post-Enlightenment world, C. S. Lewis writes, imagines space to be "a pitch-black and dead-cold vacuity. [But] it was not so in the Medieval Model." For the ancients, the heavens were neither dark, nor silent. Indeed, "if our ears were opened we should perceive, as Henryson puts it, 'every planet in his proper sphere/In moving makand har mony and sound.' (*Fables*, 1659)" (Lewis, *The Discarded Image*, 111).

gramophone and the sound film) "the great foe."[2] He worried that "perhaps this continuous tinkle, regardless of whether anyone wants to hear it or not . . . will lead to a state where all music has been consumed, worn out."[3] At one time, he says, music could be surprising, even disturbing. "But some day, it may no longer disturb; people will be as hardened to this noise as to any other."[4] As I sit typing notes for this essay, in an airport boarding gate lounge, Schoenberg's prophecy seems extraordinarily prescient. Two iPod-wearing travelers inhabit separate musical worlds to either side of me; two different sets of background music from two different eating establishments swirl behind me; the man across from me is (loudly!) discussing a business presentation on his cell phone; ceiling- and wall-mounted speakers broadcast amplified notices from both the gate agent and a public address announcer—often simultaneously. Meanwhile, immediately above me, a 50-inch flat screen television bathes me in the headline roundup from CNN—a background chatter I thought I was ignoring until I began to write the word "paradox" a moment ago, and instead found myself typing "Petraeus"—the name of the American General responsible for providing the scandal *du jour*. In this bewildering but culturally ubiquitous chaos of sound, we hear both too much and too little. Our condition, in fact, amounts to a kind of aural solipsism, in which the only voices we hear are our own. This is a double-deafness, in which we are both *isolated from* and *insulated by* sound. As he reflected on the atheism of the mid-twentieth century, Walter Ong wondered: "Could it be that God is not silent but that man is relatively deaf, his sensorium adjusted to the post-Newtonian silent universe?"[5]

In contrast to this earsplitting silence, both scripture and the pre-modern theological tradition testify to a natural world that has a voice; one that not only speaks, but *sings*. The scriptural imagery of a singing creation, and the Pythagorean cosmology of a music of the spheres, provide us with rich conceptual resources for re-imagining the world and our place in it. Moreover, these traditions suggest that practices of sound—namely, silence, song and harmony (sounding together)—have a vital role to play in the care and healing of creation.

2. Schoenberg, "The Radio," 147.

3. Ibid.

4. Ibid., 148.

5. Ong, *The Presence of the Word*, 16.

Scripture and the Singing Creation

The Bible regularly attributes speech, song and music to the nonhuman creation. Not surprisingly, it is the Old Testament songbook, the Psalms, that uses this language most frequently. Psalm 65 describes the exuberant song of hills, meadows, and valleys. The trees sing songs of praise in Psalm 96, accompanied by the sea and all it contains, the fields and all who dwell in them. Indeed, the first verse of the psalm exhorts "all the earth" to sing a new song to the Lord. Psalms 66, 69, 103 and others likewise speak of all the earth singing and praising the Lord. Psalm 98 urges the trees to clap their hands, and the mountains to sing in harmony. The scope of praise in the Old Testament, Patrick Miller observes, "is not . . . confined to human beings and human communities. All the works of God, the whole creation, the heavenly beings praise God."[6]

There are at least six further references to a singing, shouting natural world in the book of Isaiah. In what is probably the best known of these passages, the prophet looks forward to a day when the mountains and the fields will burst forth in song, while the trees clap their hands (Isa
We could add to these references the stars that sing for joy in Job 38
ing to the New Testament, when Pharisees complain about the songs of praise Jesus' followers are singing, Jesus replies that should they fall silent, the very rocks will take up the chorus. In Revelation chapter 5 a singing creation features again in one of the most remarkable scenes in scripture. There John listens with astonishment as a song begun by the twenty four elders around the throne spreads to the hosts of angels, and then continues to move out in ever widening circles, until it is taken up by "every creature in heaven and on earth and under the earth" (5:13). Paul Achtemeier de scribes the scene in appropriately poetic language:

> The heavenly hymn swells to a crescendo that threatens to burst the very walls of heaven itself, but not alone of heaven. It is a song so compelling that now all creatures must join in. Every creature in every nook and cranny, wet or dry; every creature bathed in light or hid in darkness; every creature covered with scales or clothed in fur or feathers; every creature crawling, walking, running or flying; every creature now joins in the climax of praise.[7]

6. Miller, "'Enthroned on the Praises of Israel,'" 13–14.

7. Achtemeier, "Revelation 5:1–14," 285–86.

We likewise find passages that suggest other registers sounded by the voice of creation. The earth not only sings songs of joy, but also sighs, accuses, and wails tunes of lament. In at least four places, Jeremiah speaks of the land mourning. Habakkuk makes the chilling declaration that the very stones and wood of a house built by injustice will moan within its walls (Hab 2:11).[8] And, of course, Paul, in Romans 8, speaks of the entire creation groaning.

What is the import of these references to a sounding creation? We are, of course, familiar with the idea that creation speaks. In reading passages such as these, however, we may miss the rather obvious point that speech is aural and oral—something that happens in the realm of sound. In modern society, where words are read silently more often than aloud, it is easy to equate the *physical* event of speech with the *silent* act of thought. If, however, we bypass the sounding dimension of these metaphors, then the voice of creation ceases to be something outside of me—something originating in the natural world—and instead becomes an idea inside of me—an idea I arrive at while considering nature. We may, in other words, miss a fundamental point arising from this biblical imagery, namely, that ours are not the only voices in the song of creation.

The language of song—as opposed to simply speech—underlines this point. Though it would be a mistake, we might be tempted to reduce the *act* of speech to the *ideas* spoken. Singing, however, is not susceptible to this kind of reduction. A song is not simply a carrier for some content. Song draws our attention to the act of sounding itself. A singing creation, then, is a creation that *acts*. It is not merely a vehicle by which a message is communicated; it has its own voice. Again, this is a dimension of the biblical language that is easily overlooked.

I can provide an example of this carelessness from my own classroom! In my Introduction to Theology courses, I will often point to Psalm 19 as an example of general revelation, and say something like: "The natural world is one way that God speaks to us." Of course, this is true. But Psalm 19 doesn't

8. This warning is all the more striking given the argument the prophet goes on to make against those who worship idols: "For its maker trusts in what has been made [that is, the idol], though the product is only an idol that cannot speak! Alas for you who say to the wood, 'Wake up!' to silent stone, 'Rouse yourself!' Can it teach?" (2:18–19). The idolater is foolish, not because he attributes a voice to the created world (see, for instance, Hab 3:10–11), but because he attributes a living voice to the product of his own hands. The prophet in fact speaks very directly to us: those whose world is almost entirely populated by non-living voices; who listen to voices that are only stone, steel or silicon, but have no breath in them, and cannot teach.

say "*God declares his glory to us* through the beauty of the heavens." Rather: "*the heavens declare* the glory of God"! The physical world is not simply the passive mechanism through which God speaks; instead, it has been given a voice of its own voice with which to praise God.

Not only do we translate the spoken (or sung) words in such passages into silent ideas; we also often transfer this biblical language from the do main of the aural to that of the visual.[9] So a passage like Psalm 19 be inwardly paraphrased into something like: "The heavens display God's glory, and in the beautiful skies you can see the work of God's hand." Again, this is true. The heavens are beautiful, and we do see God's skillful work on display there. But nevertheless a declaration ("the heavens *declare* glory of God") is different from a display, and one of the principal points of difference between the aural and the visual language is something like the difference between an active and a passive verb. One *makes* a declaration; a display is *made available*. I can turn my head away from a message that is displayed; I cannot turn my sense of hearing away from a word that is declared. The metaphors of hearing, then, emphasize that nature is not sim ply passively waiting to be noticed, dependent upon my act of perception; rather, it actively comes to meet me, demanding attention. The nonhuman world cries out. The language of sound then, again, draws attention to na ture as a reality that has its own integrity, rather than simply being the inert recipient of human action.

Gerhard von Rad makes this point eloquently. In passages like Psalm 148, he writes, "We encounter the idea that the world is not dumb, that it has a message . . . The world proclaims itself before God as a created thing; the heavens 'tell,' the firmament 'proclaims.'" Rad likewise urges that we not take these descriptions too lightly, writing, "What finds expression here is not simply poetic exuberance, but the idea of a real witness emanating from the world."[10] The natural world speaks to human beings about God, and more than that, it speaks alongside humanity in praise of God.

9. Of course, the psalm goes on to observe: "There is no speech, nor are there words; their voice is not heard." The psalmist in other words, acknowledges the surpris ing metaphor being used. But at the same time—almost as if anticipating our propensity to translate this form of words into a different sensory mode—the psalmist goes on to insist on just this metaphor. He continues: "*yet* their *voice* goes out through all the earth, and *their words* to the end of the world" (emphasis mine).

10. Rad, *Wisdom in Israel*, 162.

11. "Moreover, by invoking praise from the rivers and mountains, the song topples the complacent and dangerous modern view of the nonhuman world as passive,

nonhuman creation does not merely exist as a witness to humanity; it has its own praise to bring, its own commerce of worship with its creator.

This last point is another insight that emerges from attending to the specifically musical character of this biblical language. The language of song indicates that there is meant to be continuity and collaboration between the songs of praise that humanity sings and the song that nature sings. There is no sharp break between the sacred and natural world here. Praises begun in the sanctuary continue in the eyries; the songs that first sound in prairie grasses find their antiphon in the hymns of the church.

Moreover, in invoking the voice of every creature from stars to human beings, passages like Psalm 148 and Revelation 5 ally worship with a vision of universal harmony; a grand chorus. This is not simply evocative language. It suggests that worship includes a specific sort of relationship between the human and the nonhuman creation. Passages that portray a universal song describe—in fact, they insist upon—a creation in which there are (first of all) *different* voices, but (secondly) voices that nevertheless are joined together in a way that is complementary and harmonious. The voices of human beings, sun, moon and stars, birds and beasts do not need to exclude or compete with one another. All are and each is necessary to complete the grand chorus.

This mutuality is at work in another respect as well. It is the human psalmist who calls on all of nature to sing; conversely, it is in light of creation's song that human beings are urged to join the song. In Psalm 148, for instance, it is only after sun, moon and stars, sea monsters, wind, snow and hail, beasts and cattle are called into song, that the psalmist extends his invitation to kings and princes, young men and women, old men and youths.[12] The movement in Psalm 98 however is in the other direction. There, the song of lyre and trumpet (vv. 5–6) spills over to the sea and all who dwell in it, the floods and the hills (vv. 7–8). So there is a sense in which human beings lead the cosmic chorus, and there is another sense in which men and women learn to sing from listening to the song of creation. As we sing, creation joins the song; as we become aware of creation's song,

insensible—nothing more than the stage for human actors with their magisterial and often frenetic gestures. Thus the world is revealed for what it really is: in fact, not Nature at all but rather Creation, still exquisitely sensitive to the presence and will of its Maker, eager to the point of impatience for the full manifestation of God's will in human life, which is the final goal of judgment (cf. Rom. 8:19–22)" (Davis, "Rejoicing in Judgment," 171).

12. Cf. Ps 66:1–8.

we sing. Indeed, several of the passages we've mentioned suggest that the creation is more faithful than humanity in witnessing to God's goodness. Human beings may or may not praise the Lord; if however we fail in our worship, the stones will not.

The Music of the Spheres

This biblical witness finds a striking parallel in another ancient conception of the cosmos: the Pythagorean vision of the "music of the spheres." Of course Pythagoras's understanding of creation is in many ways very differ ent from the biblical picture we have been considering. The two traditions are alike however in representing the cosmos as a kind of chorus in which each element has a part to sing.

The Pythagoreans, Aristotle explained, "thought that the whole heav en was a harmony and a number."[13] This heavenly harmony, moreover, was thought to reverberate through each element of the cosmos—from the heavenly movements of the planets, to the various elements of society, to the internal movements of the human soul. Each heavenly body and earthly creature, sounds forth its own "note" and, at the same time, participates in the larger harmony. If these various elements of the cosmos are arrayed rightly, in right relation to themselves and one another, they comprise a grand universal symphony. Saint Augustine, in his early work *De Musica* describes it as the *carmen universitatis*—the song of the universe.

The Pythagoreans acknowledged that for the most part we are un able to hear this cosmic harmony. Cicero explains that this is because the celestial music has been ringing in our ears since birth, and we have grown deaf to it. (In the same way, he says, children who grow up in a village situ ated by a thundering waterfall will be oblivious to its roar.)[14] This, however,

13. Aristotle, *Metaphysics* 985b–986a (pp. 19–20).

14. Cicero, *De Re Publica* book 6. Cicero offers a dramatic account of the idea in book six of *De Re Publica*. There the character Scipio relates a dream in which he is visited by his ancestor, Africanus. Africanus leads Scipio up into the heavens, from which vantage he is able to view not only the various cities and nations of earth, but the very workings of the cosmos. As they journey, Scipio exclaims: "*Pray what is this sound that strikes my ears in so loud and agreeable a manner?* To which he replied *It is that which is called the music of the spheres, being produced by their motion and impulse; and being formed by unequal intervals, but such as are divided according to the most just proportion, it produces, by duly tempering acute with grave sounds, various concerts of harmony. For it is impossible that motions so great should be performed without any noise; and it is agreeable to nature that*

is precisely one of the reasons that music (in our ordinary, contemporary sense of the word) is valued by the ancients. If we are attentive, and if we learn to listen well, in human songs and melodies we may hear some echo of this deep harmony; the universal music to which we have grown insensible. Through music, Augustine writes, we come to know "what proportion is and how great is its authority in all things."[15] This "proportion," this relatedness of all things, could in principle be discerned in any number of places, but Augustine explains that these relations (what he calls "the powers belonging to numbers in all kinds of movements") are:

> most easily studied as they are presented in sounds, and this study furnishes a way of rising to the higher secrets of truth, by paths gradually ascending, so to speak, in which Wisdom pleasantly reveals herself, and in every step of providence meets those who love her.[16]

Music, in other words, is a school in which we learn a harmony that extends beyond human songs.

The Christian writer Boethius, drawing on this Pythagorean tradition, describes the relationship between these different kinds of "music" in a three-fold hierarchy of harmony. At the highest level is *musica mundana*. This is the music of the spheres; the harmony produced by the stars and the other heavenly bodies in their orbits. At the next level is *musica humana*, or human music. This is the harmony that governs the relationship between body and soul, between sense and reason, and between the other seemingly disparate elements that are nevertheless unified in the human person. Finally, there is *musica instrumentalis*. This is music in our contemporary sense of the word—music produced on instruments and in ordinary

the extremes on one side should produce sharp, and on the other flat sounds. For which reason the sphere of the fixed stars, being the highest, and being carried with a more rapid velocity, moves with a shrill and acute sound; whereas that of the moon, being the lowest, moves with a very flat one. As to the Earth, which makes the ninth sphere, it remains immovably fixed in the middle or lowest part of the universe. But those eight revolving circles, in which both Mercury and Venus are moved with the same celerity, give out sounds that are divided by seven distinct intervals, which is generally the regulating number of all things. This celestial harmony has been imitated by learned musicians, both on stringed instruments and with the voice, whereby they have opened to themselves a way to return to the celestial regions, as have likewise many others who have employed their sublime genius while on earth in cultivating the divine sciences" (Cicero, *The Political Works of Marcus Tullius Cicero*, 304–5; italics mine).

15. Augustine, *De Musica* 1.12.23 (p. 200).

16. Augustine, "Letter CI," 413.

song. While the three levels of music are distinct, the same proportion and harmony runs through all of them, and for this reason, sounding music potentially offers us insight into the very nature of the cosmos.[17]

This Pythagorean vision of the created world is radically different from the boldly Promethean cosmology that characterizes modernity. In the modern picture of reality, human beings are set apart from the rest of the created order by virtue of their rationality. They quite appropriately stand astride the world of mute and mindless matter, and dispose of it as seems best to them. We find a breathtaking statement of this attitude in Kant's *Conjectural Beginning of Human History*. In keeping with the "conjectural" character of the essay, Kant imagines a moment in primeval history when some human being approached a sheep and declared: "*Nature gave the skin you wear not for you but for me,* and then took it off the sheep and put it on himself."[18] The description of this notional inter-species encounter would be comical if Kant were not so intent on celebrating the declaration as a moment of great human achievement. This, he says, was "the fourth and last step that reason took in elevating the human being entirely above the society with animals."[19] At this point, humanity "became aware of the prerogative he had by nature over all animals, which he no longer saw as fellow creatures, but as means and tools at the disposal of his will for the attainment of the aims at his discretion."[20]

In the Pythagorean conception, however, the physical stuff of the cos mos is not "means and tools," but alive; neither is it mute, but rather, it sings.[21] As with the biblical conception of a singing nature, the Pythagorean

17. See Bower, "Boethius' *The Principles of Music*," esp. 48–62.

18. Kant, "Conjectural beginning of human history," 167. Frustratingly, Kant fol lows this imagined statement with a parenthetical citation of Genesis 3:21. ("And the Lord God made garments of skins for the man and for his wife, and clothed them.") In the biblical narrative, however, it is God who provides garments of skin for Adam and Eve. Moreover, it should go without saying, the biblical narrative does not portray this as a proud and auspicious episode in human history.

19. Ibid.

20. Ibid. See also Wood, "*Kant on Duties Regarding Nonrational Nature*," 189

21. Ong observes that for the ancients the cosmos was a harmony of "living celestial spheres." The emergence of "the Newtonian revolution, and its accompanying exaltation of the sense of sight at expense of hearing, spelled the end of the feeling for a vitalized universe." Sight, Ong contends, registers surfaces of things. Through sight, we encounter the world around us as objects. Sound, on the other hand suggests not a surface, but something with an interior; something that acts. With the death of the ancient cosmol ogy, Ong concludes, nature became something merely "sighted and measured"—a realm,

cosmology recognizes the created world as a reality with its own integrity. Reality is not a monologue narrated by human beings. The natural world has a voice. The musical conception of the universe situates humanity within a larger environment. In the music of the spheres, human beings sound one part within a vast chorus. Human beings are called upon to sing their own part, but also, to hear and harmonize with the other voices of creation.

In addition to this, the ancient cosmology conceives the universe embodying an exquisite set of proportions and ordered relations, and so in that sense, it is—against Kant—the very perfection of rationality (that is, to say *ratio*-nality).[22] For Boethius and the other ancient writers, it is the music that human beings make—*musica instrumentalis*—which is the least reliably ordered. The planets, for their part, move unswervingly through their orbits, faithfully sounding their part within the cosmic harmony. As in some of the biblical passages we considered earlier, it is the music of the *non-human* creation that most reliably sings its tune. The music made by human beings on the other hand, is a much "more fragile embodiment of harmony"[23] depending as it does on flawed and fallible performers. In this ancient view, we imitate the order of nature rather than impose order upon it. Nicomachus the Pythagorean (Second Century CE) writes that "among objects of perception, *the music of the planets* is considered to be the prototype of our music according as we imitate it."[24]

PYTHAGORAS BAPTIZED

In late antiquity and the middle ages, the Pythagorean vision—or at least elements of it—becomes part of the world of Christian thought. Some Christian thinkers, such as Boethius, Isidore of Seville and Cassiodorus explicitly articulate the elaborate cosmology of the Pythagoreans. More typically, Christian thinkers simply appropriated some of the principal themes and images from Greek cosmology. In particular, they drew on the image of a singing universe, the idea of a grand cosmic symphony, and the governing concepts of harmony and proportion.

---

not of activity, but of objects. Ong, *The Presence of the Word*, 227–28.

22. For an extended discussion of music, *ratio* and the ancient concept of a universe of ordered relation, see Guthrie, "Carmen Universitatis."

23. Stone-Davis, *Musical Beauty*, 30.

24. Nicomachus the Pythagorean, *The Manual of Harmonics*, 45; my emphasis.

Consider one early example from Clement of Alexandria (c. c. 215). His *Protrepticus* is a remarkable attempt to baptize the Pythagorean cosmos for the church. In Clement's cosmology, the ground bass to which all else is harmonized is Jesus Christ, or as Clement refers to him: the New Song. "Behold the might of the new song!" he writes:

> It . . . composed the universe into melodious order, and tuned the discord of the elements to harmonious arrangement, so that the whole world might become harmony . . . And this deathless strain—the support of the whole and the harmony of all—reaching from the centre to the circumference, and from the extremities to the central part, has harmonized this universal frame of things . . . Having tuned by the Holy Spirit the universe, and especially man—who, composed of body and soul, is a universe in miniature—makes melody to God on this instrument of many tones.[25]

Athanasius, writing sometime later, will also borrow Pythagorean lan guage and the idea of musical harmony to describe a beautiful and ordered world; one in which there is a unity maintained among countless diverse elements. He writes:

> Just as when one hears from afar a lyre, made up of many different strings, and wonders at their harmonious symphony . . . [that] all sound together in balanced tension; and one concludes from all this that the lyre neither operates by itself nor is played by many, but rather that there is one musician who by his art blends the sound of each string into a harmonious symphony—even though one fails to see him—so too, since there is an entirely harmonious order in the world as a whole, without things above being at odds with those below, and those below with those above, but one completed order of all; it follows that we know there is one leader and king of all reaction, not many, who illuminates and moves everything with his own light.[26]

Similarly, toward the end of the *City of God*, Augustine draws on the Pythagorean language of proportion and harmony to describe the beauty and perfection of the Heavenly City. He says:

> The peace of the Heavenly City is a perfectly ordered and perfectly harmonious fellowship in the enjoyment of God, and a mutual fellowship in God; the peace of the whole universe is the tranquillity

25. Clement of Alexandria, "Exhortation to the Heathen," 172.

26. Athanasius, "Oratio contra gentes 38," 55–56.

> of order—and order is the arrangement of things equal and unequal in a pattern which assigns to each its proper position.[27]

It would be a mistake to interpret these passages as examples of Christian theology infected by the foreign strains of Greek philosophy. Rather, in terms and images like "harmony" and the "music of the spheres," Christians of late antiquity discovered extra-biblical language by which they could summarize profoundly biblical truths. (And of course, there are plenty of parallel examples of this in Christian theology, two of the most obvious being *trinitas* and *homoousios.*) Clement and Augustine recognized in the music of the spheres an eloquent résumé of biblical teaching regarding creation. This cosmology, when read through the lens of the biblical narrative, portrays a physical creation that has its own integrity. Human beings have a voice, but so too does the rest of the created world. The cosmos is conceived of as a vast, dynamic and interconnected ecology in which each creature has a valuable part. Moreover, it imagines the creation not as a machine to be deployed but as a song to be heard and enjoyed. The creation is, in fact, the sort of thing of which the Creator would be expected to say: "it is very good," (rather than simply: "it is working properly").

Finally, the Pythagorean cosmology describes a cosmic harmony that is real, but that we cannot yet hear. We must learn to hear it. We must discern fragments of it—in the sound of the physical world, and in the practice of human music. Here too, this vision resonates with the biblical understanding. For the time being, the song of the universe includes a groaning creation; what melody it does sound goes largely unheard by a tone-deaf humanity. Those snatches of the *carmen universitatis* that we can discern, however, are bits of melody that point forward to the full realization of the song of the new creation. It is for this reason that Augustine appeals to harmony in particular when describing the *heavenly city*. The music of the spheres is "already" but "not-yet." It goes unrecognized, largely because of the dullness of humanity. In the words of the prophets, we have ears, but do not hear.[28] Boethius and Augustine, however, argue that *musica instrumentalis*—sounding music in our ordinary sense of the word—may be one means by which we are reminded of and become aware of this deeper harmony. Is there any way of making sense of this idea? Is there some respect

27. Augustine, *Concerning the City of God Against the Pagans*, 870.

28. It is interesting that this inability to *hear* is one of the more regularly repeated characterizations of a people grown dull spiritually. Cf. Jer 5:12; Isa 6:10, 43:8; Ezek 12:2; Zech 7:11; Matt 13:13; Mark 4:12, 8:18; Luke 8:10; John 12:40; Acts 28:26; Rom 11:8.

in which the domain of sound in general, and of music in particular, can make us better stewards of creation?

Singing and the Healing of Creation

It seems notable that two of the practices we most readily associate with monastic life are silence and singing. Significantly, the religious world in which the Pythagorean cosmology was Christianized was a world orga nized around regular intervals of silence and song. It may be then that one way of recovering the insights of Augustine and Boethius, and one way of responding to the biblical vision of a singing creation, is by investing our selves in these ancient spiritual disciplines of silence, singing, and harmony. What is more, I believe that these disciplines may be a means of bringing greater wholeness not only to individuals and Christian communities, but also to the rest of the created world, and to our relationship with it.

We need, first, to recover silence. As I noted at the outset, we live in a world in which it is difficult to hear; more difficult still to listen. The ob stacles to hearing well are simultaneously physical and philosophical. The two paradigmatic models of aural culture emerging from modernity are the domination of aural space (noise pollution) and the radical privatization of aural space (the iPodscape). At a philosophical level these in turn embody two problematic modern strategies for engaging with the physical world: either overriding the natural environment on the one hand, or ignoring it on the other. In one mode we impose our will on the landscape; in the other, we withdraw into an environment of our own design. Both, as I have argued, reflect a kind of environmental solipsism in which humanity reso lutely refuses all voices other than its own.

At the level of actual sense experience, these twin responses of aural domination and aural isolation are also genuine obstacles to understanding the world and our place within it. Listening turns out to be a particularly potent way of knowing our environment. In a recent *New York Times* piece, the neuroscientist Seth Horowitz warns that "Listening is a skill that we're in danger of losing, in a world of digital distraction and information overload. And yet we dare not lose it. Because listening tunes our brain to the patterns of our environment faster than any other sense."[29]

29. Horowitz, "The Science and Art of Listening," SR10. "Sound is everywhere," Horowitz writes elsewhere. "From the night chorus of frogs in the deepest rain forest to the emptiest wind-blown stretch of the Antarctic, you are surrounded by, embedded in,

The reach of our aural experience is far more extensive and, we might say, far more general than our visual experience. We hear further and in more directions than we see. We hear what is behind us, beneath us, above us, and invisible to us. What is more, as we have already pointed out, while we direct our gaze, sound is directed toward us. We can close our eyes, but we cannot close our ears. In this way, the aural world speaks against the monological pretensions of humanity—the idea that we alone have voices, and that we alone speak reality into being. Unless we become still and attentive, however, we may fail to recognize the ways our environment has been broken and damaged. One of the seminal texts of the environmental movement, *Silent Spring*, draws a pointed connection between a ruined natural world and human aural insensitivity:

> Over increasingly large areas of the United States, spring now comes unheralded by the return of the birds, and the early mornings are strangely silent where once they were filled with the beauty of bird song. This sudden silencing of the song of the birds, this obliteration of the color and beauty and interest they lend to our world have come about swiftly, insidiously, and unnoticed by those whose communities are as yet unaffected.[30]

Of course, as we have already observed, the practices of silence and careful listening are not only environmentally useful; they are also Christian virtues. Silently attending to our environment is an act of humility and hospitality. By our silence we acknowledge the presence of another, one who has a voice and who has something we need to hear. Silence may sometimes be misunderstood (or misguidedly practiced) as a withdrawing into oneself. Bonhoeffer however points out the "essential relationship of silence to the Word":

> Silence is the simple stillness of the individual under the Word of God. We are silent before hearing the Word because our thoughts are already directed to the Word, as a child is quiet when he enters

---

and molded by sound and vibration. Anywhere there is energy, including the depths of intergalactic space, is a vibratory region. Some are richer than others, but none are totally silent." In a strange way the ancients were right: the heavens are not silent. The highest note we are aware of is apparently the vibration of a Cesium atom, which trills away at 9,192,631,770 cycles per second (as compared with the standard concert pitch of A, at 440 cycles per second). The lowest notes we know of are the pulses of sound emanating from black holes—which rumble out an impressive B flat 57 octaves below middle C! Horowitz, *The Universal Sense*, 3–4.

30. Carson, *Silent Spring*, 103.

> his father's room. We are silent after hearing the Word because the Word is still speaking and dwelling within us. We are silent at the beginning of the day because God should have the first word, and we are silent before going to sleep because the last word also belongs to God. We keep silence solely for the sake of the Word, and therefore not in order to show disregard for the Word but rather to honor and receive it.[31]

Bonhoeffer very wisely recognizes that we are silent not simply from a love of silence but because the God of the Bible speaks. And, we might add, our fellow human beings have voices as well; and so too, we have learned, does the nonhuman creation. Silence, then, embodies our recognition of these other voices. It is part of our active response to the singing creation portrayed in the Psalms. In silence, we show hospitality by allowing time and space for others to speak (God first of all, but also our brothers and sisters, and the rest of the created world). Silence is also an act of humility by which we "look not to our own interests but to the interests of others" (Phil 2:4). In silence we set aside our attempts to be "dictators" (from the Latin *dicere, to speak*—so, literally one who attempts to dominate by speech). Instead we become student and servant.

A second way of responding to the singing creation, is—as the Psalms suggest—by singing ourselves. Silence is necessary to hear the voice of creation, but we are not to remain silent. After speaking the world into being, in Genesis 2, God invites Adam to speak into the world as well—to name the animals, and in this way, to contribute his own voice to the song of creation. This power of the voice to carry one out into the world is another way in which sound is different from sight. Rousseau notes that "we have an organ that corresponds to that of hearing, that is, the voice. Sight has nothing like this, for though we can produce sounds, we cannot give off colors. We have therefore fuller means of cultivating hearing, by exercising its active and passive organs upon one another."[32] Through our voices, we participate, enter into, and share in the aural world. So, the philosopher Jonathan Rée suggests, our voices

> are the radiant centre of our auditory world. We can use them like torches, as a means of exploration; but whilst a beam of light can only touch the surfaces of things, our voices go out and mingle

31. Bonhoeffer, *Life Together*, 79.

32. Rousseau, *Émile*. Rée cites this passage and discusses Rousseau's treatment of hearing and the voice in the section of *I See a Voice* mentioned below.

> with all the other sounds we hear. We use them as a probe for sounding out the world, and they draw us into it, and anchor us there. We hear with our voices as well as our ears.[33]

In speech and in song, our voice becomes a part of the aural environment we perceive. As our own voice sounds, we hear our voice in its interaction with the physical environment.

This is particularly the case with respect to singing, since in singing we attend especially to the sound of the voice (rather than simply to the content of our words). Singing is a kind of ear training, in more senses than one. Singing involves an awareness of sound and an awareness of oneself in relation to one's environment. As I sing, I attend to my place within a space. I become aware of the dimensions and the kinds of surfaces in the area around me, and how it responds to my voice. If sin is "*homo incurvatus in se*" —humanity turned in upon itself—then song is potentially one means by which we are moved outside of ourselves. In song we not only extend ourselves into the world; the surrounding world is carried back to us, indeed, *into* us, along with the sound of our voice. Song then becomes a kind of training ground for acting in dialogue with my environment. It involves recognizing how the sounds that I make and the sounds that are around me relate to the space in which all of those sounds are happening. "I not only can but must hear all the sounds around me at once," Walter Ong insists. "Sound thus situates me in the midst of a world. Because it situates me in the midst of a world, sound conveys simultaneity."[34]

The word "simultaneity" is vitally important here. It suggests a third way of responding to a singing creation, and that is through embracing that venerable Pythagorean term: harmony. There is special value not simply in singing but in singing *with* others. One reason is because corporate song requires that I actively tune my voice to the voices of those around me. It demands that I be both singer and listener. In order to sing along with others, I need to hear the tempo, the pitch, the volume, the inflection and articulation of both my voice and their voices. In this way I learn to perceive and respond to other voices and the world they inhabit, in real time.

Interestingly, environmental scientists report some striking examples of this sort of aural responsiveness in bird-song:

33. Rée, *I See A Voice*, 57.

34. Ong, *The Presence of the Word*, 129.

> Recently, considerable evidence has emerged showing that anthrophony [sounds produced by human beings] can influence animal communication in a variety of ways. For example, American robins (*Tur-dus migratorius*) shift the timing of their singing in urban environments to the night . . . In song sparrows (*Melospiza melodia*), the lowest-frequency notes were higher in environments with high ambient noise . . . Brumm (2004) found that free-ranging nightingales (*Luscinia megarhynchos*) in noisier environments sing more loudly than those in quieter environments, and Slabbekoorn and Peet (2003) determined that the great tit (*Parus major*) sings at higher pitches in urban noise conditions.[35]

At one level this is a negative example—an instance, not of harmony, but of species desperately searching for open space in an increasingly crowded aural environment. At another level, however, this seems to be a Psalm 148-like instance of inter-species song, in which the nonhuman creation initiates the kind of song that human beings are also meant to sing. The birds studied are doing what animal species do—adjust their songs and the sounds they make in response to the sounds in their environment. What is lacking is a corresponding sensitivity and responsiveness among human producers of sound.

Since the 1970s, scholars in a number of disciplines have emphasized the importance of listening and sound in care of the environment. R. Mur ray Shafer of Simon Fraser University is often credited with establishing the branch of studies known as acoustical ecology or soundscape studies. Schafer, in a striking echo of Boethius, urges us to "regard the soundscape of the world as a huge musical composition, unfolding around us ceaseless ly. We are simultaneously its audience, its performers and its composers." Listening well is the first step, Schafer suggests, in "tuning the world."

35. Pijanowski et al., "Soundscape Ecology," 208.

36. Of interest at this point is the work of bioacoustician Bernie Krause. Krause studies the "biophony"—the distinctive soundscape of various physical environments. Krause also claims that animal species that thrive within any given soundscape do so in part by virtue of having carved out their own "acoustic niche." To survive, each species must find an unoccupied place in the aural bandwidth in which its own vocalizations can be heard. While the ideas of a "soundscape" and the importance of the aural environment are widely recognized, Krause's proposal of acoustic niches as an evolutionary mecha nism has had a mixed reception among biologists. See Hull, "The Noises of Nature."

37. See, for instance, Wrightson, "An Introduction to Acoustic Ecology," 11–also Pijanowski et al., "Soundscape Ecology," 203–16.

38. Schafer, *The Soundcape*, 205.

39. Schafer, *The Tuning of the World*.

begins by discerning discordant notes in the soundscape, as well as voices that are missing or being overpowered. Then, like a conductor with an orchestra, or an orchestrator working with a score, one can begin bringing out this melody, de-emphasizing that motif, adding and eliminating voices and instruments, in pursuit of an ever more satisfying sym-phony (sounding together).[40] Schafer believes that this "tuning of the soundscape"—interacting with our environment with the attention and skills of a musician—is a particularly potent way of pursuing a whole and healed environment.

Musical harmony, or singing-with, may then turn out to be (as Boethius suggests) a means by which we learn to harmonize with the grander *harmonia mundi*. Corporate song forces me to attend to my simultaneous roles as producer and receiver of sound. In this way, singing potentially models and instantiates a non-competitive way of sharing space; one that is mutually participatory without being invasive or destructive. In song, human voices and the surrounding space enter into and contribute to one another, and—what is more—this sort of attentive collaboration is revealed to be compelling and beautiful. The alternative to noise pollution and iPod isolation is harmony.

Nor is this harmony simply a matter of good manners (everyone "getting along"). Rather, the kind of non-competitive shared life we have outlined is rooted in the central mysteries of the Christian faith. In God's own person, Father, Son, and Spirit share fully in one another's lives without ceasing to be the three distinct persons of the Trinity. In the perichoretic life of the Godhead, the Father fully inhabits the Son and Spirit without ceasing to be the Father and without in any way compromising the personhood of Son or Spirit. Likewise, in the incarnation, Jesus (literally) embodies a way of being in which union does not annul distinction, and distinctiveness does not demand separation. The *homoousios* declares that perfect union between God and humanity neither diminishes the fullness of God's deity, nor abrogates the reality of human identity. The point, once again, is that the concept of "harmonized being" and the ideal of the creation as shared space are not relics of ancient cosmology nor instances of contemporary political correctness. Instead, what we have been describing is grounded in the being of God and the person of Jesus Christ.

40. For a fascinating and accessible discussion of how environmental scientists are using musical concepts see Ira Flatow's interview with Bryan Pijanowski and Bernie Krause. Pijanowski et al., "Listening to Wild Soundscapes."

It is possible to conceive the Music of the Spheres as the cosmic and creaturely expression of the kind of perichoretic unity that exists eternally in the Godhead; a profound harmony arising from the mutual indwelling of many diverse voices. One way of caring well for God's creation might be to take very seriously this symphonic conception of reality—at both the level of a world view (*Weltanschauung*) and at the level of immediate sense experience. In the case of the latter, this will mean attending carefully to the sounds of the nonhuman world around us, attending with equal care to the sounds that we make (our voices and music, our machines, structures and cities), and then pursuing a genuine *symphonia*—a sounding together—that is pleasing and allows the expression of each voice. Through silence and song we may be made more fully aware of whether we as human beings are in fact joining in with the grand theme Augustine refers to—the Song of the Universe.

Of course, the most obvious setting in which Christians employ si lence, song, and harmony is that of corporate worship. If caring well for God's earth means learning to listen and harmonize, then worship and liturgy are part of our task as stewards of creation. In a great antiphon of praise, the creation's song tunes our voices to worship the Creator, while our human praise of the Creator tunes our ears to care for creation:

> Make a joyful noise to God, all the earth;
> sing the glory of his name;
> All the earth worships you;
> they sing praises to you,
> sing praises to your name. (Psalm 65:1–2, 4)

BIBLIOGRAPHY

Achtemeier, Paul J. "Revelation 5:1–14." *Interpretation* 40, no. 3 (1986) 283–88.

Aristotle. *Metaphysics*. Translated by Hugh Lawson-Tancred. London: Penguin, 2004.

Athanasius. "Oratio contra gentes 38." In *Music in Early Christian Literature*, edited by James McKinnon, 52–56. Cambridge Readings in the Literature of Music. Cambridge: Cambridge University Press, 1987.

Augustine. *Concerning the City of God Against the Pagans*. Translated by Henry Bettenson. London: Penguin, 1984.

———. *On Music* [*De Musica*]. In *The Immortality of the Soul; The Magnitude of the Soul; On Music; The Advantage of Believing; On Faith in Things Unseen*, translated by R. C. Taliaferro, 169–379. Fathers of the Church 4; Writings of Saint Augustine 2. New York: Cima, 1947.

———. "Letter CI." In *A Select Library of The Nicene and Post-Nicene Fathers of the Christian Faith*, translated by J. G. Cunningham and edited by Philip Schaff, 1:412–14. Edinburgh: T. & T. Clark, 1994.

Bonhoeffer, Dietrich. *Life Together*. Translated by John W. Doberstein. New York: Harper & Row, 1954.

Bower, Calvin M. "Boethius' *The Principles of Music*: An Introduction, Translation, and Commentary." PhD diss., George Peabody College for Teachers, 1967.

Carson, Rachel. *Silent Spring*. New York: Houghton Mifflin Harcourt, 2002.

Cicero, Marcus Tullius. *The Political Works of Marcus Tullius Cicero: Comprising his Treatise on the Republic; and his Treatise on the Laws, Volume* 1. Translated by Francis Barham. London: Spettigue, 1841.

Clement of Alexandria. "Exhortation to the Heathen." In *Ante-Nicene Fathers: Translations of the Writings of the Fathers down to A.D. 325*, edited by Alexander Roberts and James Donaldson, 2:171–206. Edinburgh: T. & T. Clark, 1994.

Davis, Ellen F. "Rejoicing in Judgment," *Interpretation* 46, no. 2 (1992) 171–75.

Guthrie, Steven R. "Carmen Universitatis: A Theological Study of Music and Measure." PhD diss., University of St. Andrews, 2000.

Horowitz, Seth S. "The Science and Art of Listening." *The New York Times*, 11 November 2012, SR10.

———. *The Universal Sense: How Hearing Shapes the Mind*. New York: Bloomsbury, 2012.

Hull, Jeff. "The Noises of Nature." *The New York Times*, 18 February 2007. Online: http://www.nytimes.com/2007/02/18/magazine/18wwlnessay.t.html.

Kant, Immanuel. "Conjectural beginning of human history (1786)." In *Anthropology, History, and Education*, 160–75. Translated by Allen W. Wood. The Cambridge Edition of the Works of Immanuel Kant. Cambridge: Cambridge University Press, 2007.

Lewis, C. S. *The Discarded Image: An Introduction to Medieval and Renaissance Literature*. Cambridge: Cambridge University Press, 2012.

Miller, Patrick D., Jr. "'Enthroned on the Praises of Israel.' The Praise of God in Old Testament Theology." *Interpretation* 39, no. 1 (1985) 5–19.

Nicomachus the Pythagorean. *The Manual of Harmonics*. Translated by Flora R. Levin. Grand Rapids: Phanes, 1994.

Ong, Walter J. *The Presence of the Word: Some Prolegomena for Cultural and Religious History*. Minneapolis: University of Minnesota Press, 1967.

Pijanowski, Bryan C., et al. "Soundscape Ecology: The Science of Sound in the Landscape." *BioScience* 61, no. 3 (2011) 203–16.

Pijanowski, Bryan C., et al. "Listening to Wild Soundscapes." *National Public Radio, Science Friday*. Originally broadcast 22 April 2011. Online: http://www.npr.org/2011/04/22/135634388/listening-to-wild-soundscapes.

Rad, Gerhard von. *Wisdom in Israel*. London: SCM, 1993.

Rée, Jonathan. *I See A Voice: A Philosophical History of Language, Deafness and the Senses* London: Flamingo, 2000.

Rousseau, Jean-Jacques. *Émile or, Concerning Education; Extracts*. Edited by Jules Steeg. Translated by Eleanor Worthington. Boston: Ginn, Heath, 1888. N.p. Online: http://www.gutenberg.org/files/30433/30433-h/30433-h.htm.

Schafer, R. Murray. *The Soundcape: Our Sonic Environment and the Tuning of the World* Rochester: Destiny, 1994.

———. *The Tuning of the World*. New York: Knopf, 1977.

Schoenberg, Arnold. "The Radio: Reply to a Questionnaire." In *Style and Idea: Selected Writings*, 147. Berkeley: University of California Press, 1984.

Stone-Davis, Férdia J. *Musical Beauty: Negotiating the Boundary between Subject and Object*. Eugene, OR: Cascade, 2011.

Wood, Allen W. "*Kant on Duties Regarding Nonrational Nature.*" *Aristotelian Society* supplement, 72, no. 1 (1998) 189–210.

Wrightson, Kendall. "An Introduction to Acoustic Ecology." *Journal of Electroacoustic Music* 12 (2002) 11–15.

Name Index

14221915R00132

Made in the USA
San Bernardino, CA
20 August 2014